DATE DUE

TRUE PATRIOT LOVE

The Politics of Canadian Nationalism

Sylvia B. Bashevkin

Toronto
OXFORD UNIVERSITY PRESS
1991

Oxford University Press, 70 Wynford Drive, Don Mills, Ontario M3C 1J9

Toronto   Oxford   New York
Dehli   Bombay   Calcutta   Madras   Karachi   Petaling Jaya
Singapore   Hong Kong   Tokyo   Nairobi   Dar es Salaam
Cape Town   Melbourne   Auckland

and associated companies in
Berlin   Ibadan

Canadian Cataloguing in Publication Data
Bashevkin, Sylvia B.
    True patriot love

Includes bibliographic references and index.
ISBN 0-19-540810-1

1. Nationalism - Canada. 2. Political planning - Canada.
3. Canada - Politics and government.
I. Title.

FC97.B3 1991   320.5'40971   C91-095122-5
F1034.2.B3 1991

For my parents and my daughters

Contents

Illustrations   vi

Acknowledgements   vii

Preface   viii

1   Exploring the Nationalist World View   1

2   From Ideas to Policies: Three Explanatory Frameworks   39

3   Cultural Nationalism and the *Time/Reader's Digest* Bill   61

4   Investment Nationalism: The Case of the National Energy Program   83

5   The Adoption of Canada-US Free Trade   104

6   NAC's Opposition to Free Trade: The Costs and Benefits   136

7   Solitudes in Collision? Pan-Canadian and Quebec
    Nationalisms in Perspective   154

8   Epilogue: Nationalist Futures   179

Appendix A: Abbreviations   188

Appendix B: Acknowledgement of Informants   189

Index   190

Illustrations

Figures

2.1 Societal approach to public policy 42
2.2 State structures approach to public policy 45
2.3 Integrative approach to public policy 51
2.4 Specification of independent and dependent variables,
     integrative model 54
3.1 Scoring independent variables on Bill C-58 71
4.1 Scoring independent variables on National Energy Program 93
5.1 Scoring independent variables on adoption of comprehensive
     free trade policy 125

Tables

1.1 Major federal reports on cultural policy, 1951-1986 10
1.2 Major federal reports on investment policy, 1957-1972 21
3.1 Cultural nationalist attitudes, 1966-1979 73
4.1 Canadian attitudes towards energy policy, 1980-1983 95
4.2 Canadian attitudes towards extent of US investment, 1961-1987 96
4.3 Canadian attitudes towards proposed policies on foreign
     investment, 1974-1986 98
5.1 Published reports favourable to sectoral or comprehensive
     free trade, 1975-1988 106
5.2 Free trade attitudes in Canada, 1984-1988 128
6.1 Gender gap in free trade attitudes 145
7.1 Pan-Canadian nationalist attitudes by cultural group, 1977-1981 166
7.2 Quebec nationalist attitudes by cultural group, 1977-1981 167
7.3 Attitudinal differences by language and region, 1979 168
7.4 Quebec nationalist attitudes towards pan-Canadian nationalism,
     1979 170
7.5 Pan-Canadian nationalist attitudes towards Quebec nationalism,
     1979 171
7.6 Pan-Canadian and Quebec nationalists view the 'other' nationalism,
     1979 172
7.7 Attitudes towards free trade and Quebec's future in Canada,
     1990 173

Acknowledgements

This book is very much a product of human collaboration. Without the assistance of so many people who offered ideas, citations, information and their own perspectives on nationalism, I could not have completed the research for the study. My deepest thanks to each of the individuals whose names are listed in Appendix B, the acknowledgement of informants.

Writing the manuscript was made easier because my husband, Alan Levy, and three colleagues, Grace Skogstad, Evert Lindquist and Robert Vipond, offered encouragement and critical comments along the way. I am grateful to these readers for their help with the book, and to the assessors for Oxford University Press, *Canadian Public Administration*, *Canadian Public Policy* and *Comparative Political Studies*, for their advice on earlier versions of various chapters. As well, I wish to thank colleagues who commented on drafts of chapters 1, 7 and 8 at the 1988 Canadian Political Science Association meetings, the 1990 'Limitless Identities' conference at the University of Edinburgh, the 1990 political science colloquium at the University of Waterloo and the 1991 political economy workshop at the University of Toronto.

The Humanities and Social Sciences Committee and the Connaught Programme in Law and Public Policy, both at the University of Toronto, were generous in their support of this project. Research assistance by Bruce Arnold, Robert Boyd and David Docherty was financed by these grants. I appreciate both their expert work and the funding that made it possible.

At Oxford University Press, Richard Teleky was encouraging and efficient, assisted at every turn by Phyllis Wilson. As Richard predicted, Sally Livingston's efforts improved the final manuscript at the copy-editing stage.

Readers should also know about the personal background to this study. I grew up in a small New England city, and moved to Canada as a foreign student in 1977. My initial fascination with English Canadian nationalism was that of an outsider; indeed, I was an identifiable member of the 'out-group' referred to in this study. Although I have not been actively engaged in Canadian nationalist politics at any point, my personal sympathies are moderately nationalist.

My parents, Esther and Irving Bashevkin, shared with me their critical intelligence and so much more, which I have tried to bring to bear on this subject. My daughters, Dalia and Aviva, prodded me to get the book written and, in their own way, taught me a great deal about what it means to grow up in Canada. This study is dedicated to the four of them for the unusual perspective they have given me.

All errors of fact and judgement remain my own.

Preface

In the fall of 1985 the federal royal commission chaired by Donald S. Macdonald released its final report endorsing Canada-US free trade. This recommendation touched off a lengthy and heated public debate, not simply over the economic merits of free trade but also over more visceral matters of national sovereignty and Canadian identity.[1]

Balanced accounts that could explain this debate were few and far between. What were the bases of nationalist opposition to the idea of free trade? Why were anti-trade groups so critical of the implications for investment, energy and culture of a bilateral agreement? Why did proponents and opponents of free trade—frequently the only commentators on this subject—talk or, more frequently, shout past each other?

This book begins the task of analysing pan-Canadian nationalism on a political level. Rather than asking whether nationalist approaches to issues of trade, foreign investment or culture are normatively 'good' or economically beneficial —questions that have arguably been exhausted in recent years—this study examines *what* these approaches are and *how* they have influenced government action. More specifically, it considers the interplay between nationalist ideas and organizations, on the one hand, and federal politics, on the other.

The overall purpose of this research is to shed light on larger questions of social action and state response: How have nationalists shaped Canadian politics and society? How successful have they been in articulating a pan-Canadian vision of the country? To what extent has their influence been limited by the pull of competing regional, cultural and ideological identities? What are the future political prospects of pan-Canadianism?

Chapter 1 considers the outlook or world view of Canadian nationalists, identifying the origins, beliefs and limitations of their perspective. It argues that organized pan-Canadianism incorporates at least three distinct streams of thought and activism: namely, cultural, trade and investment nationalism. Each of these streams has articulated an identifiable policy agenda: namely, support for the domestic communications industry in the case of cultural nationalism; resistance to Canada-US free trade in the case of trade nationalism; and reduced foreign investment and economic control—particularly in the natural resource sector—in the case of investment nationalism. Chapter 1 defines pan-Canadianism as *the organized pursuit of a more independent and distinctive Canadian in-group on the North American continent, primarily through the introduction by the federal government of specific cultural, trade and investment policies that are designed to limit US out-group influences.*

The final section of Chapter 1 examines the limitations of this world view, suggesting that pan-Canadianism is 'wedged' by a number of problems. First, since nationalist thinking is defined by distinctions between in- and out-groups, pan-Canadianism has had to argue for the 'differentness' and, ultimately, the superiority of Canada vis-à-vis the United States. This is a difficult task, in part because the US is admired by many Canadians as a prosperous society brimming over with career opportunities, as a free and individualist democracy, as a warm, friendly place to shop and vacation. As well, kinship ties and cultural similarities—particularly between English Canada and the US—have tended to erode further the in-group/out-group distinctions that are pivotal to any nationalist world view.

Second, nationalists have tried to articulate in-group identity among members of a society who hold diverse multiple identities—whether French/English, regional, multicultural or ideological.[2] Ironically, then, nationalist views of Canadian identity have themselves been fractured and somewhat exclusive ones, refracted through particular lenses and prisms. Chapter 1 argues that the nationalist world view reflects a left-of-centre bias in favour of assertive federal government intervention in the economy, a perspective that is consistent with its modern development, primarily in Ontario, among a progressive, English-speaking constituency.[3]

Third, this discussion does *not* suggest that the modern pan-Canadian world view is politically intolerant.[4] In fact, unlike many European nationalisms of the early twentieth century, Canadian nationalism since the late 1960s has attracted considerable numbers of well-educated, socially progressive people to its ranks —people who consistently defend civil rights and cultural diversity as an integral part of their democratic politics. This pattern has created an important difficulty of its own, however, in that the nationalist tendency towards tolerance, diversity and coalition-building with other groups has had to co-exist alongside the idea of a cohesive Canadian in-group united within one Canada. In the shadow of the Meech Lake constitutional initiative, with a re-emergence of Quebec nationalism, western Canadian regionalism and efforts by aboriginal, feminist and other groups to reform federalism along more participatory lines, this tension between unity and diversity is especially clear.

Chapter 2 builds on these themes. It presents three frameworks that address the translation of nationalist ideas into federal public policies. The first of these approaches, drawn from the literature on societal groups, views policy decisions as a function of competition among organized interests. According to this view, governments act as impartial umpires among groups, whose policy influence varies with their resources, cohesion, expertise and representativeness. The second framework, a bureaucratic state perspective, rejects the notion of government as impartial umpire and instead explains policies with reference to the preferences, capacity and autonomy of administrative decision-makers.

Chapter 2 argues that both approaches overlook the importance of *nationalist ideas*, and that both neglect international and domestic political responses to these ideas. In particular, such traditional assessments of policy influence do not consider the orientation of the US government, of Canadian party elites and of Canadian media and public opinion towards nationalist arguments. Chapter 2 proposes a third framework, the integrative politics approach, which considers these variables, and suggests that neither of the first two approaches—on its own—can adequately explain federal action in the areas targeted by nationalists.

The next three chapters evaluate this proposition using one case of policy intervention by each of the major streams of pan-Canadianism. Chapters 3 and 4 consider two relatively successful attempts by cultural and investment nationalists respectively to influence federal policy: first, Bill C-58, also known as the *Time/Reader's Digest* Bill, which restricted tax deductibility for Canadian advertisers in foreign periodicals and broadcast outlets; and second, the National Energy Program, which aimed to 'Canadianize' the domestic petroleum industry. The adoption of these nationalist initiatives by the federal government would have been difficult to predict using the societal or bureaucratic frameworks alone; as argued in Chapters 3 and 4, both policies are more coherently explained using an integrative model.

Chapter 5 employs the same strategy in exploring the federal government's decision to pursue a comprehensive Canada-US free trade policy. Although nationalists and their allies were unable to block free trade during the 1980s, explaining this lack of success and the adoption of free trade again requires attention to ideas and the political response to them. The case studies presented in Chapters 3, 4 and 5 thus indicate the inadequacy of existing frameworks as applied to communications, natural resource and bilateral trade policy, at the same time as they illustrate the utility of an integrative approach.

Nationalist opposition to free trade is examined from a somewhat different perspective in Chapter 6. By the mid-1980s, the need for a societal alternative to the business coalition that endorsed this policy was clear. Efforts to develop such an alternative culminated in the establishment in 1987 of the Pro-Canada Network, a diverse coalition of approximately 35 groups that included the leading Canadian women's organization, the National Action Committee on the Status of Women (NAC). Chapter 6 examines the costs and benefits of NAC's involvement in the anti-trade coalition, arguing that these new allies of organized nationalism were themselves engaged in a high-stakes political game during the 1980s. While pan-Canadianism gained a larger and more representative social base through the Pro-Canada Network, coalition partners such as NAC faced considerable risks as well as some potential benefits from their involvement. On balance, Chapter 6 concludes that NAC's vocal opposition to free trade was consistent with the organization's main lines of development since 1972, but suggests that this strategy could politically isolate and financially weaken Canadian women's groups for some time.

Chapter 7 addresses the complicated question of how nationalists in Quebec and English Canada view each other's nationalism. Using the writings of activists in both cultures as well as public opinion data as prisms through which to evaluate this relationship, it considers possibilities for collision as well as accommodation. Chapter 7 suggests that the two nationalisms were on less of a collision course in the period of the 1980 Quebec referendum on sovereignty-association than subsequently. Debates during the late 1980s and following over free trade and the Meech Lake constitutional accord went to the heart of long-standing tensions between Anglo-Canadian and Quebec nationalisms, highlighting their unbridgeable differences over the jurisdictional primacy of the federal state (and federal/provincial relations generally) as well as over Canada's relations with the United States.

The book concludes in Chapter 8 with a speculative look at the future of English-Canadian nationalism. How has the free trade debate, with its deep polarization of pro- and anti-free trade interests, shaped the subsequent evolution of nationalist politics? Are regional, cultural and ideological limits on pan-Canadianism likely to recede in the near future? What are the prospects for a somewhat different brand of trans-national 'nationalism'?

Notes

[1] Royal Commission on the Economic Union and Development Prospects for Canada, *Report* (Ottawa: Supply and Services Canada, 1985).

[2] See Richard Johnston, *Public Opinion and Public Policy in Canada*, Royal Commission Research Studies, vol. 35 (Toronto: University of Toronto Press for Supply and Services Canada, 1986), 226.

[3] On the regional bias of English Canadian nationalism, see Daniel Drache, 'The Enigma of Canadian Nationalism', *Australian and New Zealand Journal of Sociology* 14 (1978), 310-21.

[4] On the tolerant origins of nationalist ideas in Canada, see Alexander Brady, 'The Meaning of Canadian Nationalism', *International Journal* 19 (1964), 349. Brady argues that George-Étienne Cartier's vision of Canadian nationality 'would have warmed the heart of Lord Acton'.

1 Exploring The Nationalist World View

There have been many varieties of Canadian nationalism, and, while they have all been inspired by the same nation, the manner in which the character and interests of Canada have been interpreted vary enormously.[1]

Introduction

The literature on Canadian nationalism has been dominated by the writings of committed proponents and opponents. Rather than simply lamenting the normative nature of this literature and disregarding most of it, Chapter 1 uses the ideas of pan-Canadian nationalists as evidence, or raw data. It attempts to situate their beliefs in the broader contexts of nationalism and social theory, arguing that the pan-Canadian phenomenon is defined by the same in-group/out-group distinction which characterizes many other nationalisms.

How have pan-Canadian concepts of in- and out-group developed? Max Weber's concept of world view, or *Weltanschauung*, provides a useful framework in which to address this question; it permits analysts to evaluate the ideas and limitations of a given belief system. In this case, how do nationalists view Canadian culture and identity? What are the bases of their concerns about national sovereignty and economic independence?

Using the world-view approach, Chapter 1 identifies three major domains within the nationalist outlook, beginning with its core concerns regarding identity and culture. Rather than viewing the cultural dimension of pan-Canadianism as a side-show or diversion from more important *economic* preoccupations, this discussion demonstrates that cultural matters of in-group identity have, as in other nationalisms, constituted the pivot of the pan-Canadian world view.

After examining the cultural domain, we then consider nationalist approaches to trade policy, particularly vis-à-vis the United States, and to questions of foreign investment. In each of the sections on culture, trade and investment, the main policy proposals put forward by nationalists are identified: proposals in support of the domestic communications industry, in opposition to continental free trade, and in support of Canadian control of the natural resource sector, respectively. This three-way distinction helps to bring out the unity as well as the diversity within the nationalist world view and makes the analysis of nationalist policy influence in subsequent chapters more manageable. Finally, Chapter 1 examines the limitations of the pan-Canadian world view, focussing on problems in its treatment of both in- and out-group categories.

Before turning to the main discussion, two important caveats are in order. First, this chapter does not provide a comprehensive account of all the perspectives that together constitute the pan-Canadian world view. Many of its less prominent and, in social terms, less organized elements—including the nationalist critique of Canadian foreign policy—are addressed only briefly as they relate to core concerns regarding culture, trade and investment.[2] This deliberate emphasis on principal components is not meant to demean other aspects of pan-Canadianism; rather, its purpose is to make sense of the larger belief system.

Second, Chapter 1 does not address the complex histories of individual nationalists. Although activists in each of the three modern streams have tended to endorse the ideas and efforts of their counterparts in other streams, there have been important exceptions. For example, at least one prominent investment nationalist of the 1970s later supported continental free trade.[3] Moreover, the chapter does not consider in detail the diversity and, at times, disunity that have characterized the three main strands of Anglo-Canadian nationalism. Although these stories of individuals and their sometimes conflictual relations within nationalist organizations are interesting, our focus remains the general rather than individual directions of pan-Canadianism.

Studies of Canadian Nationalism

To the extent that a literature on pan-Canadianism can be said to exist, it has been dominated by advocates and adversaries whose works present essentially normative views of the subject. Assertively pro- and anti-nationalist writers have thus competed for control of this research terrain in much the same way they have opposed each other in the public arena. Although their contributions capture the real-world flavour of many heated policy debates, from a research perspective they have built a less analytic and less systematic literature than that which exists in other areas of Canadian politics. In the words of one author, Denis Stairs, who attempted in 1981 to evaluate this field:

> The literature—to say nothing of the polemical rhetoric . . . is thematically untidy, and many—perhaps most—of the contributors are neither clear nor explicit about their basic premises and assumptions. The arguments in practice tend to overlap, and the disputants have an unsettling habit of talking past one another, serenely oblivious of the fact that they are missing their targets.[4]

Studies of foreign investment by active and publicly identified nationalists are especially numerous. They include important works by Walter Gordon, Peter C. Newman and Abraham Rotstein, the three founders of the Committee for an Independent Canada,[5] as well as by signatories to the Waffle manifesto, notably Cy Gonick, James Laxer and Mel Watkins.[6] Other books whose titles reflect clear sympathies with the nationalist position include Kari Levitt's *Silent Surrender*, Ian Lumsden's *Close the 49th Parallel Etc.*, Philip Resnick's *Land of Cain* and, since 1980, Glen Williams's *Not for Export*, Stephen Clarkson's *Canada and the Reagan Challenge* and Gordon Laxer's *Open for Business*.[7] On the other side of the spectrum, where integrationist or continentalist beliefs prevail, the volume of published output has been somewhat less, although, according to nationalists, it has been more politically influential.[8] The continentalist bookshelf includes classic studies by Goldwin Smith and Samuel Moffett, as well as the more contemporary work of Harry Johnson and Peter Brimelow.[9]

This tendency towards a normative focus was especially clear during the 1985-88 debate over Canada-US free trade. In large part, the trade debate was conducted between committed nationalists and continentalists; much of the vast outpouring of commentary pitted advocates of cultural and economic nationalist policy against proponents of an integrationist or 'harmonized' North American approach.[10] With few exceptions, only limited effort was devoted to getting behind the normative biases or beyond individual specializations in order to place the trade debate within a larger idea system known as Canadian nationalism.[11] The existence of these exceptions, however, indicates that systematic research is both possible and worthwhile. Various historical and biographical studies point towards an analytic view of nationalism,[12] as do several pieces on banking and periodicals policy—areas in which nationalist influence was considerable.[13]

Perhaps the most useful conceptual treatment of this subject can be found in Denis Stairs's 1981 article, which divided Canadian nationalism into its component parts.[14] Identifying five 'schools of protest' against continental dominance, Stairs devoted primary attention to what he termed 'diplomatic penetration', 'economic penetration' and 'philosophical penetration', and less detailed consideration to 'cultural penetration' and 'informational penetration'.[15] Stairs linked nationalist ideas about Canada both to the comparative literature on nationalism and to questions of public policy at the federal level. In a similar vein, Kim Nossal's 1985 study for the Macdonald Royal Commission evaluated the content and implications of economic nationalist arguments, using broader comparative theories of nationalism as a guide.[16]

This chapter builds on the work of Stairs and Nossal in applying comparative theories of nationalism to the Canadian case; it differs from their approach, however, in emphasizing the importance of *cultural* or identity questions within what we delineate as the nationalist world view.

Nationalist Ideas and Movements

The idea of nationalism flows from concepts of nation and national consciousness. Although some theories of nationalism—primarily those propounded by its critics—establish categories of race and ethnicity as the basis for 'nation',[17] a more useful approach from the perspective of pan-Canadianism begins with notions of in-group loyalty and sovereignty.[18] According to this view, nationalism is grounded in the distinction between members of an in-group and their loyalty to a preferably sovereign or self-determining political unit which is representative of that in-group, on the one hand, and members of an out-group who hold loyalties to any number of other sovereign or dependent units, on the other.

Following the lines of this approach, the basic 'glue' that holds together nationalist ideas and movements is in-group loyalty. Identification with other members of the in-group—whether because of pride in this present shared membership, faith in the future of the unit or memory of past experiences—and a concomitant distancing from the out-group are essential components of nationalist ideology. On the crucial level of political action, the establishment of a clear and assertive in-group category usually produces demands for national independence, self-determination and state sovereignty. As Anthony Birch has observed, nationalism at its core 'refers to a political doctrine about the organization of political authority'.[19]

Nationalist ideas are most often promulgated through political movements or, in some cases, interest group organizations. John Breuilly defines the following link between nationalist ideas and groups:

> The term 'nationalism' is used to refer to political movements seeking or exercising state power and justifying such actions with nationalist arguments. A nationalist argument is a political doctrine built upon three basic assertions: (a) There exists a nation with an explicit and peculiar character. (b) The interests and values of this nation take priority over all other interests and values. (c) The nation must be as independent as possible. This usually requires at least the attainment of political sovereignty.[20]

In situations where formal state sovereignty has already been obtained, and here Canada since 1867 is an obvious example, Breuilly suggests that nationalist pressure groups may emerge for the purpose of attempting to re-orient the ideas and policies of that established state. Such groups may

> base their claims upon some general nationalist ideology. They do not, however, seek to take control of the state. Often this is because they regard the existing state as 'their' nation-state and are seeking merely to influence its policies in ways which they believe best represent the national interest.[21]

The present study suggests that the overriding purpose of pan-Canadianism from its origins in the late nineteenth century through the present has been identical to that described by Breuilly: namely, the channelling of state action in directions that are meant to strengthen national sovereignty and to reinforce the autonomy of state institutions. In this discussion, *'pan-Canadian nationalism' refers to the organized pursuit of a more independent and distinctive Canadian in-group on the North American continent, primarily through the introduction by the federal government of specific cultural, trade and investment policies that would limit US out-group influences.*

Because the federal state is viewed as the most capable vehicle around which
to organize resistance to continental influences, its jurisdictional primacy is
central to the pan-Canadian world view. In the face of what are perceived to be
overwhelming pressures towards continental integration, nationalists have
worked to bring Canada beyond what they view as an otherwise formal, empty
and sterile political independence. The problems confronting pan-Canadianism, therefore, have not been the same as those faced in Third World struggles
for colonial independence. Instead, the difficulties in Canada have involved
identifying the in-group which activists have sought to champion under the
banner of an existing federal state, and mobilizing that in-group against the
continental out-group.

As argued in the final section of this chapter, cultural, regional and ideological
divisions within the established entity known as Canada tend to limit the influence of nationalist ideas and, indeed, have sometimes divided activists among
themselves. In analysing the limits thus imposed upon pan-Canadianism, this
book takes issue with those explanations—in many cases offered by nationalists
themselves—that claim the presumed 'failure' of this movement results from US
economic penetration.[22] Rather, it proposes that many crucial constraints on
nationalism follow from the internal *political* realities of Canada itself.

The World-View Perspective

How have Canadian nationalists defined their in-group constituency and out-
group adversaries? What concepts of national identity have developed, and how
have nationalists used these ideas in order to strengthen and mobilize a Canadian in-group?

In an essay entitled 'The Social Psychology of World Religions', Max Weber
provided one framework in which to address these questions. He argued that
the *Weltanschauung*, or world view, of individuals could be understood as an
orderly pattern rather than as a scattered, random phenomenon.[23] According
to Weber, important similarities exist in the ways in which people see the world.
These similarities frequently correspond with such identifiable social categories
as religion, class and ethnicity. Each category or group tends to hold an identifiable world view; in Weber's terms, an 'elective affinity' links groups and world
views, such that groups tend to become the 'carriers of meaning' for particular
political symbols that together comprise the world view.[24]

The manner in which researchers might study *Weltanschauungen*, and thereby
grasp the core symbols and meanings held by groups and individuals, was
explored in other essays by Weber and a second German theorist, Karl Mannheim.[25] According to both writers, world views need to be explored systematically, from objective as well as subjective perspectives.[26] In Weber's words, the
purpose of such study is to provide 'an interpretive understanding of social
action insofar as the acting individual attaches a subjective meaning to it'.[27] By

delineating the main ideas and identifying the key social groupings of political activists, Weber suggested that a meaningful representation of their actions and belief systems could be developed.

The next sections of this chapter begin to reveal the core ideas and meanings attached by Canadian nationalists to their actions. We examine the priorities that nationalists have identified for themselves and the organizational vehicles that they have established to serve as collective 'carriers of meaning'. What are the main arguments of Canadian nationalists? How have they been advanced in a group context? By posing these questions, we try to capture in a broad sense the world view of pan-Canadianism.

Cultural Nationalism

Early Treatments of Culture and Identity
Canadian nationalism in the period from 1867 through the first decades of this century is said to have stood on three key pillars. To paraphrase historian W.M. Baker, these foundations were, first, a strong psychological attachment to the imperial or British connection; second, growing resentment of the cultural and, at times, territorial threat of 'Americanization'; and, third, commitment to the development of a distinct Canadian identity through enhanced imperial ties, on the one hand, and vigilant, restrained continental ties on the other.[28] If Canadian nationalism at its point of origin can be said to have contained a core belief system or world view, then, it seems to have been an imperialist and anti-continentalist one, based primarily on *cultural* arguments.

From the perspective of the late twentieth century, the imperial dimension of early nationalism appears at first glance contradictory, or at least awkward and antiquarian. Why, in asserting the existence of Canadian selfhood and in-group identification, would nationalists have resorted to argumentation based on what we now know to have been a declining British presence? From the perspective of the turn of the century, however, imperial assertions made a great deal of sense, not only to nationalist activists but also to many members of the general public. This linkage with the British Empire was seen first of all as providing Canada with a route to prominence on the world stage. As the loyalist hero General Brock exclaims in Charles Mair's *Tecumseh: A Drama*, published in 1886,

> For I believe, in Britain's Empire, and
> In Canada, its true and loyal son,
> Who yet shall rise to greatness, and shall stand
> At England's shoulder helping her to guard
> True liberty throughout a faithless world.[29]

Second, imperialism in this period offered a direct political, military and economic counterweight to continentalism, embodied in the 'godless republic' that threatened to absorb its neighbour to the north. As Robert Craig Brown demonstrates in his study of post-Confederation attitudes, members of the Canadian elite as well as the public at large distrusted American intentions.[30] They feared that the US was a republic out of control, a chaotic, potentially very aggressive government which lacked not only the sure hand of British constitutional monarchy but also the steady direction and purpose of Canada's own National Policy. Particularly as the economic utility of the National Policy came to be questioned, a matter discussed below at greater length, the prospect of strengthened imperial relations seemed increasingly attractive.[31]

In order to foster the development of a distinctive in-group, imperial nationalists worked to delineate the bases for its identity. Leaders of the Canada First movement (established in 1868) wrote at length about the northern climate and icy land that, in their view, provided the core strength and spirit of Canada.[32] Drawing on the dominant social Darwinist and Romantic ideas of the day, George Parkin maintained that the severity of the Canadian climate would ensure national vigour, order and strength. In his words, 'it teaches foresight; it cures or kills the shiftless and improvident; history shows that in the long run it has made strong races.'[33]

This view that residents of the Dominion had conquered the frigid climate helped imperial nationalists to assert their distinctiveness from the important out-group formed by Canada's neighbour to the south. Their belief that the US was an unstable, excessively democratic society, overrun with immigrants from southern origins, prompted such activists as Colonel George Taylor Denison to argue against continental integration. In Denison's view, the Americans 'are forming a community there entirely different in its characteristics from ours'.[34] The US, in short, was a less steady and desirable ship of state than Canada.

These assertions of Canadian distinctiveness and, indeed, superiority vis-à-vis the US were linked directly with celebrations of the imperial tie. For the Canada Firsters, developing in-group identity meant exploiting the linkage with Empire, through which Canada's national destiny would be fostered rather than fettered and threatened as it was in the continental relationship. As Carl Berger explains in his lucid study of their ideas:

> imperialists contended that the history of the Dominion was essentially the story
> of material progress and the steady advance of liberty and self-government. For
> them, all Canadian history was ceaselessly moving toward one irrefragable con-
> clusion—the acquisition of full national rights and freedom within an imperial
> federation.[35]

Although this goal of imperial union was not obtained, the Canada Firsters' emphasis on cultural identity did carry through to subsequent generations of nationalists in English Canada. For example, their emphasis on northern land and climate became the artistic focal point of the Group of Seven, whose visual representation of the physical landscape constituted a 'national movement' in

Canadian painting, an explicit rejection of continental similarities in environment and culture.[36]

As well, notions of physical space and natural endowment—captured so centrally in the writings of the Canada Firsters—provided a foundation for subsequent emphases on the *protection* of territorial resources and rights. Twentieth-century nationalist preoccupations with preventing the export of water and defending Canadian sovereignty in the high Arctic, with opposing the 'extra-territorial' application of US trade law and 'Canadianizing' the oil and natural gas industries, follow logically from the spatial definition of national identity adopted late in the last century.[37]

This physical and intensely landscape-oriented definition of identity retains a pivotal place in the Anglo-Canadian world view.[38] Its continued presence helps to explain how nationalists have linked perceived *economic* threats resulting from foreign investment or continental free trade with a loss of *cultural* identity and sovereignty. If the products of the Canadian landscape or the enterprises of its territory are 'gobbled up' by foreigners, to use the nationalist imagery, then in essence the being known as Canada will no longer survive.

Moreover, in attempting to limit the influence of US periodicals by creating their own magazines, the Canada Firsters established the foundation for what remains a key nationalist policy priority: namely, Canadian control of the communications media.[39] The existence of the *University Magazine* from 1907 until 1920, when a new generation of activists established the *Canadian Forum*, reflected a conscious effort by imperial activists to replace what were seen as cultural 'instruments of "Americanization"'.[40]

The inheritors of this early cultural nationalism, however, rejected much of the imperial, racialist and conservative baggage of the Canada Firsters. The inter-war beginnings of the *Canadian Forum*, the League for Social Reconstruction (LSR), and the Canadian Radio League were important landmarks in the trend towards an increasingly progressive nationalism based in the university, journalism and arts communities.[41]

Unlike earlier nationalist efforts in English Canada, these newer organizations presented a far more reformist—at times radical—approach to Canadian identity and, especially, to the use of federal institutions to advance the cultural world view.[42] The *Forum*, which originated at the University of Toronto, began as an 'avowedly nationalist' magazine that would offer Canadian readers an alternative to American and European journals of opinion.[43] One of its most prominent contributors, Frank Underhill, announced the formation of the League for Social Reconstruction in the pages of the *Forum*.[44] The League set out to offer Canadian critics of capitalism their own Fabian Society; it provided a domestic incubator of many ideas that were later incorporated in the Regina Manifesto of the Cooperative Commonwealth Federation (CCF).[45]

Although the nationalist credentials of Underhill, the LSR and the CCF were each questioned from time to time, all shared a strong belief in the importance of federal state action, particularly in the field of communications policy.[46] Reflected most clearly in the mandate of the Radio League, this belief derived from a fundamental commitment to public as opposed to private ownership, as demonstrated in pressure to create the Canadian Broadcasting Corporation (CBC) and National Film Board (NFB) during the 1930s. As Ramsay Cook has argued, the cultural nationalism of the early Canadian left followed directly from a belief in the necessity and benevolence of federal involvement:

> It is not merely that the state alone has the resources necessary to finance cultural survival, though that is important; it is also that a statist or socialist approach to culture would in itself be evidence that Canadian culture is different from the free enterprise culture of the United States.[47]

In the oft-quoted words of Graham Spry, the straightforward choice confronting cultural nationalists in the 1930s was 'the State or the United States'.[48]

Modern Cultural Nationalism

Given this background, it is not surprising that much of the impetus for a renewed cultural nationalism in the years following the Second World War came from progressive academics and artists, who successfully pressed for a series of federal government studies. The 1951 Report of the Royal Commission on National Development in the Arts, Letters and Sciences (Massey-Lévesque report) articulated much of what has become the modern cultural nationalist world view, including the belief that the influence of the US communications industry in Canada was excessive.[49] As summarized in Table 1.1, the report recommended a series of policies to encourage independent cultural development (including the establishment of the Canada Council and greater funding for the CBC and NFB) and to limit 'alien' and specifically American media penetration, notably through controls on television content.[50]

The idea that a direct threat to Canadian cultural life was posed by US broadcasts and periodicals was developed further in the Fowler (1957) and O'Leary (1961) reports, respectively.[51] Like Massey-Lévesque, these commissions maintained that national identity was endangered by weak and underfunded Canadian cultural institutions and by spillover from an assortment of US media. The federal government, it was argued, should devote greater policy attention and more budgetary resources to strengthening domestic cultural enterprises, notably the CBC, and to restricting the American cultural presence. Otherwise, according to this view, the influence of foreign magazines, books, radio, television, newspapers, films and other media would ultimately jeopardize Canada's continued existence.[52]

The ability of cultural nationalists to act on these ideas, however, was limited as long as their positions were expressed only in royal commission reports, and as long as few organizational vehicles existed other than the CBC and NFB.[53] Both problems were clear by the 1970s, when a flood of nationalist books and orga-

TABLE 1.1 MAJOR FEDERAL REPORTS ON CULTURAL POLICY, 1951-1986

NAME	DATE OF FINAL REPORT	MAIN RECOMMENDATIONS	IMPLEMENTATION
Royal Commission on National Development in the Arts, Letters and Sciences (Massey-Lévesque)	1951	• Limit US cultural influences • Increase funding for CBC, NFB • Establish Canada Council	• Canadian TV content regulated, 1961 • Canada Council established, 1957
Royal Commission on Broadcasting (Fowler)	1957	• Ensure Canadian-owned TV and radio across country • Secure long-term CBC funding • Establish Board of Broadcast Governors (BBG)	• Foreign ownership of non-cable TV regulated, 1958 • BBG established, 1958
Royal Commission on Publications (O'Leary)	1961	• Impose less favourable advertising and postage rates on US publications, especially *Time* and *Reader's Digest*	• New Canadian editions of US magazines prohibited, *Time* and *Reader's Digest* exempt, 1965
Special Senate Committee on Mass Media (Davey)	1970	• Implement O'Leary Commission recommendations regarding *Time* and *Reader's Digest*	• Tax exemptions eliminated for Canadian firms advertising in Canadian editions of foreign publications, 1976
Federal Cultural Policy Review Committee (Applebaum-Hébert)	1982	• Reduce CBC, NFB production • Allow ministerial control of Canada Council and other cultural agencies	• Major reductions in federal financing of CBC, 1984-1990
Task Force on Broadcasting Policy (Caplan-Sauvageau)	1986	• Increase funding for CBC • Create new public TV channels • Increase Canadian programming on private channels	• CBC / Newsworld established, 1989

nizations—many of which linked concerns about culture with demands for limits on foreign investment—began to emerge, and when nationalist opinion, according to mass-level surveys, peaked.[54] Not surprisingly, this process coincided with the emergence of other new social movements in Canada, including student, environmental, peace and feminist activism, and with an awakening elsewhere in the world to problems of US economic control.[55] In many respects, then, the growth of nationalism in progressive circles in English Canada during the late 1960s and following reflected the frustration of both liberals and socialists with the continental limits on their designs. In the cultural field, for example, US ownership, control and media spillover were viewed as major obstacles to the kinds of changes that artists and writers wanted to effect.[56]

One of the most important statements of cultural nationalist thinking in this period can be found in Margaret Atwood's 1972 study entitled *Survival*, which maintained that

> Canada is an unknown territory for the people who live in it . . . I'm talking about Canada as a state of mind, as the space you inhabit not just with your body but with your head . . . For the members of a country or a culture, shared knowledge of their place, their here, is not a luxury but a necessity. Without that knowledge, we will not survive.[57]

Atwood attempted to define the 'here' of Canada using its literature as a guide. She argued that survival, or 'hanging on, staying alive', was Canada's central symbol.[58] For Atwood, survival in the cold, harsh climate and unforgiving landscape, where death at the hands of nature's brutal winters was common, defined Canadian literature. Although she did not link this theme explicitly with the ideas of the Canada Firsters, Atwood's thesis in *Survival* and the plot line in her 1972 novel *Surfacing* echoed older themes regarding the essence of Canada as lying in its coldness and landscape, and the threat that Americanization posed to this territorial identity.[59]

A more radical statement of modern cultural nationalism appeared in Susan Crean's 1976 book, *Who's Afraid of Canadian Culture*.[60] In what began as a study of artistic touring groups, Crean developed a forceful critique not only of American influence on Canadian media, education and the arts, but also of the willingness of Canadian elites to abandon their culture 'to a continental economy that favours US monopolies'.[61] Crean argued vigorously *against* the dominance of what she termed 'Official Culture' in Canada, preferring instead a more independent, grass-roots form of cultural life.[62]

Part of what Crean was arguing for had been created, at least in formal organizational terms, by the late 1970s. Independent publishing houses such as Lorimer, New Press and House of Anansi, as well as cultural groups including the Writers' Union of Canada, the Independent Publishers' Association and the Council of Canadian Film-makers, were established during this period.[63] Closely related to their growth were efforts to include the study of Canada's culture and history within educational curricula. In particular, a series of pieces by James Steele and Robin Mathews on the 'takeover of the mind' within Canadian universities, together with articles about Americanization in various academic disciplines, argued that foreign scholars and foreign approaches were dominating university life.[64] As Steele and Mathews wrote:

> We are presently conferring degrees upon Canadian students who are often so ignorant of their own country that they are a disgrace to it, and an indictment of the degree granting institutions from which they come. More than in any other country, because of the proximity of the United States and its often oppressive influence on many aspects of Canadian life, studies in the Canadian experience should be available to every Canadian student in the fullest range and at the highest academic level possible.[65]

In large part, this problem of intellectual dependency was attributed to the influx of American-trained and, in many cases, American-born Ph.D.s to Canada.[66]

The assumption that Canadian identity was threatened directly by cultural spillover from the US had thus come full circle. Like the Canada Firsters, cultural nationalists one hundred years later were setting out—in the words of an influential report on Canadian studies by T.H.B. Symons—'to know ourselves'.[67]

Communications Policy

Nationalist efforts to define and explain Canadian identity have, since the late nineteenth century, been accompanied by parallel efforts to defend that distinctiveness. Particularly because of the cross-border transmission of US television signals, modern proponents of a cultural nationalist world view developed a specific set of policy demands regarding federal regulation of the communications media. Since the success of one of these proposals (Bill C-58, also known as the *Time/Reader's Digest* Bill) is explored in greater detail in Chapter 3, this section is confined to an examination of the ideas behind the policies.

Beliefs that new communications technologies were fundamentally re-shaping Western civilization, and that the penetration of modern mass media held very damaging implications for Canadian identity, grew increasingly popular among nationalists during the 1960s and following.[68] Based to some extent on the theoretical work of George Grant and Marshall McLuhan,[69] both then at Ontario universities, cultural nationalists proposed a series of federal policies that would restrict foreign influence in both the print and broadcast media. One of the first of these policies, following from the 1951 Massey-Lévesque report, involved the regulation of Canadian versus non-Canadian television content, while a second, following from the 1957 Fowler Commission, concerned limitations on foreign ownership of non-cable television.[70] This second policy, primarily addressed towards American broadcasters, complemented nationalist proposals to secure increased and long-term funding for the CBC, and to constrain the expansion of Canadian private-sector broadcasting.

Promoted by cultural groups including the various incarnations of the Canadian Radio League, these positions turn on a long-standing tension between 'the two dominant forces shaping the Canadian broadcasting system—nationalism and the belief in the market system'.[71] As Frank Peers describes the nationalist position,

> The second [force], unless it is checked by the first, will clearly lead to a subordination of the Canadian system to the American, if not complete absorption. Nationalism has been a protection, ensuring that the Canadian community will retain some possibility of directing broadcasting in a way that will serve our own particular ends.[72]

In other words, the defensive or what Peers terms 'protectionist' orientation of nationalist broadcasting policy mirrors offensive efforts to strengthen domestic cultural institutions (notably the CBC) and, through them, Canadian identity.

A similar set of ideas can be seen in nationalist proposals regarding the print media. With reference to foreign periodicals, a concern of cultural nationalists since the Canada Firsters, the O'Leary report recommended that tariff and tax amendments be introduced so as to limit the dominance of such magazines as *Time* and *Reader's Digest*.[73] The rationale behind these proposals was as follows: If the entry into Canada of special editions of foreign publications were limited (through amendments to the Customs Act) and if tax exemptions for Canadian advertisers in foreign periodicals were eliminated (by changes to the Income Tax Act), then the independent Canadian magazine industry would be strengthened.[74] A virtually identical strategy to limit foreign ownership of book publishers was proposed in a series of commission reports.[75] As in the case of periodicals and broadcasting, the nationalist approach to book publishing emphasized controls on foreign, primarily US, investment and, concomitantly, incentives for Canadian-owned and -produced culture.

Taken as a group, these proposals reflected the cultural nationalist view that Canadian identity was threatened by continental influences. At least since the 1930s, the corollary to this belief held that federal government intervention was appropriate and necessary in order to foster in-group culture and, at the same time, to restrict media spillover from the out-group located south of the forty-ninth parallel.

Trade Nationalism

From Confederation to King
According to the nationalist world view, Canada's trading relationship with the United States is closely linked with questions of cultural identity. Can members of the Canadian in-group develop open, free or unrestricted continental trading relations and still retain their distinctiveness? According to pan-Canadianism since the period of the National Policy, the answer is emphatically negative.

The reasons for this opposition to continental free trade—and, conversely, support for tariffs and enhanced multilateral trade—follow from a basic nationalist distrust of liberal or neo-classical economics. The *laissez-faire* operation of international markets, according to trade nationalists, ultimately leads small economies like that of Canada to be dominated by larger ones, notably that of the United States. Lacking an independent economic life, it is argued, Canada would no longer control its national destiny, would eventually lose all vestiges of an autonomous culture and identity and, ultimately, would be submerged within the continental out-group.

The origins of this approach to trade policy can be discerned in the period of Confederation itself. During the mid-nineteenth century, Canada did not spring forth from a popular uprising against imperial oppression; in the absence of a revolutionary experience to establish its foundations, the country adopted a political surrogate in the National Policy.[76] Under the terms of this nation-building vehicle, early Conservative governments established a system of protective tariffs as well as a transcontinental railway. The purposes of the National Policy were at least three-fold: first, to ensure east-west economic integration among the founding provinces of the Dominion; second, to establish the groundwork for what Donald Smiley terms 'the acquisition and subsequent development of a Western hinterland'; and third, to strengthen imperial ties and thus thwart the possibility of invasion and absorption by the US.[77] As a whole, the National Policy constituted an ambitious effort to foster east-west and minimize north-south integration.

With reference to pan-Canadianism, the National Policy is significant because it defined what would become a basic parameter of this world view for at least the next one hundred years. The Macdonald-Cartier vision of an assertive federal state that shaped economic development and, through its ties with railway and industrial interests, functioned essentially as the architect of economic life, created a virtual identity between federal state action and national interest. This key role played by the central government provided a sturdy basis for nationalist assumptions to the effect that *in-group loyalty equalled commitment to an assertive, economically intervenionist, highly regulative federal state*.

Although the tariff system within the National Policy was designed to enhance state autonomy by fostering domestic production, its effects were somewhat contradictory. According to many analysts, protective tariffs encouraged foreign as well as Canadian industrialists to build plants *behind* the tariff wall. Michael Bliss, for example, has argued that large-scale foreign investment and branch-plant development in Canada are attributable not to the post-war Liberal policies of C.D. Howe and Mackenzie King, but rather to the very protectionist terms of the Conservatives' own National Policy.[78]

Other effects of the tariff system were also clear by the turn of the century. Farmers in western Canada, for example, demanded that protectionism be eliminated in order to lower the cost of manufactured goods and permit free trade in 'natural products'.[79] Arguing that they were the victims of a National Policy bias in favour of central Canadian business interests, agricultural groups found a favourable reception among Liberal elites. In particular, Wilfrid Laurier leaned towards free trade, with its promise of increased markets, economic prosperity and, not least of all, political support in western Canada.[80]

By provoking a head-on confrontation with supporters of the National Policy, Laurier's willingness to test the limits of public support for tariffs proved disastrous on at least two occasions. Business nationalism, which during this period combined opposition to continental free trade with support for protectionism under the banner of the Conservative party, was firmly entrenched among industrialists in Toronto and Montreal. As well, it retained a powerful imperial element, immortalized in Sir John A. Macdonald's 1891 statement 'A British subject I was born and a British subject I will die,' and presented strong economic arguments that the Canadian market for manufactured goods was too small and fragile to function without protective tariffs.[81]

The full flowering of business opposition to free trade occurred during the 1911 federal election campaign, when Laurier's Liberal government was forced to defend a specific reciprocity agreement that had been negotiated with the US. In many respects, as J.L. Granatstein suggests, events in this early period 'defined the rhetoric and set the terms of the [trade] debate that continues to this day'.[82] Laurier's announcement of a continental trade agreement, primarily in natural products, was attacked directly by eighteen prominent Toronto Liberals in a statement published in the *Mail and Empire*. Known as the Manifesto of the Toronto Eighteen, this document offered ten reasons why business nationalists opposed reciprocity. These included the absence of a government mandate to negotiate free trade, as well as the threats to economic prosperity and 'national unity' posed by any abrogation of the National Policy.[83] Above all, the Manifesto argued, reciprocity would weaken 'the ties which bind Canada to the Empire' and risk a wholly undesirable 'political union with the United States'.[84] Its signatories would not permit east-west trade ties, fostered by protective tariffs, and the imperial connection that gave political identity to the Dominion to be severed at the same time—and certainly not by an agreement that 'would eventually lead to Canada's absorption into the United States'.[85]

The well-financed opposition of business nationalists, combined with extensive disunity in the Liberal party, helped to ensure a Conservative victory in 1911. Nationalist organizations including the Canadian National League (directed by Z.A. Lash of the Toronto Eighteen) and the Canadian Home Manufacturers' Association (established by the Canadian Manufacturers' Association, or CMA) in Toronto, and the Anti-Reciprocity League in Montreal circulated vast amounts of literature against free trade. According to historical accounts, pamphlets produced by the Home Manufacturers were funded by approximately $70,000 from the CMA and were distributed 'to some three hundred daily and weekly papers, which regularly printed their prepared copy'.[86]

In English Canada, this campaign against free trade succeeded in defining the 1911 elections in nationalist terms that were advantageous to the Conservatives. As party leader Robert Borden emphasized in his final speech to an audience in

Halifax, 'This [reciprocity] compact, made in secret and without mandate, points indeed to a new path. We must decide whether the spirit of Canadianism or Continentalism shall prevail on the northern half of this continent.'[87] In Quebec, the 1911 election turned on a more curious and, according to some, 'unholy' alliance.[88] By mobilizing opposition to Laurier's allegedly imperialist Naval Bill of 1910, Conservative and *Nationaliste* forces coalesced (calling themselves *Autonomistes*) and attracted strong support using an appeal that was essentially the reverse of the pro-imperial, anti-reciprocity strategy adopted in English Canada.[89]

The advent of the First World War, however, substantially altered the ways in which Anglo-Canadian nationalists could articulate their position. Critics of reciprocity, like cultural nationalists in the same period, tended to set aside or at least downplay the imperial connection, in part because the war had severely strained the British economy—thus making it difficult for Canada to rely on imperial sources of finished products, military defence or investment capital. According to Granatstein's interpretation, British weakness beginning in this era essentially 'forced Canada into the arms of the United States'; continental defence and economic links began to deepen as the imperial alternatives that Canada had pursued since the era of the National Policy disappeared.[90] As well, the imperial pillar of the nationalist world view seemed to be a social anachronism, as increasing numbers of immigrants were arriving in Canada from non-French, non-English backgrounds.[91]

Nationalism confronted these challenges at a time when most of the Western world was slipping into economic recession. The Great Depression meant unemployment for millions of Canadians and, under the circumstances, a succession of federal governments considered tariff reductions as a means of easing job losses. In both 1935 and 1938, Canada and the US agreed to limit tariffs despite the continued opposition of business interests.[92] The Manufacturers' Association and other groups that sought to protect their status in the Canadian market were unable to prevail during the 1930s, in part because of the particular economic conditions of the Depression and in part because the trade agreements in question involved selective tariff reductions rather than full-scale reciprocity.[93]

Trade nationalists continued to argue through the post-war years that the Canadian market for finished products was tiny, vulnerable and in need of tariff protection. The political risks entailed in opposing this position were clear in 1947-48, when Prime Minister William Lyon Mackenzie King withdrew from continental free trade talks. In March 1948, King confided to his diary: 'I would no more think of at my time of life and at this stage of my career attempting any movement of the kind than I would of flying to the South Pole.'[94]

Post-War Trade Debates

King's unwillingness to risk continental free trade and the conflict it would precipitate with business interests—notably the Manufacturers' Association—

was mirrored in the actions of successive Liberal and Conservative governments. Even though international pressures for tariff reduction increased under the terms of the General Agreement on Tariffs and Trade, and while periodic trade and balance-of-payments problems arose with the US, the nationalist world view continued to shape trade debate in Canada during the 1950s and 1960s. Federal governments did recognize, however, Canada's increasing integration into what was becoming a North American market; for example, the Diefenbaker government promised in 1957 to shift this pattern through increased trade with Great Britain, and the Pearson government agreed in 1964 to a managed sectoral trade agreement known as the Auto Pact.[95] Even as business groups continued to argue that industry and the larger national interest required tariffs, their position on continental trade was subject to increased scrutiny. Liberal economists including Harry Johnson, a Canadian teaching at the University of Chicago, claimed that free trade would promote economic growth and efficiency, provide a larger market for Canadian goods and prevent the US from levelling tariffs against Canadian exports. As well, Johnson questioned whether free trade necessarily entailed a loss of national identity:

> Nations have in the past practised free trade, or at least had lower barriers to trade than they now have, without losing their national identity or feeling an overwhelming urge to submerge themselves in political union with a larger country. If it were true that economic integration leads to a loss of identity, how could one explain the survival of minority and regional groups inside national boundaries, such as the Scots and Welsh in the United Kingdom or the French Canadians and Nova Scotians in Canada?[96]

Combined with global economic changes, the views of Johnson and others ultimately weakened support for tariffs and strengthened support for free trade among leading advocates of trade nationalism. In 1984, for example, the Canadian Manufacturers' Association reversed its position on free trade, a change described in one account as 'an historic shift in the climate of business opinion'.[97]

As the commitment of organized business interests was weakening, many of the same modern nationalists who endorsed limits on American media influence and (as discussed below) on foreign direct investment assumed the mantle of trade nationalism. Like their predecessors in the trade stream, most rejected *laissez-faire* economics and maintained that tariffs were essential to Canadian independence. Writing in the aftermath of the 1971 surcharge on processed materials imposed by President Richard Nixon, for example, Peter C. Newman argued that tariffs constituted 'the economy's only protection against unlimited competition from the industrial giant south of the border'.[98] Continental free trade meant that Canada would become the 'hinterland supply house for the US industrial machine', the plentiful source of natural resources that could otherwise foster Canadian economic independence.[99] Foreshadowing much of the debate over the 1988 Canada-US Free Trade Agreement, Newman warned in 1971 that American finished products would overrun the Canadian market, that Canadian manufactured goods would continue to be more expensive than their US counterparts, and that the removal of tariffs 'inevitably would be followed by "harmonization" of the two countries' monetary, fiscal and social policies . . . It would be the end of the Canadian dream.'[100]

Opposition to free trade in the late twentieth century thus paralleled in many respects the older lines of pro-tariff and anti-reciprocity argumentation. Struggling against what were seen as powerful forces of market absorption, modern trade nationalists echoed the Manifesto of the Toronto Eighteen in maintaining that the free flow of goods and services offered no guarantee of Canadian independence. Indeed, as demonstrated below in Chapter 5, free trade remained the nemesis of nationalists through the 1980s; it entailed the potentially fatal weakening of an actor that had defined Confederation from its point of origin—namely, the assertive, economically interventionist federal state that regulated and moderated market forces.

By the 1980s the Manufacturers' Association and most of Canadian business had adopted a much different approach. Involved in pursuing global trading opportunities, these interests were no longer comfortable with protectionist regulation in their home market. Yet, even though the traditional carriers of the nationalist world view had changed sides, their distrust of liberal economics remained intact among a new generation of trade nationalists. Like cultural and investment activists in this same period, the latter tended towards ideologically progressive, left-of-centre views; they distrusted market mechanisms and endorsed state intervention to minimize US out-group influences over many aspects of Canadian life.[101]

Investment Nationalism

Nationalist views regarding foreign investment developed for the most part *after* nationalist positions on culture and trade had been well established. Although opposition to foreign investment, especially direct investment by multinational corporations based in the United States, dominated nationalist discourse during the 1960s and 1970s, this position constituted a relatively late addition to the pan-Canadian world view. Coming long after the Canada Firsters and the reciprocity debate of 1911, pressure to limit foreign economic control built on older concerns regarding loss of national sovereignty and independence. As argued below, however, modern nationalist beliefs regarding foreign investment tended to divide internally along left/right ideological lines (this was not so much the case with respect to culture and trade).

Early statements of nationalist unease with foreign investment appeared during the 1920s and 1930s in the pages of the *Canadian Forum* and in sections of a book-length study by the League for Social Reconstruction.[102] These writings reflected disquiet over the extent of foreign and notably US investment in the natural resource and manufacturing sectors, and were among the first to argue that foreign-controlled branch plants in these industries resulted from the Canadian tariff system. Moreover, early statements of the investment nationalist position highlighted an important shift then occurring in the type and origin of foreign capital in Canada; rather than deriving mostly from British portfolio interests, as in the past, new capital following 1920 arrived primarily from the United States in the form of direct investment.[103] A 1926 editorial in the *Forum*, entitled 'Peaceful Penetration', suggested the main lines of what was to become the investment nationalist perspective:

> If this flow of capital from the United States to Canada continues at the same rate for another ten years, practically all of our manufacturing plants and the greater part of our mines and timber limits will be owned or controlled by American capital . . . Once American capital assumes a dominant position in our industrial life it is idle to imagine that we can retain complete control over our political destiny.[104]

These statements about foreign investment, however, did not challenge increasingly close patterns of co-operation between Canada and the US. Symbolized by the signing in 1941 of the Hyde Park Agreement, which established joint military production, and by the prominence of C.D. Howe in a succession of Liberal cabinets, patterns of continental investment as well as trade became *more* rather than *less* integrated.[105] From the nationalist perspective, Howe was a key villain in this integration process, functioning as the willing and anxious comprador suitor to US direct investment.[106] For his own part, Howe believed that government and business could work together to create a stable employment environment for Canadian workers; he maintained that foreign investment was immensely preferable to no investment at all.[107] In Howe's words: 'Canada has welcomed the participation of American and other foreign capital in its industrial expansion. In Canada foreign investors are treated the same as domestic investors.'[108]

This effort to encourage business (including foreign direct) investment and to foster 'good neighbour' relations with the US as part of the Western alliance during the Cold War did not come under sustained scrutiny until the mid-1950s.[109] The year 1956 was crucial in many respects; it saw the divisive parliamentary debate over a trans-Canada pipeline from Alberta to Montreal as well as the release of the preliminary report of the Royal Commission on Canada's Economic Prospects (Gordon report).[110] The pipeline debate was important in refining the nationalist arguments of Conservative leader John Diefenbaker; by objecting to joint US participation in the Trans-Canada Pipe Lines firm that Howe had established to oversee the project, Diefenbaker drew attention to issues of foreign economic control.[111]

As well, Diefenbaker's arguments raised broader questions about national identity. Elaborated in the writings of historian Donald Creighton and philosopher George Grant, conservative nationalism of the late 1950s and following maintained that Canada was becoming 'a branch-plant satellite' under the tutelage of what Grant termed 'the party of the ruling class', the Liberals.[112] In his influential *Lament for a Nation*, published in 1965, Grant worried that the Liberals would be unable 'to maintain some independence of the American empire'; 'this lament mourns the end of Canada as a sovereign state.'[113] Many of Grant's ideas, especially his view that a submissive 'branch-plant mentality' had developed after the Second World War, formed one intellectual foundation for modern investment nationalism.[114]

The Gordon report, released in its final form in November 1957, presented the beginnings of what was to become the liberal or moderate version of this world view. An accountant, the scion of an affluent Toronto family, Walter Gordon presented a careful, well-documented study of the consequences and extent (then estimated at about 40 per cent) of foreign ownership in Canada. His report reflected a growing but still minority unease: as summarized in Table 1.2, it proposed a series of measures to increase Canadian shareholding and representation at senior levels in foreign subsidiaries, and recommended disclosure laws that would reveal the operations of branch-plant enterprises.[115]

This moderate or, in the words of Denis Smith, 'gentle' investment nationalism was pursued further in the 1963 budget of the Pearson government.[116] As Finance Minister, Gordon proposed a 30 per cent tax on non-resident takeovers of Canadian firms. This measure was withdrawn a few days later under severe pressure from many sources, including the president of the Montreal Stock Exchange, the US ambassador to Canada, major editorial writers, and conservative members of the Pearson cabinet who opposed interventionist—and especially nationalist—economic policies.[117]

Gordon subsequently resigned from the Liberal cabinet, but he rejoined it in 1967 to sponsor, through a ministerial committee on foreign investment, what ultimately became the Task Force on Foreign Ownership and the Structure of Canadian Industry. Chaired by Melville Watkins, a political economist at the University of Toronto, this task force considered the benefits and costs of foreign investment and echoed the Gordon report in endorsing new disclosure laws and additional shareholding by Canadians.[118] In response to concerns over the application in Canada of US trade law (notably the Trading with the Enemy Act), the Watkins task force recommended legislation to prevent the exercise of extraterritoriality. Finally, the 1968 report proposed the creation of two new federal agencies, one to direct domestic investment in Canadian industry (established in 1971 as the Canada Development Corporation) and the second to co-ordinate policy towards multinational firms.[119]

The Watkins task force is probably best known, however, for raising the expectations of investment nationalists, who were subsequently frustrated by what they perceived to be the inaction of the Trudeau government. As a result, two new organizational vehicles were established to pressure for nationalist investment

TABLE 1.2   MAJOR FEDERAL REPORTS ON INVESTMENT POLICY, 1957–1972

NAME	DATE OF FINAL REPORT	MAIN RECOMMENDATIONS	IMPLEMENTATION
Royal Commission on Canada's Economic Prospects (Gordon)	1957	• Limit foreign and especially US economic control via • Increased number of Canadians in senior positions in multinational corporations (MNCs) • Increased Canadian suppliers of and ownership in MNCs • Disclosure laws re. operations of Canadian subsidiaries	• Tax on corporate dividends to non-Canadians, 1960, 1963
Foreign Ownership and the Structure of Canadian Industry (Watkins)	1968	• Establish agency to monitor MNCs • Establish agency to encourage Canadian investment (Canada Development Corp., CDC) • Prevent application of US trade laws in Canada (extra-territoriality)	• Foreign takeovers blocked by Cabinet in uranium and oil industries, 1969 & 1971 • CDC established, 1971
Standing Committee on External Affairs and National Defence (Wahn)	1970	• Establish 51 per cent Canadian ownership target in economy	
Foreign Direct Investment in Canada (Gray)	1972	• Establish agency to screen foreign investment	• Foreign Investment Review Agency (FIRA) established, 1973

policies.[120] The first of these groups, the Waffle wing in the New Democratic Party, emerged in 1969 under the leadership of Watkins and James Laxer, another Toronto-based political economist. Along with Cy Gonick, Gad Horowitz and other Waffle activists, Watkins and Laxer viewed themselves as radical heirs of the *Forum* tradition of socially progressive nationalism, and of the Canadian political economy tradition of Harold Innis, which warned against the dangers of a dependent 'staple' or resource-extracting economy.[121] Moreover, because Wafflers believed that the goals of economic nationalism and socialism were inseparable, they suspected that even the limited reforms recommended by the Watkins report would not be pursued by a Liberal government.[122]

Writing in a new generation of nationalist periodicals, including *Canadian Dimension* and *This Magazine is About Schools*, Wafflers proposed a distinctly Canadian social movement—independent of the New Left in the US—to lead the country towards both independence and socialism. Their 1969 statement, entitled 'For an Independent Socialist Canada' and known as the Waffle Manifesto, focussed on foreign control and proposed a socialist response to Americanization:

> American corporate capitalism is the dominant factor shaping Canadian society. In Canada American economic control operates through the formidable medium of the multi-national corporation. The Canadian corporate elite has opted for a junior partnership with these American enterprises. Canada has been reduced to a resource base and consumer market within the American empire . . . Relevant instruments for bringing the Canadian economy under Canadian ownership and control and for altering the priorities established by corporate capitalism are to hand. They include extensive public control over investment and nationalization of the commanding heights of the economy, such as the key resources industries, finance and credit, and industries strategic to planning our economy.[123]

Statements by the Waffle were equally critical of US control of trade unions in Canada. Following from efforts during the same period to establish an independent Canadian union movement, Wafflers emphasized the significance of autonomy in working-class organizations that were, in many cases, affiliates of US-based internationals.[124]

At its peak during the early 1970s, the Waffle operated its own mailing list of approximately 1,500 names and sponsored James Laxer's campaign for the federal NDP leadership.[125] His loss in 1971 to the candidate of the party and union establishments, David Lewis, marked the beginning of a vigorous purge of Waffle influence both within the federal NDP and, under the direction of Lewis's son Stephen, in the Ontario party.

A second organizational response to the Watkins report was the establishment in September 1970 of the Committee for an Independent Canada. Founded by Walter Gordon, who had retired from federal politics in 1968, Peter C. Newman, then editor-in-chief of the *Toronto Star*, and Abraham Rotstein, then editor of the *Canadian Forum* and professor of political economy at the University of Toronto, the Committee aimed to steer investment nationalism towards a moderate ground, away from the radical and politically marginal turf inhabited by the Waffle.[126] In Rotstein's words: 'It was clear to those of us who founded the Committee that many people in Canada were not going to move in the direction of socialism as a precondition for independence. In our view, we needed a more broadly based movement.'[127] The Committee for an Independent Canada focussed initially on gathering support for a petition that demanded government action on foreign investment. As a coalition of prominent Liberals, notably Walter Gordon, and Conservatives, including Toronto lawyer Eddie Goodman, the group arranged a brief meeting with Prime Minister Trudeau in June 1971, at which the petition and approximately 170,000 signatures were presented.[128]

The growing tide of public concern regarding foreign investment, raised in the Gordon and Watkins reports and reinforced by the activities and prolific writings of Waffle and Committee participants, moved towards a crest in this period.[129] The Arctic voyage of the *USS Manhattan* in 1969 renewed questions about territorial sovereignty, the Wahn report of 1970 reiterated earlier royal commission and task force recommendations regarding the need for controls on investment and extra-territoriality and, perhaps most damaging of all, the 1971 Nixon surcharge on processed materials revealed for many Canadians the failings of exceptionalism or any 'special relationship' with the US.[130]

Given this environment, the Trudeau government agreed to respond in part to one of the Watkins task force's recommendations. In 1971, the Liberals established the Canada Development Corporation (CDC), a state holding company designed to operate as a profit-seeking private enterprise.[131] In introducing the enabling legislation, Finance Minister Edgar Benson stated that Canadian entrepreneurs would steer the CDC 'to areas of critical importance in economic development', notably high technology and natural resources, thus bolstering Canadian control in key sectors.[132]

Public concern regarding foreign control increased through the mid-1970s despite the creation of the CDC. Investment nationalists of all ideological varieties maintained that the holding company was only a partial response to fundamental problems of industrial development. As articulated in the 1972 report of the Task Force on Foreign Investment, headed by Liberal MP Herb Gray, external economic control was continuing to grow, causing Canada to assume the characteristics of a truncated, dependent, branch-plant economy.[133] The Gray report estimated that foreign investment had reached 60 per cent in the manufacturing sector and 90 per cent in the rubber and petroleum industries.

Entitled *Foreign Direct Investment in Canada*, the report presented yet another statement of liberal investment nationalism. It recommended administrative review of all new investment by a federal screening agency: firms would be required to demonstrate the *need* for and *innovativeness* of their products in Canada, the *technology* that would be introduced, the *jobs* that would result and the resultant *procurement* of supplies and services in Canada.[134] Overall, the Gray report concluded that foreign investments that did not offer a net contribution to the Canadian economy should be vetoed by the federal screening agency.

By 1972, the moderate or liberal nationalist view of foreign investment had thus congealed: it maintained that increasing ownership, control and direction of the economy by non-Canadian interests meant that the country would gradually cease to be sovereign. According to this outlook, foreign investment threatened Canadian independence because it converted important sectors of the economy—especially manufacturing and natural resources—into dependencies of foreign corporations. The Gray report pressed this position one step further, demanding a national industrial strategy within which to guide and plan federal screening decisions. Radical investment nationalists went further still, of course, by linking economic independence to the broader process of socialist transformation.[135]

In 1973, a Liberal minority government introduced legislation to create the Foreign Investment Review Agency (FIRA).[136] Like the CDC as it was implemented following the Watkins report, FIRA as established after the Gray report received only lukewarm support from investment nationalists. As Walter Gordon later observed:

> I do not think that either of these initiatives amounts to very much. The CDC was launched with considerable reservations and changes from the original concept. FIRA, in my humble opinion, is basically a big joke on the Canadian public.[137]

According to its moderate and radical critics, FIRA lacked straightforward criteria for assessing foreign investment and, furthermore, was not attached to any overarching national industrial strategy.[138]

Although investment nationalists were frustrated with what seemed to be their lack of influence on government policy, opinion polls from this same period suggest that nationalists did shape public attitudes. Gallup surveys show that approximately 71 per cent of Canadians in 1975 believed that the country had enough US investment, compared with a level of 52 per cent in 1961.[139] These levels generally declined through the 1980s, when Conservative Prime Minister Brian Mulroney replaced FIRA with Investment Canada and declared that Canada was 'open for business'.[140]

Natural Resource Policy

Just as communications policy was a prominent concern of cultural nationalists, natural resource policy commanded a pivotal and in many respects parallel position among investment nationalists. Because it connected older ideas about the territorial and natural endowments that defined Canada with a fundamental concern that Canadians were losing control of key economic sectors, the natural resource issue represented a rallying-point for investment nationalists of all ideological stripes.[141] The specific details of their influence on energy policy during the 1970s and early 1980s are discussed at length in Chapter 4; this section considers only the general beliefs underlying that pressure.

The Waffle Manifesto was one of the first published statements to argue that majority foreign control in the natural resource industry required a shift in the direction of 'Canadianization'.[142] This view was later presented in more moderate terms by the Committee for an Independent Canada, and was propelled to the political forefront by a number of events including the attempted foreign takeovers of Denison Mines in 1969 and Home Oil in 1971 (both of which were blocked by the federal cabinet), the 1973 OPEC oil embargo and lengthy debates over the Mackenzie Valley pipeline proposal. The basic idea that domestic energy reserves should not be controlled by subsidiaries of US multinational corporations was not new,[143] but it was given new force in the Gray report, which argued that continued dependence on the extraction of natural resources—while offering some economic stability—produced a 'truncated' or abbreviated form of industrial development.[144]

The 1974 creation of Petro-Canada was a partial response to nationalist concerns about domestic control and technological development in this sector; subsequently, in 1980, the National Energy Program (NEP) took these same beliefs further still. Building on older investment arguments, the NEP proposed to increase Canadian ownership and control of the oil industry to 50 per cent by 1990 (termed 'opportunity'), to ensure oil self-sufficiency by 1990 ('security') and 'to establish a petroleum pricing and revenue-sharing regime that recognizes the requirements of *fairness* to all Canadians no matter where they live'.[145]

In embarking on what Glen Toner describes as 'an interventionist, nationalist and centralist political and policy initiative', the federal Liberal government was warmly applauded by most investment nationalists.[146] The NEP was harshly criticized, however, by supporters of a more *laissez-faire*, decentralist and regionalist approach to economic policy. It is to these broader conflicts surrounding the pan-Canadian world view that we now turn our attention.

The Limits of Nationalist Discourse

This brief review of resource policy points towards a number of problems that have acted as limits or brakes on the nationalist world view. These problems have tended to restrict the practical application of important nationalist ideas in Canada, including the intensely territorial definition of national identity which they provide and their attention to the asymmetry of Canada-US relations in many fields.

Boldly stated, pan-Canadianism faces serious problems in its treatment of both in-group and out-group categories. The ability of this perspective to differentiate between Canadians and Americans and to generate a convincing sense of 'Canadianness' has been problematic. As a result, the nationalist world view remains a minority perspective at most times, an outlook that is limited by the pull of competing political identities within Canada and by the reality of broader continental and global influences.

Pan-Canadianism has not had an easy task with reference to the continental out-group. In arguing for the distinctiveness of Canada on the North American continent, it has relied on arguments dating back to the Canada Firsters regarding the chaotic, undisciplined and unattractive republicanism of the United States. By painting Canada as a more calm and consensual democracy, defined by its harsher and colder landscape, and anchored to firm British notions of parliamentary government and constitutional monarchy, the nationalist world view has attempted to assert the inherent differentness and, indeed, inferiority of the US out-group.

While conceptually this argument seems straightforward, putting it into operation is more difficult. Canadians may be convinced that the US has more crime, urban decay, drug abuse, guns and poverty—as nationalists were quick to claim during the 1985-88 free trade debate—but many also admire elements of American society. Whether they believe that the US offers greater opportunities for professional advancement, that it is somehow more 'free' and innovative, or that it is simply a warm and friendly place that differs little from Canada, the effect remains clear.[147] Nationalists have a hard time distinguishing between in- and out-group when the out-group seems quite similar and quite attractive to considerable numbers among the in-group.

Even within this in-group category, moreover, the nationalist world view has faced major problems. Above all, it has attempted to define identity among members of a society who hold multiple identities—whether French/English, regional, multicultural, ideological or otherwise. Nationalist views of Canada tend to reflect the particular identities of the carriers of this world view and, with few exceptions, these perspectives have been distinctly centralist, central Canadian and interventionist.[148] With even fewer exceptions, the voices of this nationalism have been overwhelmingly English Canadian.[149] Each of these identities has shaped the character of pan-Canadian nationalism, and each has in some respect limited its influence.

One crucial problem follows from the pan-Canadian preference for strong federal government as opposed to jurisdictional decentralization. Kim Nossal observes that 'the state is critical to the nationalist perspective, because it is cast as the primary vehicle for asserting and maintaining the separate existence of the nation'.[150] Faced with what they see as a looming threat of continental integration, pan-Canadian nationalists have viewed aggressive action by a powerful federal government as the best possible in-group bulwark against out-group interference.

Pan-Canadianism thus rests its case on a vision of federal supremacy and authority that is at odds with the decentralist reality of Confederation in the late twentieth century. Particularly with reference to federal regulation in the communications and natural resource fields, the equation that this world view posits between national interest and federal action, and its virtual exclusion of 'province' as a relevant unit of analysis, leave it wide open to challenge.[151] Donald Smiley summarized this 'major deficiency' of pan-Canadianism as follows: 'it fails to come to grips with the federal dimension of Canada and in particular [with] provincial economic nationalisms and the complications of the federal-provincial division of powers over economic matters.'[152] Conflicting perceptions of federalism were clearly evident in debates over the National Energy Program, when provinces that produced oil (notably Alberta) rejected what seemed to be a federal jurisdictional and fiscal grab concealed under the cloak of investment nationalism.[153]

Debates over the NEP revealed other limitations in the pan-Canadian world view. Given that the federal criterion of 'fairness' distinguished between mostly western oil-producing regions and primarily central Canadian consuming areas, the NEP tended to reinforce older perceptions that nationalism was conceived in, and for the purpose of benefitting, Ontario's interests. Pan-Canadianism thus remained constrained through the 1980s by its conception of a single national interest and a single national identity, and by its assertion that both were appropriately advanced through active federal regulation.[154]

One of the most severe indictments of pan-Canadianism from a regional perspective is presented by David Elkins and Richard Simeon. In *Small Worlds: Provinces and Parties in Canadian Political Life*, Elkins and Simeon state quite directly that 'the richness and multiple dimensions of regional diversity mean that no vision of a homogeneous "One Canada" is either possible or desirable.'[155] In other words, the unitary perspective of pan-Canadianism negates what Elkins and Simeon view as the regional essence of national identity.

Questions of cultural bias also follow from this discussion of the pan-Canadian world view. Clearly, modern nationalist writers and activists have held far more sympathetic views of Quebec than did the Canada Firsters.[156] In fact, as argued in the Preface to this book, modern nationalists reflect an exceptionally tolerant, open-minded and socially progressive perspective. However, their emphasis on what Elkins and Simeon refer to as the 'One Canada' thesis means that the concurrent ambitions of Quebec nationalists have posed enormous conceptual—not to mention political—difficulties.

Writing in 1966, Frank Underhill observed that English Canadian nationalists were 'a little bit romantic' in their efforts to unite French and English cultures within a single national project.[157] Like the authors of the Waffle Manifesto, the founders of the Committee for an Independent Canada actively sought support in Quebec and, for a time, *Le Devoir* editor Claude Ryan was an active participant in the CIC.[158] Yet by the fall of 1971, following the release of a leaked version of the Gray report, Ryan had lost patience with what he saw as a tendency to 'ignore almost completely the existence of two different societies in Canada'.[159] Ryan went on to build a career in Quebec provincial politics, while his English Canadian colleagues in the Committee debated how pan-Canadianism could be reconciled with the reality of an increasingly independentist Quebec national-ism.[160] It seemed that commitment to a strong federal government as the prin-cipal political vehicle of the in-group meant that pan-Canadianism would continue to reject demands for decentralization from regional interests in western Canada and, above all, from Quebec nationalists.[161] (Chapter 7 will return to this complex relationship between Quebec and English Canadian nationalisms.)

Finally, pan-Canadianism has in each period of its development contained a particular set of ideological lenses or filters. In the era of the Canada Firsters and reciprocity, according to Carl Berger, its flavour was distinctly tory: 'these imperialists adhered, sometimes in an inarticulate way, to the traditional con-servative conceptions which envisaged society as composed of functionally and organically related parts knit together by the impalpable filaments of mutual obligation and history.'[162]

With the growth of cultural nationalism in progressive circles during the 1920s and 1930s, the emergence of modern pan-Canadianism as a distinctly left-of-centre phenomenon was set in motion. Although a stream of trade nationalism existed in the business community, at least until the Canadian Manufacturers' Association changed its position in 1984, and although a tory nationalist streak was present in the ideas of John Diefenbaker, Donald Creighton and George Grant, it is clear that the organized mainstream of mod-ern pan-Canadianism would remain ideologically left-of-centre.[163] Most na-tionalists, particularly since the end of the Second World War, endorsed assertive federal intervention to defend national culture, to resist continental trade flows and to assert domestic economic control in the face of growing foreign investment. In short, the pan-Canadian world view has tended to reject laissez-faire economics—a pattern that helps to explain the opposition status of nationalist interests following the election of market-oriented Conservative governments during the 1980s.

This ideological colouring meant that pan-Canadian nationalism became po-litically wedged during the same decade. At the federal level, New Democrats and Liberals both advocated interventionist policies, meaning that nationalist ideas at times became a focal point for competition between the two main opposition parties. This wedging within larger political struggles, particularly on the free trade issue in the years 1985-88, meant that the public face of pan-Canadian nationalism seemed identifiably left—as well as centralist, En-glish-speaking, and central Canadian.

In short, the nationalist world view had equated a powerful, interventionist federal state with the defence of in-group interests. In so doing, it risked nar-rowing its support base among that same in-group.

In Chapters 2 through 5, we explore the policy implications of pan-Canadian ideas, returning once again to the limits of this perspective in Chapters 6 through 8.

Notes

[1]Carl Berger, *The Sense of Power: Studies in the Ideas of Canadian Imperialism, 1867-1914* (Toronto: University of Toronto Press, 1970), 9.

[2]On the nationalist critique of Canadian foreign policy, see Stephen Clarkson (ed.), *An Independent Foreign Policy for Canada* (Toronto: McClelland and Stewart, 1968).

[3]See Eddie Goodman, *Life of the Party: The Memoirs of Eddie Goodman* (Toronto: Key Porter, 1988), chap. 17.

[4]Denis Stairs, 'North American Continentalism: Perspectives and Policies in Canada', in David M. Cameron (ed.), *Regionalism and Supranationalism* (Montreal: Institute for Research on Public Policy, 1981), 85.

[5]Walter L. Gordon's contributions include the Royal Commission on Canada's Economic Prospects, *Final Report* (Gordon Report; Ottawa: Queen's Printer, 1957); *Troubled Canada: The Need for New Domestic Policies* (Toronto: McClelland and Stewart, 1961); *A Choice for Canada: Independence or Colonial Status* (Toronto: McClelland and Stewart, 1966); *Storm Signals: New Economic Policies for Canada* (Toronto: McClelland and Stewart, 1975); *A Political Memoir* (Toronto: McClelland and Stewart, 1977); and *What is Happening to Canada* (Toronto: McClelland and Stewart, 1978).

Peter C. Newman's publications in this area include *Renegade in Power: The Diefenbaker Years* (Toronto: McClelland and Stewart, 1963); 'The U.S. and Us: A Four-Part Report', *Maclean's* (6 June 1964); *The Distemper of Our Times: Canadian Politics in Transition, 1963-1968* (Toronto: McClelland and Stewart, 1968); 'Economic Union with the U.S. Would Doom Canada', *Toronto Star* (9 Oct. 1971); and *Sometimes a Great Nation: Will Canada Belong to the 21st Century?* (Toronto: McClelland and Stewart, 1988), 13-39.

Abraham Rotstein's writings include two studies co-edited with Gary Lax: *Independence: The Canadian Challenge* (Toronto: Committee for an Independent Canada, 1972) and *Getting it Back: A Program for Canadian Independence* (Toronto: Clarke, Irwin, 1974); as well as *The Precarious Homestead* (Toronto: New Press, 1973); 'Canada: The New Nationalism', *Foreign Affairs* 55 (1976), 97-118; 'Is There an English-Canadian Nationalism?' *Journal of Canadian Studies* 13 (1978), 109-18; and *Rebuilding from Within: Remedies for Canada's Ailing Economy* (Toronto: Lorimer, 1984).

[6]Cy Gonick's publications include 'Foreign Ownership and Political Decay', in Ian Lumsden (ed.), *Close the 49th Parallel Etc.: The Americanization of Canada* (Toronto: University of Toronto Press, 1970), 43-73; *Inflation or Depression: The Continuing Crisis of the Canadian Economy* (Toronto: Lorimer, 1975); and *The Great Economic Debate* (Toronto: Lorimer, 1987).

James Laxer's writings include *The Energy Poker Game* (Toronto: New Press, 1970); 'Introduction to the Political Economy of Canada', in Robert M. Laxer (ed.), *(Canada) Ltd.: The Political Economy of Dependency* (Toronto: McClelland and Stewart, 1973), 26-41; *Oil and Gas* (Toronto: Lorimer, 1983); *Rethinking the Economy* (Toronto: NC Press, 1984); and *Leap of Faith: Free Trade and the Future of Canada* (Edmonton: Hurtig, 1986).

Mel Watkins's contributions include *Foreign Ownership and the Structure of Canadian Industry: Report of the Task Force on the Structure of Canadian Industry* (Watkins Report; Ottawa: Queen's Printer, 1968); 'The Dismal State of Economics in Canada', in Lumsden (ed.), *Close the 49th Parallel Etc.*, 197-208; 'The Multi-National Corporation and Socialism', in Laurier LaPierre et al., *Essays on the Left* (Toronto: McClelland and Stewart, 1971), 201-8; 'The Staple Theory Revisited', *Journal of Canadian Studies* 12 (1977); and 'The Case Against United States-Canada Free Trade', *Canada-United States Law Journal* 10 (1985), 89-96.

[7]Kari Levitt, *Silent Surrender: The Multinational Corporation in Canada.* (Toronto: Gage, 1970); Ian Lumsden (ed.), *Close the 49th Parallel Etc.: The Americanization of Canada* (Toronto: University of Toronto Press, 1970); Philip Resnick, *The Land of Cain: Class and Nationalism in English Canada, 1945-1975* (Vancouver: New Star, 1977); Glen Williams, *Not for Export: Toward a Political Economy of Canada's Arrested Industrialization* (Toronto: McClelland and Stewart, 1986); Stephen Clarkson, *Canada and the Reagan Challenge: Crisis in the Canadian-American Relationship* (Toronto: Lorimer, 1985); and Gordon Laxer, *Open for Business: The Roots of Foreign Ownership in Canada* (Toronto: Oxford University Press, 1989).

[8]Stephen Clarkson, 'Anti-Nationalism in Canada: The Ideology of Mainstream Economics', *Canadian Review of Studies in Nationalism* 5 (1978), argues that pan-Canadian nationalism is not a governing but rather a minority, opposition ideology, while continentalism is the reverse (45-65).

[9]Goldwin Smith, *Canada and the Canadian Question* (Toronto: University of Toronto Press, 1971; rpt of 1891 ed.); Samuel E. Moffett, *The Americanization of Canada* (Toronto: University of Toronto Press, 1972; rpt of 1907 ed.); Harry G. Johnson, *The Canadian Quandary* (Toronto: McGraw-Hill, 1963); and Peter Brimelow, *The Patriot Game: Canada and the Canadian Question Revisited* (Toronto: Key Porter, 1986).

[10]Publications generally opposed to the trade agreement included Laxer, *Leap of Faith*; John W. Warnock, *Free Trade and the New Right Agenda* (Vancouver: New Star, 1988); Duncan Cameron (ed.), *The Free Trade Papers* (Toronto: Lorimer, 1986); Cameron (ed.), *The Free Trade Deal* (Toronto: Lorimer, 1988); and Laurier LaPierre (ed.), *If You Love this Country* (Toronto: McClelland and Stewart, 1988). Studies favourable to the agreement included John Crispo (ed.), *Free Trade: The Real Story* (Toronto: Gage, 1988); Gilbert Winham, *Trading with Canada: The Canada-U.S. Free Trade Agreement* (New York: Twentieth Century Fund, 1988); Richard Lipsey and Murray Smith, *Taking the Initiative: Canada's Trade Options in a Turbulent World* (Toronto: C.D. Howe Institute, 1985); and Earle Gray (ed.), *Free Trade, Free Canada: How Free Trade Will Make Canada Stronger* (Woodville, Ont.: Canadian Speeches, 1988).

[11]One of the few exceptions to this pattern was Kim Richard Nossal, 'Economic Nationalism and Continental Integration: Assumptions, Arguments and Advocacies', in Denis Stairs and Gilbert R. Winham (eds), *The Politics of Canada's Economic Relationship with the United States*, Royal Commission Research Studies, vol. 29 (Toronto: University of Toronto Press for Supply and Services Canada, 1985), 55-94.

[12]On the 1911 election, see W.M. Baker, 'A Case Study of Anti-Americanism in English-Speaking Canada: The Election Campaign of 1911', *Canadian Historical Review* 51 (1970), 426-49; Paul Stevens (ed.), *The 1911 General Election: A Study in Canadian Politics* (Toronto: Copp Clark, 1970); and Robert Craig Brown and Ramsay Cook, *Canada 1896-1921: A Nation Transformed* (Toronto: McClelland and Stewart, 1974), 180-7.

Other contributions to this literature include Berger, *The Sense of Power*; Peter H. Russell (ed.), *Nationalism in Canada* (Toronto: McGraw-Hill, 1966); Ramsay Cook, *The Maple Leaf Forever: Essays on Nationalism and Politics in Canada* (Toronto: Macmillan, 1971); Cook, *Canada, Quebec and the Uses of Nationalism* (Toronto: McClelland and Stewart, 1986); J.L. Granatstein, 'Free Trade Between Canada and the United States: The Issue that Will not Go Away', in Stairs and Winham (eds.), *The Politics of Canada's Economic Relationship with the United States*, 11-54; R.D. Cuff and J.L. Granatstein, *Ties That Bind: Canadian-American Relations in Wartime from the Great War to the Cold War* (Toronto: Hakkert, 1977); and Denis Smith, *Gentle Patriot: A Political Biography of Walter Gordon* (Edmonton: Hurtig, 1973).

[13]See John Fayerweather, *Foreign Investment in Canada: Prospects for a National Policy* (Toronto: Oxford University Press, 1974); Fayerweather, *The Mercantile Bank Affair: A Case Study of Canadian Nationalism and a Multinational Firm* (New York: New York University Press, 1974); and Isaiah A. Litvak and Christopher J. Maule, *Cultural Sovereignty: The Time and Reader's Digest Case in Canada* (New York: Praeger, 1974).

[14]Stairs, 'North American Continentalism'.

[15]Ibid., 86.

[16]Nossal, 'Economic Nationalism and Continental Integration', 59-62.

[17]On ethnic and racial approaches to nationalism, see Elie Kedourie, *Nationalism* (2nd ed.; London: Hutchinson, 1961); and Louis L. Snyder, *The Idea of Racialism* (Princeton: Princeton University Press, 1962). A critique of Kedourie's ideas is presented in Anthony H. Birch, *Nationalism and National Integration* (London: Unwin Hyman, 1989), 30-4. Birch spent much of his academic career in Canada, but focusses on questions of nationalism and national integration in Canada through the lens of Quebec nationalism; he refers only obliquely to the existence of other nationalisms in the country.

[18]This alternative to racial and ethnic approaches is drawn from Nossal, 'Economic Nationalism and Continental Integration', 59-62.

[19]Birch, Nationalism and National Integration, 4.

[20]John Breuilly, Nationalism and the State (Manchester: Manchester University Press, 1982), 3.

[21]Ibid., 11.

[22]I thus take issue with views that Canadian class structure or the international affiliations of leading trade unions by themselves explain the weakness of pan-Canadianism. See, for example, D. Drache, 'The Canadian Bourgeoisie and its National Consciousness', in Lumsden (ed.)., Close the 49th Parallel Etc., 3-25; Gary Teeple, 'Introduction', in Teeple (ed.), Capitalism and the National Question in Canada (Toronto: University of Toronto Press, 1972), x-xv; and G. Laxer, Open for Business. For a political explanation that is closer to the argument of this study, see Drache's later work, including 'The Enigma of Canadian Nationalism', Australian and New Zealand Journal of Sociology 14 (1978), 310-21.

[23]Max Weber, 'The Social Psychology of World Religions', in From Max Weber: Essays in Sociology, trans. Hans H. Gerth and C. Wright Mills (New York: Oxford University Press, 1946).

[24]Ibid., 284-5.

[25]Max Weber, 'The Fundamental Concepts of Sociology', in The Theory of Social and Economic Organization, trans. A.M. Henderson and Talcott Parsons (New York: Free Press, 1964); and Karl Mannheim, 'On the Interpretation of Weltanschauung', in Kurt H. Wolff (ed.), From Karl Mannheim (New York: Oxford University Press, 1971), 8-58.

[26]Mannheim added a third 'stratum of meaning', which he termed 'documentary or evidential meaning'. See Mannheim, 'On the Interpretation of Weltanschauung', 19 and, for explanation, Wolff, 'Introduction' to From Karl Mannheim, xix-xx.

[27]Weber, 'The Fundamental Concepts of Sociology', 88.

[28]Baker, 'A Case Study of Anti-Americanism in English-Speaking Canada'. An important dissident voice in this period was that of Henri Bourassa, founder of Le Devoir, who clearly rejected the imperial connection. Bourassa's brand of pan-Canadianism was predicated on Anglo-French unity, resistance to Americanization, and opposition to imperial domination. See Bourassa's writings in H.D. Forbes (ed.), Canadian Political Thought (Toronto: Oxford University Press, 1985), 177-93.

[29]Mair as quoted in Berger, The Sense of Power, 65.

[30]Robert Craig Brown, 'Canadian Opinion After Confederation, 1867-1914', in S.F. Wise and Robert Craig Brown, Canada Views the United States: Nineteenth-Century Political Attitudes (Toronto: Macmillan, 1967), 98-120. See also Berger, The Sense of Power, chap. 6.

[31]See Craig Brown, 'The Nationalism of the National Policy', in Russell (ed.), Nationalism in Canada, 155-63.

[32]Carl Berger, 'The True North Strong and Free', in Russell (ed.), Nationalism in Canada, 3-26. See also Michael Burgess, 'Canadian Imperialism as Nationalism: The Legacy and Significance of the Imperial Federation Movement in Canada', in Burgess (ed.), Canadian Federalism: Past, Present and Future (Leicester University Press, 1990).

[33]Parkin as quoted in Berger, 'True North Strong and Free', 9.

[34]Denison as quoted in Berger, The Sense of Power, 164.

[35]Ibid., 109.

[36]See J. Russell Harper, Painting in Canada: A History (2nd ed.; Toronto: University of Toronto Press, 1977), chap. 22; and Ramsay Cook, 'Cultural Nationalism in Canada', in Janice L. Murray (ed.), Canadian Cultural Nationalism (New York: New York University Press, 1977), 27-9. Cook's essay also appears in his Canada, Quebec and the Uses of Nationalism, chap. 8.

[37]At least one leading nationalist despaired of this legacy. Abraham Rotstein described the territorial or spatial preoccupations of English-Canadian nationalism as 'mappism', and argued that these concerns tended to overshadow urgent cultural and economic questions. See Rotstein, 'Is There an English-Canadian Nationalism?'

[38]For one example, see Newman, 'Foreword' to *Sometimes a Great Nation*.

[39]See Litvak and Maule, *Cultural Sovereignty*.

[40]Berger, *The Sense of Power*, 154.

[41]On these developments, see J.L. Granatstein and Peter Stevens (eds), *Forum: Canadian Life and Letters, 1920-1970* (Toronto: University of Toronto Press, 1972); and Michiel Horn, *The League for Social Reconstruction: Intellectual Origins of the Democratic Left in Canada, 1930-1942* (Toronto: University of Toronto Press, 1980).

[42]On nationalist organizations as vehicles for modernizing reform, particularly with reference to Quebec, see Charles Taylor, 'Nationalism and the Political Intelligentsia', *Queen's Quarterly* 72 (1965), 150-68.

[43]Granatstein and Stevens, 'Preface' to *Forum*, xiii.

[44]Frank H. Underhill, 'The League for Social Reconstruction', *Canadian Forum* (April 1932), reprinted in Granatstein and Stevens (eds), *Forum*, 98-9.

[45]See ibid. as well as Horn, *The League for Social Reconstruction*.

[46]On the complicated fate of pan-Canadianism in the political left in this period, see Peter Karl Kresl, 'Before the Deluge: Canadians on Foreign Ownership, 1920-1955', *American Review of Canadian Studies* 6 (1976), 86-125; and, more generally, Drache, 'The Enigma of Canadian Nationalism'.

[47]Cook, 'Cultural Nationalism in Canada', 17. More recent treatments of this issue can be found in Marc Raboy, *Missed Opportunities: The Story of Canada's Broadcasting Policy* (Montreal: McGill-Queen's University Press, 1990); and Richard Collins, *Culture, Communication and National Identity: The Case of Canadian Television* (Toronto: University of Toronto Press, 1990).

[48]Spry as quoted in Cook, 'Cultural Nationalism in Canada', 17. On the variety of other cultural organizations established during the 1920s and 1930s, see Horn, *The League for Social Reconstruction*; Litvak and Maule, *Cultural Sovereignty*, chap. 2; and Margaret Prang, 'The Origins of Public Broadcasting in Canada,' *Canadian Historical Review* 46 (1965).

[49]Royal Commission on National Development in the Arts, Letters and Sciences, *Report* (Massey-Lévesque Report; Ottawa: Queen's Printer, 1951).

[50]Ibid., 18. For a critique of the Massey-Lévesque view of American culture as 'alien', see Frank H. Underhill, 'Notes on the Massey Report', *Canadian Forum* (August 1951), reprinted in Granatstein and Stevens (eds), *Forum*, 271-4. The subsequent report of the O'Leary Commission also rejected the view 'that the culture of the American people is in some way an alien culture', but did agree that Canada is different and thus should be reported through 'Canadian eyes'. See Royal Commission on Publications, *Report* (Ottawa: Queen's Printer, 1961), 6, 70-1.

[51]Royal Commission on Broadcasting, *Report* (Fowler Report; Ottawa: Queen's Printer, 1957); and Royal Commission on Publications, *Report* (O'Leary Report; Ottawa: Queen's Printer, 1961).

[52]For an unofficial statement of this same view during the 1960s, see Frank Peers, 'The Nationalist Dilemma in Canadian Broadcasting', in Russell (ed.), *Nationalism in Canada*, 252-5. On the political context of cultural policy, see Bernard Ostry, *The Cultural Connection* (Toronto: McClelland and Stewart, 1978).

[53]In addition to the Massey-Lévesque, Fowler and O'Leary reports were the three-volume *Report* of the Special Senate Committee on Mass Media (Davey Committee; Ottawa: Queen's Printer, 1970), and the Ontario Royal Commission on Book Publishing, *Canadian Publishers and Canadian Publishing* (Toronto: Queen's Printer for Ontario, 1972).

[54]See Sylvia Bashevkin, 'Does Public Opinion Matter? The Adoption of Federal Royal Commission and Task Force Recommendations on the National Question, 1951-1987', *Canadian Public Administration* 31 (1988), 396-400.

[55]See Jean-Jacques Servan-Schreiber, *The American Challenge* (trans. of *Le Défi américain*; New York: Atheneum, 1969).

[56]Many activists interviewed for this study stated that they were not nationalists at the outset; rather, they had reluctantly reached the conclusion that their commitments to liberal internationalism,

socialism or, more recently, organized feminism were thwarted by the realities of US influence in Canada. Interviews with Paul Audley, 7 June 1990; Maude Barlow, 14 Oct. 1989; Gerald Caplan, 25 May 1990; Stephen Clarkson, 8 Aug. 1990; Marjorie Cohen, 26 Aug. 1988; Daniel Drache, 28 June 1990; James Laxer, 28 Sept. 1990.

[57]Margaret Atwood, *Survival: A Thematic Guide to Canadian Literature* (Toronto: House of Anansi, 1972), 18-19.

[58]Ibid., 33.

[59]Atwood also referred in *Survival* to the 'Canada Last opponents' of nationalism. See ibid., 17; and Atwood, *Surfacing* (Toronto: McClelland and Stewart, 1972).

[60]S.M. Crean, *Who's Afraid of Canadian Culture* (Don Mills, Ont.: General Publishing, 1976).

[61]Ibid., 5.

[62]Ibid., 10.

[63]For an overview of these developments, see M. Patricia Hindley, Gail M. Martin and Jean McNulty, *The Tangled Net: Basic Issues in Canadian Communications* (Vancouver: J.J. Douglas, 1977); Paul Audley, *Canada's Cultural Industries* (Toronto: Lorimer, 1983); and Mary Vipond, *The Mass Media in Canada* (Toronto: Lorimer, 1989).

[64]James Steele and Robin Mathews, 'The Universities: Takeover of the Mind', in Lumsden (ed.), *Close the 49th Parallel Etc.*, 169-78; Ellen and Neal Wood, 'Canada and the American Science of Politics', in Lumsden (ed.), 179-95; Watkins, 'The Dismal State of Economics in Canada', in Lumsden (ed.), 197-208; and Lynn Trainor, 'Science in Canada—American Style', in Lumsden (ed.), 241-55.

[65]Steele and Mathews, 'The Universities', 174.

[66]Ibid., 176. Steele and Mathews helped to organize a successful campaign for legislation to limit the hiring of non-Canadian faculty by Canadian universities.

[67]T.H.B. Symons, *To Know Ourselves: The Report of the Commission on Canadian Studies* (Ottawa: Association of Universities and Colleges of Canada, 1975).

[68]See, for example, Abraham Rotstein and Melville H. Watkins, 'The Outer Man: Technology and Alienation', *Canadian Forum* (August 1965), reprinted in Granatstein and Stevens (eds), *Forum*, 384-6; and Rotstein, 'Running from Paradise', *Canadian Forum* (May 1969), reprinted in Granatstein and Stevens (eds), *Forum*, 420-4.

[69]George Grant's most influential works in this period were *Lament for a Nation: The Defeat of Canadian Nationalism* (Toronto: McClelland and Stewart, 1965) and *Technology and Empire* (Toronto: Anansi, 1968). Although McLuhan's concerns about technological change, notably the alienation of individuals in an age of machines, were adopted by nationalists, his opinions regarding nationalist efforts were far from favourable. See Matie Molinaro, Corinne McLuhan and William Toye (eds), *Letters of Marshall McLuhan* (Toronto: Oxford University Press, 1987), esp. letter dated 1967 to Tom Easterbrook; and Philip Marchand, *Marshall McLuhan: The Medium and the Messenger* (Toronto: Random House, 1989).

[70]The latter recommendation was implemented in 1958, while the former, regarding content laws, was initiated in 1961. The Fowler Commission report is assessed in Thelma H. McCormack, 'Canada's Royal Commission on Broadcasting', *Public Opinion Quarterly* 23 (1959), 92-100. On the development of broadcasting policy, see Collins, *Culture, Communication and National Identity*; Raboy, *Missed Opportunities*; Frank W. Peers, *The Politics of Canadian Broadcasting* (Toronto: University of Toronto Press, 1969); Peers, *The Public Eye: Television and the Politics of Canadian Broadcasting, 1952-1968* (Toronto: University of Toronto Press, 1979); David Ellis, *Evolution of the Canadian Broadcasting System* (Ottawa: Supply and Services Canada, 1979); and Herschel Hardin, *Closed Circuits: The Sellout of Canadian Television* (Vancouver: Douglas and McIntyre, 1985). For an interesting spoof of content regulations, see Mordecai Richler, *The Incomparable Atuk* (Toronto: McClelland and Stewart, 1963).

[71]The Canadian Radio League, established in October 1930, served as the model for more recent cultural nationalist organizations including the Friends of Public Broadcasting, which changed its

name in 1988 to the Friends of Canadian Broadcasting. See Prang, 'The Origins of Public Broadcasting in Canada'; and Raboy, *Missed Opportunities*, chaps. 1, 7.

[72]Peers, 'The Nationalist Dilemma in Canadian Broadcasting', 265. For a more recent evaluation of the nationalist model of cultural policy, see Thelma McCormack, 'Culture and the State', *Canadian Public Policy* 10 (1984), 267-77.

[73]See Litvak and Maule, *Cultural Sovereignty*, chaps 1-4.

[74]Ibid., and John R. LoGalbo, 'The Time and Reader's Digest Bill: C-58 and Canadian Cultural Nationalism', *New York University Journal of International Law and Politics* 9 (1976), 237-75.

[75]See especially the *Report* of the Special Senate Committee (Davey Report) as well as Audley, *Canada's Cultural Industries*, chap. 3; Crean, *Who's Afraid of Canadian Culture*, chap. 6; and Hindley et al., *The Tangled Net*, chap. 2. In 1985, the federal Conservative government announced what came to be known as the Baie Comeau policy, which emphasized the importance of Canadian control in the publishing industry. For an assessment of Baie Comeau and other Conservative initiatives, see Stephen Godfrey, 'Is Culture Truly Excluded from Free Trade?' *Globe and Mail* (20 Jan. 1990).

[76]See Brown, 'The Nationalism of the National Policy'; Donald Smiley, 'Canada and the Quest for a National Policy', *Canadian Journal of Political Science* 8 (1975), 40-62; and the critique of nationalist 'myth-making' in Michael Bliss, *The Evolution of Industrial Policies in Canada: An Historical Survey* (Ottawa: Economic Council of Canada, 1982).

[77]Smiley, 'Canada and the Quest for a National Policy', 42.

[78]Michael Bliss, 'Canadianizing American Business: The Roots of the Branch Plant', in Lumsden (ed.), *Close the 49th Parallel Etc.*, 26-42.

[79·]'Natural products' included agricultural goods and farm machinery. See Granatstein, 'Free Trade between Canada and the United States', 21.

[80]The origins of the reciprocity agreement are difficult to identify, however. According to Stevens, *The 1911 General Election*, 'Laurier seems to have committed himself and his party to reciprocity as much by accident as by design' (1).

[81]Macdonald as quoted in Granatstein, 'Free Trade between Canada and the United States', 19.

[82]Ibid., 12.

[83·]'Manifesto of the Toronto Eighteen', reprinted in Stevens (ed.), *The 1911 General Election*, 66.

[84·]Ibid.

[85]Stevens, 'Introduction' to *The 1911 General Election*, 2.

[86]Brown and Cook, *Canada 1896-1921*, 181. The same monetary figure appears in Michael Bliss, *A Living Profit: Studies in the Social History of Canadian Business, 1883-1911* (Toronto: McClelland and Stewart, 1974), 112.

[87]Borden's speech as reprinted in Stevens (ed.), *The 1911 General Election*, 88.

[88]Stevens, *The 1911 General Election*, 147.

[89]See J. Murray Beck, *Pendulum of Power: Canada's Federal Elections* (Scarborough, Ont.: Prentice-Hall, 1968), 129-33. Henri Bourassa, editor of *Le Devoir*, was a prominent opponent of the Naval Bill in Quebec.

[90]J.L. Granatstein, *How Britain's Weakness Forced Canada into the Arms of the United States* (Toronto: University of Toronto Press, 1989).

[91]See Berger, *The Sense of Power*, chap. 5.

[92]See Ian M. Drummond and Norman Hillmer, *Negotiating Freer Trade: The United Kingdom, the United States, Canada, and the Trade Agreements of 1938* (Waterloo: Wilfrid Laurier University Press, 1989).

[93]See Granatstein, 'Free Trade between Canada and the United States', 28-33.

[94]King as quoted in ibid., 42.

[95]Diefenbaker's promise to increase Canadian trade with Great Britain by 15 per cent had no effect and, according to Granatstein, 'died quickly'. See Granatstein, 'Free Trade between Canada and the

United States', 43. On the larger question of Diefenbaker's ineffectiveness as prime minister, see Newman, *Renegade in Power*. The relationship of the Auto Pact to free trade is discussed in Granatstein, 'Free Trade between Canada and the United States', 46-7. As discussed below in Chapter 3, American pressure on the Canadian cabinet to secure a sectoral agreement helps to explain tax exemptions granted to *Time* and *Reader's Digest* during the 1960s.

[96]Johnson, *The Canadian Quandary*, 14. A special issue of the *Canadian Journal of Economics* (Winter 1978) was devoted to Johnson's contribution. For subsequent arguments in favour of free trade, see Peyton Lyon, *Canada-United States Free Trade and Canadian Independence*, Economic Council Research Study (Ottawa: Information Canada, 1975); and Economic Council of Canada, *Looking Outward: A New Trade Strategy for Canada* (Ottawa: Information Canada, 1975). For a nationalist critique of this view, see Clarkson, 'Anti-Nationalism in Canada'.

[97]Michael Bliss, *Northern Enterprise: Five Centuries of Canadian Business* (Toronto: McClelland and Stewart, 1987), 583. See also I.A. Litvak, 'Freer Trade with the U.S.: The Conflicting Views of Canadian Business', *Business Quarterly* 51 (1986), 22-32.

[98]Peter C. Newman, 'Economic Union with the U.S. Would Doom Canada', *Toronto Star* (9 Oct. 1971), reprinted in Rotstein and Lax (eds)., *Independence*, 49.

[99]Ibid.

[100]Ibid., 53.

[101]This perspective is reflected, for example, in Cameron (ed.), *The Free Trade Deal*; and in Daniel P. Drache, 'The Mulroney-Reagan Accord: The Economics of Continental Power', in Marc Gold and David Leyton-Brown (eds), *Trade-offs on Free Trade* (Toronto: Carswell, 1988), 79-88.

[102]See Kresl, 'Before the Deluge', 88-90. The LSR study was entitled *Social Planning for Canada* (Toronto: League for Social Reconstruction, 1935).

[103]For a thorough treatment of trends in foreign investment, see A.E. Safarian, *Foreign Ownership of Canadian Industry* (2nd ed.; Toronto: University of Toronto Press, 1973). Safarian's 'Introduction' distinguishes clearly between portfolio and direct investment.

[104]'Peaceful Penetration', *Canadian Forum* (February 1926), reprinted in Granatstein and Stevens (eds), *Forum*, 36-7.

[105]The Hyde Park Agreement is analysed in Cuff and Granatstein, *Ties That Bind*, chap. 4.

[106]See J. Laxer, 'Introduction to the Political Economy of Canada', 34; and David A. Wolfe, 'Economic Growth and Foreign Investment: A Perspective on Canadian Economic Policy, 1945-1957', *Journal of Canadian Studies* 13 (1978), 3-20.

[107]On Howe's pragmatism, see Robert Bothwell and William Kilbourn, *C.D. Howe: A Biography* (Toronto: McClelland and Stewart, 1979).

[108]Howe's 1954 speech to a Boston audience, as quoted in Wolfe, 'Economic Growth and Foreign Investment', 13.

[109]On the background to this period and its implications for nationalism, see Denis Smith, *Diplomacy of Fear: Canada and the Cold War, 1941-1948* (Toronto: University of Toronto Press, 1988).

[110]Royal Commission on Canada's Economic Prospects, *Report*. For accounts of the pipeline debate, see William Kilbourn, *Pipeline: Trans-Canada and the Great Debate, A History of Business and Politics* (Toronto: Clarke Irwin, 1970); and H.G. Thorburn, 'Parliament and Policy-Making: The Case of the Trans-Canada Gas Pipeline', *Canadian Journal of Economics and Political Science* 23 (1957), 516-31.

[111]See Newman, *Renegade in Power*; and Glen Toner, 'Oil, Gas, and Integration: A Review of Five Major Federal Energy Decisions', in Jon H. Pammett and Brian W. Tomlin (eds), *The Integration Question* (Don Mills, Ont.: Addison-Wesley, 1984), 227-30.

[112]Grant, *Lament for a Nation*, 90, 4. Creighton's conservative nationalism is reflected in his books *Canada's First Century, 1867-1967* (Toronto: Macmillan, 1970); *The Forked Road* (Toronto: McClelland and Stewart, 1976); *The Passionate Observer: Selected Writings* (Toronto: McClelland and Stewart, 1980); and especially *Towards the Discovery of Canada* (Toronto: Macmillan, 1972).

[113]Grant, *Lament for a Nation*, vii, 2.

[114]Ibid., 41. See also Peter C. Emberley (ed.), *By Loving Our Own: George Grant and the Legacy of Lament for a Nation* (Ottawa: Carleton University Press, 1990). Grant's ideas also helped to shape the nationalist critique of Canadian foreign policy. See, for example, Clarkson (ed.), *An Independent Foreign Policy for Canada*, the third volume in a series by the University League for Social Reform. This study and others culminated in a review of government policy and the 1972 announcement by External Affairs Minister Mitchell Sharp of Canada's 'Third Option'. See Sharp, 'Canadian-U.S. Relations: Options for the Future', *International Perspectives* (1972), 1-24; and Stairs, 'North American Continentalism'. 86-9.

[115]Royal Commission on the Economic Union, *Report*.

[116]Smith, *Gentle Patriot*.

[117]See ibid., 179; and Gordon, *A Political Memoir*, chap. 8. One of Gordon's fiercest opponents was Eric Kierans, then president of the Montreal Stock Exchange, who later became a nationalist of sorts. See John N. McDougall, 'Nationalism, Liberalism and the Political Economy of Eric Kierans', *Journal of Canadian Studies* 25 (1990), 44-71. Mitchell Sharp, an anti-nationalist at the time in the Pearson cabinet, evolved in a direction similar to that of Kierans. It should be noted that Gordon's proposed 15% tax on corporate dividends to non-residents and his depreciation advantage for Canadian firms did hold, and that a subsequent battle in cabinet over foreign control in the banking industry (the Mercantile Bank case, 1966-67) was resolved in favour of the nationalist position. See Fayerweather, *The Mercantile Bank Affair*.

[118]Task Force on Foreign Ownership and the Structure of Canadian Industry, *Report*; and Royal Commission on Canada's Economic Prospects, *Report*. A major intellectual influence on the Watkins task force was Stephen Hymer, 'Foreign Direct Investment and the National Economic Interest', in Russell (ed.), *Nationalism in Canada*, 191-202.

[119]Task Force on Foreign Ownership and the Structure of Canadian Industry, *Report*; Smith, *Gentle Patriot*, 346; and Gordon, *A Political Memoir*, 312.

[120]See Mel Watkins, 'Once Upon a Time: The Waffle Story', *This Magazine* (March-April 1989), 28-30.

[121]The importance of Innis's contribution is reflected in Mel Watkins, 'The Innis Tradition in Canadian Political Economy', *Canadian Journal of Political and Social Theory* 6 (1982), 12-34; Watkins, 'Resources and Underdevelopment', in R.M. Laxer (ed.), *Canada Ltd*, 107-26; and Watkins, 'The Staple Theory Revisited'. *The intellectual legacy of this ferment included a revitalized political economy tradition within Canadian social science and the establishment in 1979 of Studies in Political Economy*. For an overview of these developments, see Wallace Clement and Glen Williams (eds), *The New Canadian Political Economy* (Kingston: McGill-Queen's University Press, 1989).

[122]See Robert Hackett, "Pie in the Sky:" A History of the Ontario Waffle', *Canadian Dimension* (October/November 1980); and John Bullen, 'The Ontario Waffle and the Struggle for an Independent Socialist Canada: Conflict within the NDP', *Canadian Historical Review* 64 (1983), 188-215.

[123]Waffle Manifesto as reprinted in Forbes (ed.), *Canadian Political Thought*, 402, 405.

[124]The Confederation of Canadian Unions was established as an independent trade union umbrella organization in the late 1960s. For a sympathetic account of efforts to build the CCU, see Rick Salutin, *Kent Rowley, the Organizer: A Canadian Union Life* (Toronto: Lorimer, 1980). Salutin joined the CCU as an organizer in 1970, and shared the working-class nationalism of Rowley and Madeleine Parent. Interview with Rick Salutin, 22 Aug. 1990.

[125]Bullen, 'The Ontario Waffle and the Struggle for an Independent Socialist Canada', 200.

[126]See Christina Newman, 'Growing Up Reluctantly', *Maclean's* (August 1972), 58; Gordon, *A Political Memoir*, 315-16; and Goodman, *Life of the Party*, 294-7.

[127]Interview with Abraham Rotstein, 28 June 1989.

[128]See Gordon, *A Political Memoir*, 316-17.

[129]For a listing of some of these publications, see notes 5 and 6 above.

[130]See Donald Barry, 'The Politics of "Exceptionalism": Canada and the United States as a Distinctive

International Relationship,' *Dalhousie Review* 60 (1980), 114-37.

[131]See Jeanne Kirk Laux and Maureen Appel Molot, *State Capitalism: Public Enterprise in Canada* (Ithaca: Cornell University Press, 1988), 94-8; and Stephen Brooks, 'The State as Entrepreneur: From CDC to CDIC,' *Canadian Public Administration* 26 (1983), 525-43.

[132]Benson as quoted in Brooks, 'The State as Entrepreneur', 529.

[133]*Foreign Direct Investment in Canada* (Gray Report; Ottawa: Information Canada, 1972). It should be noted that a leaked version of the Gray Report was published in the December 1971 issue of the *Canadian Forum*, edited at the time by Abraham Rotstein.

[134]*See Foreign Direct Investment in Canada.*

[135]On the relationship between foreign investment and industrial strategy, see ibid., 442-3; and Richard D. French, *How Ottawa Decides: Planning and Industrial Policy-Making, 1968-1980* (Ottawa: Canadian Institute for Economic Policy, 1980), chaps 5, 6.

[136]Earlier efforts to introduce a more limited screening mechanism died on the order paper at the dissolution of parliament in 1972.

[137]Letter dated 19 March 1976 by Gordon to Stephen Clarkson, as quoted in Clarkson, 'Canadian-American Relations: Anti-Nationalist Myths and Colonial Realities', in Wallace Gagne (ed.), *Nationalism, Technology and the Future of Canada* (Toronto: Macmillan, 1976), 121.

[138]FIRA was also criticized by Charles J. McMillan, who later became a senior policy advisor to the Conservative government that dismantled FIRA and replaced it with Investment Canada. See McMillan, 'After the Gray Report: The Tortuous Evolution of Foreign Investment Policy', *McGill Law Journal* 20 (1974), 213-60. A somewhat different critical view of FIRA is presented in Carl Beigie, 'Foreign Investment in Canada: The Shading is Gray', *Columbia Journal of World Business* 7 (1972), 23-32.

[139]See Bashevkin, 'Does Public Opinion Matter', Table 4.

[140]On the change from FIRA to Investment Canada, see Arpad Abonyi, 'Government Participation in Investment Development', in Andrew B. Gollner and Daniel Salée (eds), *Canada Under Mulroney: An End-of-Term Report* (Montreal: Véhicule Press, 1988), 158-85; and Elizabeth Smythe, 'From Investment Canada to National Treatment: Canada's Foreign Investment Regime and the Canada-United States Free Trade Agreement', paper presented at Canadian Political Science Association meetings, Laval University, 1989, 8-32.

[141]The key sectors of particular concern to investment nationalists were, in addition to natural resources, the financial sector; mass communications, and particularly broadcasting; transportation; and power generation. See Litvak and Maule, 'Interest-Group Tactics and Foreign Investment', 627-9.

[142]See 'The Waffle Manifesto', in Forbes (ed.), *Canadian Political Thought*, 402-5.

[143]For a history of these positions, see John N. McDougall, *Fuels and the National Policy* (Toronto: Butterworths, 1982).

[144]*Foreign Direct Investment in Canada.*

[145]Official aims of the NEP as announced 28 Oct. 1980, reprinted in G. Bruce Doern and Glen Toner, *The Politics of Energy: The Development and Implementation of the* NEP (Toronto: Methuen, 1985), 4. Emphasis in original.

[146]Toner, 'Oil, Gas, and Integration', 238. Moderate and left nationalists tended to support the NEP, although some of the latter feared the centralist and regional consequences of the policy. See Cy Gonick, 'NEPMEN and Other Nationalists', *Canadian Dimension* (August-September 1981); and Philip Resnick, 'The Maturing of Canadian Capitalism', *Our Generation* 15 (1982).

[147]Data on these cross-border perceptions are presented in 'Special Report: Portrait of Two Nations', *Maclean's* (3 July 1989 and 25 June 1990).

[148]Obvious exceptions to this Ontario voice have included John Diefenbaker and Mel Hurtig, a publisher based in Edmonton who was active in the Committee for an Independent Canada and instrumental in organizing opposition to free trade during the 1980s.

[149]One of the only French voices in nationalist activism was that of Claude Ryan, then editor of *Le*

Devoir, who co-chaired the Committee for an Independent Canada in 1971 with Jack McClelland.

[150]Nossal, 'Economic Nationalism and Continental Integration', 60.

[151]See Hindley et al., *The Tangled Net*, 167; and Raboy, *Missed Opportunities*.

[152]Smiley, 'Canada and the Quest for a National Policy', 60. Daniel Drache presents a similar argument in 'The Enigma of Canadian Nationalism'.

[153]See David Milne, *Tug of War: Ottawa and the Provinces Under Trudeau and Mulroney* (Toronto: Lorimer, 1986), chap. 3.

[154]One of the few exceptions to this view of a single Canadian identity can be found in Crean, *Who's Afraid of Canadian Culture*, 278. Crean argues that nationalists should 'resist European and American concepts of national culture being a single, unified entity, because it obviously does not fit our heterogeneous and highly regionalized "national" culture. All too often, those who have set out in search of the Canadian identity have been looking for something that does not exist: Canadian culture as it would be if Canada were the centre of an empire.' See also Drache, 'The Enigma of Canadian Nationalism'.

[155]David J. Elkins and Richard Simeon, *Small Worlds: Provinces and Parties in Canadian Political Life* (Toronto: Methuen, 1980), x.

[156]On the cultural outlook of imperial nationalism, see Berger, *The Sense of Power*, 57.

[157]Frank Underhill, 'Foreword' to Russell (ed.), *Nationalism in Canada*, xvii.

[158]At the time that the Committee for an Independent Canada was formally established in September 1971, its founding co-chairmen were Ryan and Toronto publisher Jack McClelland. See *Historical Sketch of the Committee for an Independent Canada* (Kingston, Ont.: Queen's University Archives, August 1985).

[159]Claude Ryan, 'The Gray Report and Quebec', in Rotstein and Lax (eds), *Independence*, 172. Ryan's article was originally published in *Le Devoir*.

[160]Some activists in the Committee viewed Quebec nationalism as a threat to Canadian unity and hence pan-Canadianism, while others saw it as a parallel and in many respects inspiring movement. The treatment of Quebec nationalism also posed problems for the Waffle, according to Bullen, 'The Ontario Waffle and the Struggle for an Independent Socialist Canada', 194, 202. Some veterans of these two groups, notably Watkins and Rotstein, worked together to create the Committee for a New Constitution to pressure for a sympathetic pan-Canadian response to Quebec nationalism. See 'Canada and Quebec: A Proposal for a New Constitution', *Canadian Forum* (June-July 1977), 4-5.

[161]See Kenneth McRoberts, *Quebec: Social Change and Political Crisis* (3rd ed.; Toronto: McClelland and Stewart, 1988), 400-4, on the implications of this issue for the Meech Lake Accord.

[162]Berger, *The Sense of Power*, 197.

[163]This ideological colouration, however, stood in rather stark contrast to the highly educated and relatively affluent socio-economic status of leading nationalist activists. For critical perspectives on the middle-class nature of pan-Canadianism, see Albert Breton, 'The Economics of Nationalism', *Journal of Political Economy* 72 (1964), 376-86; Brimelow, *The Patriot Game*; S.D. Clark, 'Canada and her Great Neighbour', in S.D. Clark, *The Developing Canadian Community* (2nd ed.; Toronto: University of Toronto Press, 1968), 221-32; Johnson, *The Canadian Quandary*; and Safarian, *Foreign Ownership of Canadian Industry*, preface.

2 | From Ideas To Policies: Three Explanatory Frameworks

It would be a mistake to evoke the image of Canada as a seething colony struggling to break loose. Canada bears rather the signs of a successful lobotomy to which it has assented. The routine of daily existence is comfortable, decent and sane.[1]

Introduction

Ideas, as political activists frequently point out, constitute more than simply ends in themselves. Running with those ideas, translating a particular world view into concrete public actions and policies, is a challenge that has long confronted all kinds of political interests—including the diverse entity known as Canadian nationalism.

This chapter presents three approaches to the conversion of nationalist ideas into federal policies. Each framework or model is then employed in Chapters 3 through 5 to analyse the efforts made since the mid-1970s by cultural nationalists, to shape communications policy; by investment nationalists, to 'Canadianize' the natural resource sector; and by trade nationalists, to oppose Canada-US free trade. To borrow from Abraham Rotstein's imagery in the epigraph above, the purpose of this section is to evaluate how effectively modern nationalists have put their ideas into action, thus challenging what they view as Canada's 'lobotomized' condition.

The chapter begins with the group approach, one of the best-known conceptual frameworks in the social sciences and the one that at first glance seems most appropriate to a study of organized nationalism. A societal groups model and a series of researchable propositions regarding policy influence are distilled from this literature. Using the bureaucratic state literature as a reference point, the following section presents a second framework, which responds to weaknesses in the societal view, along with a corresponding set of research propositions. Finally, in light of problems in both the societal and bureaucratic approaches, an inclusive or *integrative* view is developed. This third model builds on the argument that a societal framework focusses exclusively on the attributes of organized groups, while a bureaucratic approach is narrowly concerned with the attributes of public administrations. Even if the two are merged in a combined state-society or network model, important limitations remain.

Chapter 2 maintains that dominant explanatory frameworks overlook the power of political ideas as well as the influence of political actors (in contrast to societal or bureaucratic players). With reference to pan-Canadianism, neither of the first two approaches questions how ideas within the nationalist world view fare among political decision-makers—whether in Canada or the United States—or, for that matter, how these ideas resonate in the media and mass public. Neither questions the translation of ideas into policies, assuming instead that societal or bureaucratic variables are by themselves sufficient to tell the story. In taking issue with prevailing approaches, Chapter 2 develops the following research propositions: first, that neither the societal nor the bureaucratic framework on its own explains the impact of Anglo-Canadian nationalism; and second, that understanding the influence of ideas is crucial to assessing policy outcomes.

In short, this chapter sets out three approaches that, to use Graham Allison's imagery, each provide a 'conceptual lens' through which to view nationalist influence.[2] The utility of the different frameworks or lenses will become clearer in the next three chapters, where each is applied; suffice it to say at this point that merging societal and bureaucratic variables with a critical focus on the political impact of nationalist ideas (in the integrative model) provides a useful framework for policy research.

Since this study compares not only the utility of competing theoretical models but also the effectiveness of nationalists across policy fields, a case study design is employed in Chapters 3 through 5.[3] Two instances of nationalist policy success are considered in Chapters 3 and 4: Bill C-58, known as the *Time/Reader's Digest* Bill, as an instrument of cultural policy, and the National Energy Program, as a vehicle for investment nationalism. By way of contrast, Chapter 5 examines the major struggle between nationalists and continentalists over Canada-US free trade, a policy that nationalists vigorously opposed. As implied by this summary, Chapters 3 through 5 do not address government action in policy areas other than culture, investment and trade nor do they consider nationalist intervention in cases other than the three cited here.

This effort to explain the conversion of ideas into action differs from previous attempts to analyse Canadian nationalism in two important respects. First, Chapters 3 through 5 compare nationalist influence across policy sectors using a design which resembles William Coleman's approach to business interest groups.[4] Rather than trying to determine whether activists 'won' or 'lost' on the basis of a single test case—for example, the outcome of the 1985-88 free trade debate—this study tries to provide a more rigorous and balanced assessment of nationalist influence on government policy. Second, Chapters 2 through 5 link the various dimensions of the world view explored in Chapter 1 with analytic questions of policy influence, thus juxtaposing abstract ideas with the real world of political action. Nationalism, we suggest, is far more than simply a set of sterile rhetorical ideas; to its adherents, it is a compelling world view that demands realization on the policy stage.

The Societal Approach

Many early efforts to assess policy influence evolved from a fundamental unease in the United States with what was known as the 'power elite' school. Represented by the post-war writings of C. Wright Mills, Floyd Hunter and other sociologists, the power elite stream maintained that a small, cohesive and at times covert elite controlled American government, thus limiting the opportunities available to non-elites for political participation.[5] The development of a competing conceptual framework that rejected power elite assumptions began in full force during the 1950s and early 1960s, when David Truman and Robert Dahl published major statements of a societal or group perspective.[6] Since the work of Truman and Dahl helped to define the parameters of this research tradition, we shall begin with a brief review of their ideas.

One of the most direct statements of the thesis that organized public groups rather than covert private elites shaped government decisions was presented in 1951 by David Truman. In *The Governmental Process*, he argued that struggles among competing groups formed the essence of democratic politics; the major function of government, in his view, was to establish and maintain orderly relations among them.[7] Truman defined an organized interest as 'any group that, on the basis of one or more shared attitudes, makes certain claims upon other groups in the society for the establishment, maintenance, or enhancement of forms of behavior that are implied by the shared attitudes'.[8] In other words, beliefs common to the adherents of an organized group formed the basis for interaction with competing groups. According to Truman, government regulated this interaction in such a way as to produce stable inter-group relations and social equilibrium. The existence of multiple points of political access for diverse interests meant that group participation in public policy-making was virtually assured.

This pluralist notion of open, balanced competition among groups was advanced further in the work of Robert Dahl. In a pivotal study of local politics in New Haven, Connecticut, Dahl argued that no single power elite but rather a set of influential groups shaped municipal decision-making.[9] Following the lines of his earlier *Preface to Democratic Theory*, Dahl treated government decisions in New Haven as responses to the varied demands of organized groups.[10]

In explaining the extent to which collective demands were satisfied, both Truman and Dahl emphasized the importance of internal group characteristics, especially organizational resources. Dahl, for example, noted that the socio-economic status, media access and education of group leaders played an important role in determining policy influence.[11] Similarly, Truman maintained that the 'strategic social position' of groups, as well as their internal organizational cohesion, helped to explain success in the policy arena.[12]

While neither Dahl nor Truman developed a concrete model of the societal paradigm, their work and that of subsequent writers suggests that four basic variables determine policy success. As outlined in Figure 2.1, these factors are

FIGURE 2.1   **SOCIETAL APPROACH TO PUBLIC POLICY**

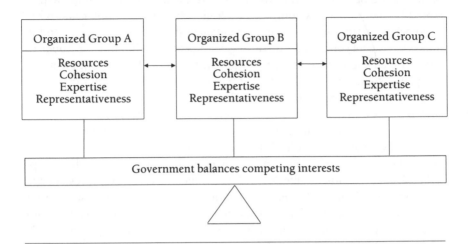

group resources, cohesion, expertise and representativeness. Each has a specific relationship to governmental action: *group resources*, in that the extent of financial and human resources controlled by a group would be positively associated with policy influence; *group cohesion*, in that the degree of organizational control, discipline and unity would be positively related to policy success; *group expertise*, in that policy and administrative knowledge would be positively associated with organizational influence; and *representativeness*, in that a favourable 'strategic position' or comprehensive group standing in a policy domain would be positively related to its success.[13]

It must be noted that these propositions follow from a literature that, for the most part, assumes between-group competition to be open, fair and ultimately resolved in favour of the interest with the highest level of resources, cohesion, expertise and representativeness. Hence it can be hypothesized that if Group A has extensive resources but only moderate cohesion, expertise and representativeness, then it is less likely to achieve its policy objectives than a competing Group B that commands extensive resources as well as high cohesion, expertise and representativeness. Group A, in turn, would be more likely to obtain policy success than a competing Group C that had only limited resources, cohesion, expertise and representativeness.

The Bureaucratic Framework

Just as the societal view developed in reaction to power-elite studies, so too have subsequent approaches evolved in response to this group model. In particular, critics have taken issue with its treatment of challenging or innovative issue areas that were not already on the public agenda. Peter Bachrach and Morton Baratz, drawing on E.E. Schattschneider's notion that 'some issues are organized into politics while others are organized out',[14] propose that the traditional group focus overlooks 'non-decisions', a realm beyond the *status quo* policy arena in which organized interests are unlikely to obtain open and unfettered access.[15]

Following Schattschneider's observation, further questions have been raised about the extent to which inter-group competition is consistent with social equality. As neo- or post-pluralist writers acknowledge, societal interests often compete in an unbalanced manner, just as the state frequently intervenes to accommodate groups in a manner that reinforces existing inequalities.[16] Arguing that governmental and specifically bureaucratic actors can pursue their own interests in the policy process, proponents of what has been termed a 'state-centred' view maintain that institutional preferences shape policy outcomes more directly than do simple group attributes.

Theda Skocpol has been one principal advocate of a state-centred approach. In *States and Social Revolutions*, published in 1979, Skocpol argued for greater attention to 'the specific interrelations of class and state structures and the complex interplay over time of domestic and international developments'.[17] This plea for 'bringing the state back in' to political analysis formed the pivot of Skocpol's contribution in 1985 to a text she co-edited with Peter Evans and Dietrich Rueschemeyer. Entitled *Bringing the State Back In*, this collection helped to set in motion the growth of a counter-pluralist, essentially statist approach to public policy.[18]

Among researchers who had become frustrated with the societal paradigm, the emergence of an alternative theoretical framework provided a welcome change. As John Ikenberry and his colleagues suggest in their overview of US trade policy, the societal approach was limited by its view of

> policy outcomes on any particular issue [as] a function of the varying ability of groups to organize and give their interests prominence in the policy process. In this approach, government institutions essentially provide an arena for group competition, and do not exert a significant impact on the decisions that emerge.[19]

If societal theorists claimed that policy success was determined by the outcome of open, free-market competition among competing groups, then critics in the bureaucratic state stream maintained that institutional structures provided far more than simply a fixed landscape for group interaction. Instead, state actors often intervened to direct policy outcomes in a manner consistent with their own institutional interests and abilities.[20]

The challenge of specifying the effects of institutional factors was taken up in a number of case studies of US and comparative public policy. The work of Peter Katzenstein, Stephen Krasner and others identified three specific dimensions of institutional influence on policy outcomes: namely, state preferences, capacity and autonomy.[21] The first of these concepts, state preferences, is illustrated in studies of US national security policy by Krasner and by Graham Allison.[22] Both works suggest that key foreign policy decision-makers may develop interests or preferences that are distinct from and potentially at odds with those of group actors. Instead of viewing policy outcomes as passively driven by societal interests, then, this segment of the literature perceives state actors as actively driving the policy process—wearing an identifiably institutional rather than societal set of lenses.

Second, the bureaucratic literature has elaborated a concept of institutional capacity. This variable, together with the notion of state autonomy, helps to rein in preferences by defining the limits of bureaucratic action. With reference to institutional capacity, state theorists have borrowed from the societal literature an emphasis on resources, in this case the administrative resources that state elites can mobilize in the policy process.[23] Capacity is thus defined as the ability of the bureaucratic state to execute its actions and, logically, depends on its ability to concentrate, co-ordinate and exploit governmental resources.[24] Finally, this literature has introduced autonomy as a further brake on institutional action. Bureaucratic elites may be variously dependent on or independent of societal groups, such that those state officials who possess extensive autonomy are likely to formulate goals and pursue them with little reference to societal influences.[25]

As in the case of the societal approach, authors who employ a bureaucratic view have not produced a concrete policy model. The work of Katzenstein, however, on strong and weak states, combined with the literature cited thus far on institutional influences, suggests a model along the lines of Figure 2.2. Implicit within the terms of this framework is the notion that bureaucratic elites can hold preferences that are distinct from those of societal actors. The former are able to direct policy-making along paths congruent with these preferences to the extent that they are capable of mobilizing resources to execute actions, and to the degree that they are autonomous—that is, independent of societal actors.

In terms of specific propositions, the bureaucratic approach suggests that a highly capable and autonomous state unit A that possessed distinct preferences would be more effective in policy terms than a less capable and autonomous unit B whose preferences were unclear. Moreover, in comparing interactions with societal groups, state unit A would be more likely to dominate and to control organized interests than unit B, since A could be expected to direct its various strengths towards controlling the institutional environment, shaping policy issues or mobilizing new social actors in a manner not available to unit B.[26]

Comparing across administrative units, then, clear bureaucratic preferences and conducive conditions of capacity and autonomy would tend to produce policy action consistent with state preferences (+,+,+), while unclear preferences and minimally conducive levels of capacity and autonomy would yield state inaction (-,-,-). Often, however, more complex conditions prevail; for example, one can imagine well-focussed administrative preferences combined

FIGURE 2.2   STATE STRUCTURES APPROACH TO PUBLIC POLICY

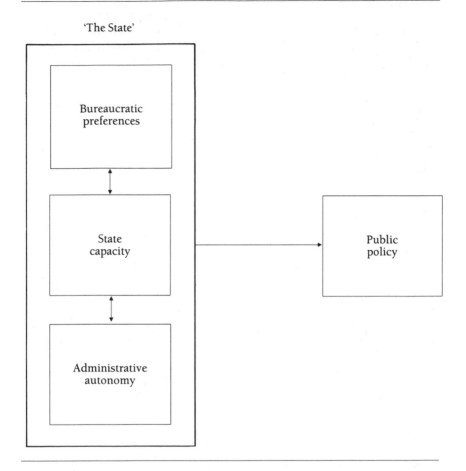

with limited capacity and autonomy (+,-,-) or unclear preferences combined with low capacity and high autonomy (-,-,+).[27]

Chapters 3 through 5 employ this simple scheme of pluses and minuses to develop policy predictions using the bureaucratic framework. Three positive scores on the criteria of preference, capacity and autonomy are posited to produce strong, direct state action in a direction consistent with bureacratic preferences. Mixed results are expected to lead to more limited and less direct action, and three negative scores to state policy inaction.

Critiques of the Bureaucratic Framework

A number of criticisms have been raised in response to this approach, particularly as it has been used in policy studies in the US. On one level, critics maintain that bureaucratic research falls considerably short of its conceptual promise. Robert Putnam, for example, observes that rather than taking account of international factors (as implied in Skocpol's early summary of the statist view), applications of this perspective are often limited to an exclusively domestic purview.[28] As a student of both comparative politics and international relations, Putnam argues that domestic public policy is only partially explained by reference to domestic environments. As he writes:

> Domestic politics and international relations are often somehow entangled, but our theories have not yet sorted out the puzzling tangle. It is fruitless to debate whether domestic politics really determine international relations, or the reverse. The answer to that question is clearly, 'Both, sometimes' . . . the crucial point [is] that central decision-makers ('the state') must be concerned simultaneously with domestic and international pressures.[29]

Putnam's effort to view international and domestic politics as a two-level game provides one way of approaching this problem.

An equally serious difficulty follows from this literature's treatments of 'the state', or politics broadly construed. Although notions of bureaucratic preference, state capacity and institutional autonomy have helped to make the state a more manageable and disaggregated concept, they have also created what one critic describes as 'a kind of public administration approach to politics writ large'.[30] By focussing virtually exclusively on bureaucratic determinants of governmental action, research in the statist tradition has obscured other influences on public policy. For example, the potentially very meaningful role of political parties, public opinion and interest groups has been overshadowed by an overwhelming focus on administrative factors—even though in some sectors, at some times, the former may well be driving the latter. Putnam summarizes this crucial weakness as follows:

> A more adequate account . . . must stress *politics*: parties, social classes, interest groups (both economic and noneconomic), legislators, and even public opinion and elections, not simply executive officials and institutional arrangements.[31]

By merging systematic consideration of domestic political variables with a recognition that international as well as bureaucratic factors may also be relevant, Putnam suggests that useful predictive statements about government action can be derived.

A third set of criticisms of the bureaucratic view, and one that is equally relevant to the societal approach, begins with an emphasis on political ideas. Rather than viewing policy outcomes as a function simply of group or state attributes, an idea-based framework questions what beliefs or preferences dominate a given political environment at a given time. The work of Jane Jenson on the 'universe of political discourse' is especially helpful; Jenson argues that the ability of organizations and movements to achieve their objectives is shaped in large part by the outcome of ideological struggle. That is, new social formations often challenge the boundaries of public discussion, and are successful to the extent that they

> overcome the resistance of political formations already in place and effectively acting as guardians of the political discourse. Since the universe of political discourse acts as a gatekeeper, excluded actors may not be able to construct a collective identity at all.[32]

Jenson's comparative research on women's movements demonstrates the significance of ideas to policy success. Whereas organized feminism in some cultures was able to enter the universe of political discourse and advance its claims in a substantive way, it was far less 'heard' and far less influential in other environments.[33]

Although they do not employ Jenson's terminology, applied policy research by Paul Sabatier (on advocacy coalitions) and Emery Roe (on narrative stories and 'anti-stories') explores the ways in which ideas shape the terms of public debate.[34] How well articulated is a given set of political ideas? To what extent does it—or, conversely, some competing set of ideas—tend to influence elite and public opinion? How sympathetically is a particular position treated in the media?

These questions about the impact of ideas on politics go beyond traditional categories of societal and bureaucratic analysis. When merged with Putnam's critique of the international and domestic political limits of an institutional framework, they point towards an integrative and idea-oriented approach to policy research. Such an approach would consider both groups and bureaucrats, but not at the exclusion of a crucial ideas/politics nexus. The impact of ideas, arguments and beliefs—such as those that constitute the pan-Canadian world view—on *political* elites in both the US and Canada, and on Canadian public and media opinion, are essential to such a formulation. In an integrative framework, ideas and political receptivity to them matter a great deal.

The Canadian Research Tradition

Some of the groundwork for an integrative policy approach is already present in the Canadian literature. For the most part, political science in Canada has retained its interest in institutional or state perspectives while adopting elements of the societal approach; the latter has constituted more of an addition to than a replacement of classical government interests.[35] Since the state, in this respect, was never 'out' of Canadian political research, the demands of Skocpol and others to 'bring the state back in' to the US discipline were viewed as less pressing north of the forty-ninth parallel.[36]

The co-existence of statist and societal approaches is reflected most clearly in the interest group literature. Early on, Paul Pross, whose work established the contours of Canadian research on organized interests, distinguished between what he termed institutionalized and issue-oriented groups.[37] By acknowledging that differing *types* of interests approach the policy process differently, in part as a result of their disparate relations with institutional actors, Pross laid the groundwork for subsequent efforts to specify these variations. In William Coleman's work on business interests, for example, Pross's categories helped to establish a further distinction between groups that engage in policy advocacy and those that proceed to the level of policy participation.[38] Similarly, an edited study by Coleman and Grace Skogstad points towards a more inclusive perspective than that provided in either the societal or bureaucratic literatures. In their concluding essay, Coleman and Skogstad argue that international and domestic political influences shape group-state relations to a degree that can no longer be ignored in policy research.[39]

A further step towards integrating societal and bureaucratic perspectives can be found in the work of Michael Atkinson and William Coleman. In their study of federal industrial policy, Atkinson and Coleman focus on policy networks at the sectoral, rather than macro- or whole-state, level. They propose that these networks, defined as linkages or interactions between societal and state actors within a given sector, directly shape federal government action.[40] On a more theoretical level, Alan Cairns has challenged political scientists to understand the mingling or counter-penetration of societal with state variables. In maintaining that a 'web of state-society interdependencies' in Canada links 'politicized societies caught in webs of interdependence with the state' with an 'embedded state tied down by its multiple linkages with society', Cairns provides an ultimatum of sorts for integrative research.[41]

Yet neither Cairns nor writers in the societal stream has focussed clearly on the domestic and international *political* variables identified by Robert Putnam, nor on the questions about *ideas* raised by Jane Jenson. It is for this reason that a third analytic framework is introduced in the next section.

An Integrative Approach

Even at first glance, the study of government policy in the areas targeted by Canadian nationalists seems to demand a more sophisticated analytic framework than that provided in either the societal or bureaucratic literatures. If policy success, as societal theorists suggest, is simply a matter of marshalling domestic group attributes to the point that they exceed those of competing domestic interests, then what about policy debates that involve actors based outside national (or in-group) boundaries? How would group analysts explain outcomes in which the array of organized interests was relatively stable over time, yet government action seemed to veer suddenly in a direction favourable to resource-poor groups? Both questions are relevant to the study of federal policy action in the cultural, investment and trade areas targeted by organized nationalists in Canada, and neither would seem to be answerable using a societal framework.

Equally difficult questions follow from the use of a bureaucratic view on its own. Are public administrators the sole or even the key architects of state preferences vis-à-vis nationalist policy issues? Do not partisan and, especially, cabinet and backroom actors help to shape and articulate these positions? Is there not *some* relationship between the preferences of domestic governmental elites, on the one hand, and constraints imposed by the international environment and domestic opinion, on the other? Given its emphasis on the administrative dimension of policy action, these kinds of political considerations receive little attention in the bureaucratic literature.

Even using the state-society web posited by Cairns and others, much of the ideological and political resonance of nationalist policy debate seems lost. Can the influence of nationalism on federal policy be analysed adequately with reference to groups, bureaucracies and the networks between them—and *without* reference to politicians? How autonomous, in an international and, especially, a continental sense, are either organized interests or administrative elites in Canada? Is there no bounded 'universe of political discourse', to use Jenson's terminology, within which policy debates and decisions unfold?

In studying the translation of nationalist ideas into governmental action, the need to move beyond the two frameworks specified in Figures 2.1 and 2.2 is in many respects self-evident. Much of what pan-Canadianism has sought to accomplish in the fields of cultural, trade and investment policy holds direct implications for relations with the continental out-group, the United States, and the US government is therefore likely to take some interest in Canadian policy debates over these matters.[42] As suggested in Chapter 1, pan-Canadian beliefs regarding foreign media spillover, foreign direct investment and the dangers of continental free trade speak directly to questions of Canada-US relations. Because nationalist ideas resonate beyond national boundaries, US government response to pan-Canadian arguments must be considered in explaining policy outcomes.

Chapter 1 also illustrated the need to consider domestic variables beyond those specified in the first two models. Questions of national identity and its defence through cultural, trade and investment policy are intensely *political*; within the nationalist world view, these are visceral issues of in-group autonomy and viability. Most of the major debates over Canadian communications, investment and trade policy have unfolded as intensely partisan and ideological struggles, and commanded considerable public and media attention.[43] In short, far more than societal and bureaucratic variables appear to be engaged on the nationalist policy landscape.

Explaining government policy in areas central to the nationalist world view thus requires attention to three key variables. Each follows from the argument that ideas matter, that political responses to the nationalist world view are essential to understanding policy influence. First, we need to consider the response of international actors, especially the US government, to nationalist arguments. In simple terms, where does Washington officially stand on a given proposal, and how extensively does it intervene to advance the US position? Second, the degree of receptivity to nationalist ideas within the Canadian party system is important. To put the matter directly, is the parliamentary leadership of the governing federal party on balance nationalist or continentalist?[44] Third, research must consider domestic attitudes towards nationalist ideas, as reflected in media and mass-level opinion. How supportive are media treatments of nationalist proposals? Does the public hold sympathetic views?

One way of addressing these political factors without ignoring the contributions of the first two models is to list the variables that follow from each conceptual starting point. With reference to the societal approach, the main factors identified thus far are: (1) internal group resources, especially personnel and financial means; (2) internal group unity or cohesion; (3) group expertise vis-à-vis a specific policy issue; and (4) group representativeness within a given policy domain. Those following from the bureaucratic literature are: (5) bureaucratic policy preferences; (6) bureaucratic capacity, or the ability of administrative actors to execute their actions; and (7) state autonomy, or independence from societal interests. The first four variables can be said to constitute a societal cluster, and the second three a bureaucratic cluster.

Critical political variables that pertain to nationalist ideas and are neglected in both clusters are: (8) international influences, particularly US government positions towards Canadian nationalist arguments; (9) domestic partisan factors, especially the receptivity to nationalist ideas in the parliamentary elite of the governing federal party; and (10) attitudes towards nationalist arguments as reflected in Canadian media and public opinion. These last three factors form an ideas/politics cluster and, together with the societal and bureaucratic clusters, constitute the core of an integrative approach.

Although ten variables may seem unwieldy, they can be conceived heuristically within a simplified policy model. As summarized in Figure 2.3, nationalist policy ideas have usually originated among an organized interest in the cultural, trade or investment stream. Once articulated, these arguments have confronted a variety of external interests including international and, notably, US governmental actors, as well as competing domestic interests. Government actors inside the 'black box'—the bureaucratic and parliamentary decision-makers—engage in debate over nationalist proposals.[45] Some of these black box actors may be sympathetically disposed to, or even actively involved in articulating the nationalist position, while others may be opposed or indifferent to this view.

Following the lines of Figure 2.3, nationalist ideas can be shaped and reshaped as a result of interaction with the partisan and bureaucratic actors in the black box, and as a result of interaction with and among international and competing group players. Operating inside a larger attitudinal environment whose domestic parameters are defined by media and mass-level opinion, the

FIGURE 2.3   **INTEGRATIVE APPROACH TO PUBLIC POLICY**

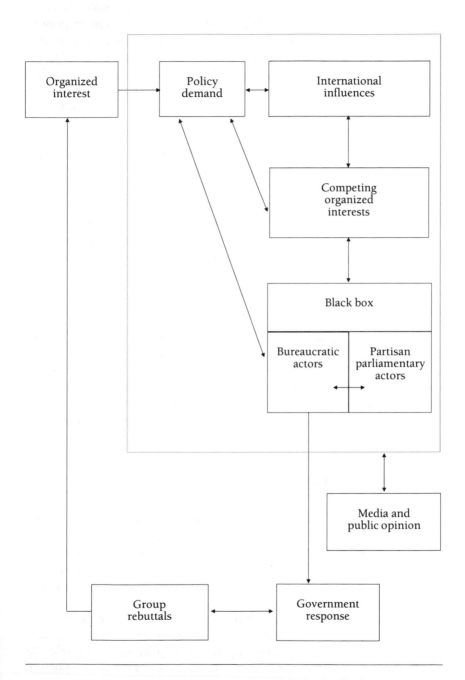

black box, international, competing group and sponsoring group actors usually interact to produce a governmental response, whether legislative or administrative, followed by a series of group 'rebuttals'. These updated nationalist positions may reflect a somewhat different view from that which was advanced prior to the black box phase. As the two-way arrows suggest, interaction could occur at this point between black box decision-makers and group actors. Finally, as a last step in what is here viewed as an ongoing cycle of nationalist position, policy interaction, governmental response, group rebuttal and the feedback patterns therein, the organized interest generally re-groups to work towards new ideas and proposals.

It should be emphasized that this model, like all models, presents an extremely simplified version of complex political realities. It overlooks such important nuances as the communication of policy ideas. Is the argumentation heard? How is it communicated, and by whom? These questions are of more than passing interest to students of nationalism, since activists in the cultural stream in particular have argued that foreign and 'comprador' owners of the Canadian communications media purposefully filter out nationalist perspectives.[46] Similarly, the model begs fundamental questions of political access. Are group demands placed on the policy agenda inside the black box? Or, to borrow from Bachrach and Baratz, are these matters diverted off the main agenda to symbolic status as 'non-issues', perhaps marginalized in the context of royal commissions, task forces and the like?[47]

Such problems of message and access are minimized in this study through the use of a control on chronological time. Each of the policy cases considered in Chapters 3 through 5 unfolded since the early 1970s, during a period when nationalist ideas were an integral part of Canadian political discourse and were resonant to varying degrees in public opinion. As a result, elements of the nationalist world view were likely to have been communicated and at least some political access assured.[48]

Research Propositions

This discussion has argued that the utility of societal and bureaucratic frameworks on their own is limited. Given their failure to consider the role of ideas and particularly the intersection between ideas and political actors, it is proposed that neither view can adequately explain government policy in the areas targeted by organized nationalists. In short, the limitations of the societal and bureaucratic models are expected to be evident in the case studies presented in Chapters 3 through 5.

As an alternative that builds on the first two frameworks, the integrative model yields the following propositions: First, for ideas to be reflected in public policy, political support is necessary. This support can originate among variables $X8$ through $X10$ of Figure 2.4; that is, among domestic and international political elites as well as in domestic public and media opinion. Without political support from at least one of these three sources, nationalist ideas are unlikely to influence public policy—regardless of their standing among societal and bureaucratic actors.

Second, if policy action is viewed in terms of likelihood or, to use the mathematical shorthand, probability, then a 50 per cent likelihood of a given outcome requires that at least half the factors (in this case , 5 out of 10) be 'on side'. Similarly, the probability of no action in a given direction requires at least half the factors (in this case, 5 out of 10) to be 'off side' or unfavourable. Policy influence can thus be defined as a mathematical probability that equals the arithmetic sum of the individual probabilities of the ten explanatory variables listed above. Using simple notation where 'p' stands for probability, the likelihood of policy action, or Y, can be defined as

$$p(Y) = p(X1) + p(X2) + \ldots + p(X10) \qquad \text{or}$$

$$p(Y) = \sum_{i=1}^{10} p(Xi)$$

If the ten explanatory variables are considered as part of an integrative web, then this web can be arrayed along a continuum from conditions that are *highly conducive* to governmental action, through *moderately* or *somewhat conducive* conditions, to *minimally conducive* or not very likely circumstances.

Figure 2.4 presents a further specification of the integrative model. Examples of the kinds of X-variable circumstances or conditions that are expected to provide high (upper horizontal stripe), moderate (middle horizontal stripe) and low (lower horizontal stripe) probabilities of governmental action are detailed in this figure. Each of the ten explanatory variables is derived from the list of factors elaborated above, and each is part of either the societal, bureaucratic or ideas/politics cluster.

The specific propositions that follow from Figure 2.4 are quite straightforward. For example, beginning in the upper left-hand corner with the societal cluster, the first independent variable (X1), group resources, suggests that extensive nationalist resources combined with limited competing group resources are likely to be correlated with government action in a pro-nationalist direction. In more general terms, the greater the financial and human resources controlled by an organized interest, and the more limited the resources of its competitors, then the higher the probability of the first group's policy influence.

Since these individual propositions follow logically from the summary in Figure 2.4, it is not necessary to review each in detail. Rather, it is more useful to consider the ten X variables again as part of an integrative web. Bearing in mind that actual policy conditions do not usually coincide with any of the three

FIGURE 2.4   SPECIFICATION OF INDEPENDENT AND DEPENDENT VARIABLES, INTEGRATIVE MODEL

	SOCIETAL CLUSTER				BUREAUCRATIC CLUSTER			IDEAS/POLITICS CLUSTER			DEPENDENT VARIABLE, Y
	Group resources X_1	Group cohesion X_2	Group expertise X_3	Group representativeness X_4	Bureaucratic preferences X_5	Bureaucratic capacity X_6	Bureaucratic autonomy X_7	International influences X_8	Partisan actors X_9	Media, public opinion X_{10}	Likelihood of policy influence
	Extensive financial and human resources; limited competing group resources	Strong organizational control, discipline and unity; low competing group cohesion	Outstanding policy and administrative expertise; low competing group expertise	Comprehensive representation of policy domain; low competing group representation	Bureaucratic actors supportive of policy proposal	Bureaucratic actors highly capable of executing actions	Bureaucratic actors highly independent of societal influences	US government supportive of policy proposal	Leadership of governing party supportive of policy proposal	Positive, favourable to policy proposal	Very likely, conditions highly conducive
	Moderate financial and human resources; moderate competing group resources	Moderate organizational control, discipline and unity; moderate competing group cohesion	Moderate policy and administrative expertise; moderate competing group expertise	Moderate representation of policy domain; moderate competing group representation	Bureaucratic actors indifferent to policy proposal	Bureaucratic actors moderately capable of executing actions	Bureaucratic actors somewhat independent of societal influences	US government indifferent to policy proposal	Leadership of governing party divided; some support for policy proposal	Mixed, moderate support for policy proposal	Somewhat likely, conditions moderately conducive
	Limited financial and human resources; strong competing group resources	Weak organizational control, discipline and unity; high competing group cohesion	Limited policy and administrative expertise; high competing group expertise	Limited representation of policy domain; high competing group representation	Bureaucratic actors opposed to policy proposal	Bureaucratic actors not capable of executing actions	Bureaucratic actors not independent of societal influences	US government opposed to policy proposal	Leadership of governing party opposed to policy proposal	Negative, unfavourable to policy proposal	Not very likely, conditions minimally conducive

horizontal 'stripes' in Figure 2.4, the likelihood of governmental action (Y) in a given direction can be described as the additive sum of individual X probabilities. Government action favourable to nationalist interests would then be most likely if 10 out of 10, or 100 per cent, of the independent variables were scored as favourable or upper-stripe conditions, and lowest if 10 out of 10, or 100 per cent, were scored in the category of minimally conducive or lower-stripe conditions.

Obviously, most policy cases do not conform to either of these circumstances, and would instead present a mixture of highly conducive, moderately conducive and minimally conducive conditions. Adding together the scores in each category and dividing by a denominator of 10 would then yield a common-sense prediction of government action. For example, 7 out of 10 highly favourable or upper-stripe scores could be interpreted as a 70 per cent or moderately high probability of policy success for the societal group in question, 3 out of 10 upper-stripe scores as a 30 per cent or relatively low probability, and so on. Parallel with this, 7 out of 10 minimally favourable scores could be viewed as a 70 per cent or moderately high probability of policy failure, meaning government inaction with respect to societal demands, and so on. Scores clustered in the middle or moderate category can be viewed as indicators of either/or situations, meaning 'saw-offs' between success and failure. For example, 7 out of 10 moderate or middle-stripe scores could be interpreted as a 70 per cent or moderately high probability of policy saw-off.

The first proposition identified in this section, however, maintains that *political* support for nationalist *ideas* is crucial, and suggests that not all variables in the integrative framework are of equal importance. We propose that highly or moderately conducive conditions on variables X8, X9 or X10 are essential to ensuring policy success, such that the complete absence of political support on variables X8 through X10 would render scores on variables X1 through X7 politically meaningless. In other words, even highly conducive societal and bureaucratic conditions, on their own, are unlikely to convert nationalist ideas into concrete federal policies.

In light of this probability approach, each of the ten variables in the integrative model is analysed and scored in Chapters 3 through 5 using data from specific policy instances. One case study involves cultural nationalist efforts (the *Time/Reader's Digest* Bill), one is relevant to foreign investment (the National Energy Program) and the last concerns comprehensive free trade with the US. This design permits an evaluation of the societal (Figure 2.1), bureaucratic (Figure 2.2) and integrative (Figures 2.3 and 2.4) frameworks as they apply to each of the three instances.

Selection of Cases

Before turning to the case studies, it is important to explain the criteria that guided their selection. First, each had to be critical or salient to organized nationalist interests, whether in the cultural, trade or investment stream, and each had to hold the sustained interest of nationalist activists. Minor, short-term and less significant policy debates were not analysed because they would have tended to bias a number of measures in both the societal and integrative frameworks. Concerns that were low on the agenda of an organized interest would probably *not* have commanded much in the way of either resources or expertise; moreover, only limited internal cohesion and policy representativeness would be expected in such circumstances. As a corollary to the propositions that accompany the first and third models, then, the following may be added: societal interests are less likely to obtain policy influence on issues of limited internal importance than on those of sustained salience.

Second, each policy case had to unfold during a particular chronological period: that is, after the organizational birth of modern pan-Canadianism in the late 1960s and early 1970s, when such groups as the Waffle and the Committee for an Independent Canada had begun to articulate publicly a variety of nationalist ideas. Selecting earlier cases, such as the Mercantile Bank affair of 1966-67, would again have biased the measurement of internal group characteristics in a negative direction, since nationalism in an organized sense was then in its infancy. Furthermore, at least one dimension of variable X10 in the integrative model (namely, mass-level opinion) would have been difficult to measure in cases prior to the early 1970s, given the absence of an identifiable group position to 'lead' the public on this issue.[49]

Finally, cases had to be the subject of some previous secondary research. This condition was imposed in order to facilitate application of the models—especially the third one, which requires attention to 30 independent variables or 10 in each of three case studies. The existence of a secondary literature meant that the policy in question had already been approached by other analysts, making this effort more manageable than if only primary materials had been available.

These criteria produce two fairly clear-cut decisions regarding cases. The controversy over Canadian versus foreign cultural influences in the fields of publishing and broadcasting, which culminated in the 1976 passage of Bill C-58 (the *Time/Reader's Digest* Bill), was the focus of concerted nationalist activity for a number of years during the mid-1970s, thus meeting the salience and time criteria. Furthermore, because Bill C-58 has been a subject of considerable academic interest, there exists a very useful secondary literature from which to draw.[50] Similarly, the debate during 1985-88 over continental free trade was of crucial and sustained importance to nationalist organizations, and conforms to the chronological condition. Although the secondary literature on free trade remains limited, abundant primary sources are available.[51]

Selecting a policy case from the foreign investment stream of pan-Canadianism is more difficult. The Canada Development Corporation (CDC) would have been difficult to justify on the grounds of time, since organized nationalist groups had only begun to form when the CDC was created in 1971. The Foreign Investment Review Agency (FIRA) and Petro-Canada, both of which were established after the CDC, are more relevant in chronological terms, yet neither FIRA nor Petro-Canada has been the subject of sustained interest among both nationalists and scholars.[52] One of the only cases that meets all three criteria is the National Energy Program (NEP), introduced in 1980. Increasing Canadian control in the natural resource sector was a major priority of investment nationalists through the 1970s and 1980s. The NEP thus meets the chronological criteria, and is the subject of a rich and diverse secondary literature.[53] Moreover, debates about the NEP highlighted deep-seated regional and ideological questions about the character of nationalism in English Canada, issues that were raised in Chapter 1 and are pursued below in the Epilogue.

Chapter 3 uses this conceptual base to evaluate the cultural politics of Bill C-58; questions of investment and trade are then considered in Chapters 4 and 5, respectively.

Notes

[1]Abraham Rotstein, 'Canada: The New Nationalism', *Foreign Affairs* 55 (1976), 98.

[2]Graham T. Allison, *Essence of Decision: Explaining the Cuban Missile Crisis* (Boston: Little Brown, 1971), v.

[3]On the utility of a case study design for 'how' and 'why' questions, see Robert K. Yin, *Case Study Research* (Beverly Hills: Sage, 1984).

[4]William D. Coleman, *Business and Politics: A Study of Collective Action* (Toronto: University of Toronto Press, 1988). A cross-sectoral design is also employed in Michael M. Atkinson and William D. Coleman, *The State, Business, and Industrial Change in Canada* (Toronto: University of Toronto Press, 1989).

[5]See C. Wright Mills, *The Power Elite* (New York: Oxford University Press, 1956); and Floyd Hunter, *Community Power Structure* (New York: Doubleday, 1953).

[6]See David B. Truman, *The Governmental Process: Political Interests and Public Opinion* (New York: Knopf, 1951); Robert A. Dahl, *A Preface to Democratic Theory* (Chicago: University of Chicago Press, 1956); Dahl, 'A Critique of the Ruling Elite Model', *American Political Science Review* 52 (1958), 463-9; and Dahl, *Who Governs? Democracy and Power in an American City* (New Haven: Yale University Press, 1961). Much of their work was grounded in the earlier pluralist theories of Arthur F. Bentley, *The Process of Government* (Evanston: Principia Press, 1949).

[7]Truman, *The Governmental Process*, chaps. 1-3.

[8]Ibid., 33.

[9]Dahl, *Who Governs?*

[10]Dahl, *A Preface to Democratic Theory*.

[11]Dahl, *Who Governs?*.

[12]Truman, *The Governmental Process*.

[13]Ibid.

[14]E.E. Schattschneider, *The Semi-Sovereign People: A Realist's View of Democracy in America* (New York: Holt, Rinehart and Winston, 1960), 71.

[15]See Peter Bachrach and Morton Baratz, 'The Two Faces of Power', *American Political Science Review* 56 (1962), 947-52; Bachrach and Baratz, 'Decisions and Nondecisions: An Analytical Framework', *American Political Science Review* 57 (1963), 641-51; and Bachrach and Baratz, *Power and Poverty:*

Theory and Practice (New York: Oxford University Press, 1970). In *Power and Poverty*, Bachrach and Baratz define a 'non-decision' as a 'decision that results in the suppression or thwarting of a latent or mainfest challenge to the values or interests of the decision-maker' (44).

[16]See A. Paul Pross, *Group Politics and Public Policy* (Toronto: Oxford University Press, 1986), chap. 10.

[17]Theda Skocpol, *States and Social Revolutions: A Comparative Analysis of France, Russia, and China* (Cambridge: Cambridge University Press, 1979), xiii.

[18]Theda Skocpol, 'Bringing the State Back In: Strategies of Analysis in Current Research', in Peter B. Evans, Dietrich Rueschemeyer, and Theda Skocpol (eds), *Bringing the State Back In* (Cambridge: Cambridge University Press, 1985).

[19]G. John Ikenberry, David A. Lake and Michael Mastanduno, 'Introduction: Approaches to Explaining American Foreign Economic Policy', in Ikenberry, Lake and Mastanduno (eds), *The State and American Foreign Economic Policy* (Ithaca: Cornell University Press, 1988), 7.

[20]For a useful summary of the state structures view, see ibid., 9-14.

[21]See Peter J. Katzenstein (ed.), *Between Power and Plenty: Foreign Economic Policies of Advanced Industrial States* (Madison: University of Wisconsin Press, 1978); Katzenstein, *Small States in World Markets: Industrial Policy in Europe* (Ithaca: Cornell University Press, 1986); Stephen Krasner, *Defending the National Interest* (Princeton: Princeton University Press, 1978); Eric A. Nordlinger, *On the Autonomy of the Democratic State* (Cambridge: Harvard University Press, 1981); and James A. Caparaso (ed.), *The Elusive State: International and Comparative Perspectives* (Newbury Park, CA: Sage, 1989).

[22]Krasner, *Defending the National Interest*, and Allison, *Essence of Decision*.

[23]Ikenberry et al., 'Introduction', 12.

[24]This definition is drawn from Grace Skogstad, 'The State, Organized Interests and Trade Policy: The Impact of Institutions', paper presented at Canadian Political Science Association meetings, University of Victoria, 1990, 3.

[25]Ibid.; 10-11, and Katzenstein, *Small States in World Markets*. For a definition of sectoral autonomy, see Atkinson and Coleman, *The State, Business, and Industrial Change in Canada*, 80.

[26]For a further discussion of these possibilities, see Ikenberry et al., 'Introduction', 12-13.

[27]For a more thorough treatment of variation among bureaucratic variables, see William D. Coleman and Grace Skogstad, 'Introduction', in Coleman and Skogstad (eds.), *Policy Communities and Public Policy in Canada: A Structural Approach* (Toronto: Copp Clark Pitman, 1990), 5-7.

[28]Robert D. Putnam, 'Diplomacy and Domestic Politics: The Logic of Two-Level Games', *International Organization* 42 (1988), 430-3.

[29]Ibid., 427, 431.

[30]Frances Fox Piven, 'Review of Margaret Weir, Ann Shola Orloff and Theda Skocpol (eds), *The Politics of Social Policy in the United States*', *American Political Science Review* 83 (1989), 1041.

[31]Putnam, 'Diplomacy and Domestic Politics', 432; emphasis in original. A very similar position is argued in Gabriel A. Almond, 'The Return to the State', *American Political Science Review* 82 (1988), 871-82.

[32]Jane Jenson, 'Changing Discourse, Changing Agendas: Political Rights and Reproductive Policies in France', in Mary Fainsod Katzenstein and Carol McClurg Mueller (eds), *The Women's Movements of the United States and Western Europe* (Philadelphia: Temple University Press, 1987), 66.

[33]Ibid., 68-86.

[34]See Paul A. Sabatier, 'Knowledge, Policy-Oriented Learning, and Policy Change', *Knowledge: Creation, Diffusion, Utilization* 8 (1987), 649-92; and Emery M. Roe, 'Narrative Analysis for the Policy Analyst: A Case Study of the 1980-1982 Medly Controversy in California', *Journal of Policy Analysis and Management* 8 (1989), 251-73.

[35]See Alan C. Cairns, 'Alternative Styles in the Study of Canadian Politics', *Canadian Journal of Political*

Science 7 (1974), 101-28; and Donald Smiley, 'Must Canadian Political Science Be a Miniature Replica?' *Journal of Canadian Studies* 9 (1974), 31-42.

[36]Skocpol, 'Bringing the State Back In'.

[37]See A. Paul Pross (ed.), *Pressure Group Behaviour in Canadian Politics* (Toronto: McGraw Hill, 1975); and Pross, *Group Politics and Public Policy*.

[38]Coleman, *Business and Politics*, chaps 2, 3.

[39]William D. Coleman and Grace Skogstad, 'Conclusion', in Coleman and Skogstad (eds), *Policy Communities and Public Policy in Canada*, 312-27.

[40]See Atkinson and Coleman, *The State, Business, and Industrial Change in Canada*, 77-8.

[41]Alan C. Cairns, 'The Embedded State: State-Society Relations in Canada', in Keith Banting (ed.), *State and Society: Canada in Comparative Perspective*, Royal Commission Research Studies, vol. 31 (Toronto: University of Toronto Press for Supply and Services Canada, 1986), 55.

[42]See Charles F. Doran and John H. Sigler (eds), *Canada and the United States: Enduring Friendship, Persistent Stress* (Englewood Cliffs, NJ: Prentice-Hall, 1985); John W. Holmes, *Life with Uncle: The Canadian-American Relationship* (Toronto: University of Toronto Press, 1981); and David Leyton-Brown, *Weathering the Storm: Canada-U.S. Relations* (Toronto: Canadian-American Committee, 1985).

[43]On the centrality of nationalist-continentalist tensions to Canadian political debate, see Stephen Clarkson, 'Anti-Nationalism in Canada: The Ideology of Mainstream Economics', *Canadian Review of Studies in Nationalism* 5 (1978), 45-65; John H. Redekop, 'Continentalism: The Key to Canadian Politics', in Redekop (ed.), *Approaches to Canadian Politics* (2nd ed.; Scarborough, Ont.: Prentice-Hall, 1983), 32-64; and Roger Gibbins, *Conflict and Unity: An Introduction to Canadian Political Life* (2nd ed.; Toronto: Nelson Canada, 1990), chap. 5.

[44]Much of this receptivity may be dependent on the legislative vulnerability of the governing party, specifically whether it is in a majority or minority situation, and whether it is facing an imminent election.

[45]One of the most prominent applications of systems theory to political science is Karl Deutsch, *A Systems Analysis of Political Life* (New York: Wiley, 1965). For an application of this view to Canadian politics, see Richard J. Van Loon and Michael S. Whittington, *The Canadian Political System* (Toronto: McGraw-Hill Ryerson, 1987).

[46]See S.M. Crean, *Who's Afraid of Canadian Culture* (Don Mills, Ont.: General Publishing, 1976).

[47]Bachrach and Baratz, 'The Two Faces of Power'; and Bachrach and Baratz, 'Decisions and Nondecisions'. Jane Jenson addresses problems of exclusion and marginalization as well in her work on the 'universe of political discourse'. See Jenson, 'Changing Discourse, Changing Agendas'.

[48]To use the language of the regulation school, nationalist discourse would have likely been included in the prevailing societal paradigm by this point. See Jane Jenson, 'Paradigms and Political Discourse: Protective Legislation in France and the United States Before 1914', *Canadian Journal of Political Science* 22 (1989), 235-58.

[49]Studies of nationalist policy influence during an earlier period thus employ a somewhat different approach. See, for example, John Fayerweather, *The Mercantile Bank Affair: A Case Study of Canadian Nationalism and a Multinational Firm* (New York: New York University Press, 1974), chap. 5.

[50]This research includes Theodore Hagelin and Hudson Janisch, 'The Border Broadcasting Dispute in Context', in Canadian-U.S. Conference on Communications Policy, *Cultures in Collision: The Interaction of Canadian and U.S. Television Broadcast Policies* (New York: Praeger, 1984), 40-99; Isaiah A. Litvak and Christopher J. Maule, 'Bill C-58 and the Regulation of Periodicals', *International Journal* 36 (1980-81), 70-90; Litvak and Maule, *Cultural Sovereignty: The Time and Reader's Digest Case in Canada* (New York: Praeger, 1974); John R. LoGalbo, 'The Time and Reader's Digest Bill: C-58 and Canadian Cultural Nationalism', *New York University Journal of International Law and Politics* 9 (1976), 237-75; and Katherine Swinton, 'Advertising and Canadian Cable Television—A Problem in International Communications Law', *Osgoode Hall Law Journal* 15 (1977), 543-90.

[51]Analyses of the trade debate and literature include David Leyton-Brown, 'The Canada-U.S. Free Trade Agreement', in Andrew B. Gollner and Daniel Salée (eds), *Canada Under Mulroney* (Montreal: Véhicule Press, 1988), 103-18; and Kenneth Woodside, 'The Canada-United States Free Trade Agreement', *Canadian Journal of Political Science* 22 (1989), 155-70. The voluminous primary literature that debated the merits of the idea of free trade and the actual bilateral agreement is referred to in Chapters 5 and 6.

[52]As indicated by Walter Gordon's observation in Chapter 1, nationalists tended to dismiss both FIRA and the CDC as government 'window-dressing' early in the course of both debates. On the CDC, see William Andrew Dimma, 'The Canada Development Corporation: Diffident Experiment on a Large Scale' (D.B.A. Thesis, Harvard University, 1973). In the case of Petro-Canada, little research is available other than Larry Pratt, 'Petro-Canada', in Allan Tupper and G. Bruce Doern (eds), *Public Corporations and Public Policy in Canada* (Montreal: Institute for Research on Public Policy, 1981), 95-148.

[53]Studies that address the NEP include Leyton-Brown, *Weathering the Storm*; Stephen Clarkson, *Canada and the Reagan Challenge* (Toronto: Lorimer, 1985); G. Bruce Doern and Glen Toner, *The Politics of Energy: The Development and Implementation of the NEP* (Toronto: Methuen, 1985); Peter Foster, *The Sorcerer's Apprentices: Canada's Super-Bureaucrats and the Energy Mess* (Toronto: Collins, 1982); Barbara Jenkins, 'Reexamining the "Obsolescing Bargain": A Study of Canada's National Energy Program', *International Organization* 40 (1986), 139-65; and David Milne, *Tug of War: Ottawa and the Provinces under Trudeau and Mulroney* (Toronto: Lorimer, 1986).

3 | Cultural Nationalism and the Time/Reader's Digest Bill

Cultural survival is perhaps the most critical problem our generation of Canadians will have to face, and it may be it can be achieved only by using all the means at our command.[1]

Introduction

Through the prism of their world view, Canadian nationalists since the late 1960s have tried to influence federal public policy in diverse ways. Cultural activists have worked to shape communications policy so as to strengthen domestic culture and limit media overflow from the United States, while trade and investment nationalists have sought to reduce foreign and increase domestic economic control.

This chapter considers one instance of government action in communications policy that was relatively favourable to nationalist interests: namely, Bill C-58, or the *Time/Reader's Digest* Bill. The purpose of the case study is two-fold: first, to compare the ability of societal, bureaucratic and integrative frameworks to explain the introduction of the policy; and second, to assess the impact of nationalists in a policy area in which their ideas appeared to be influential.

With reference to the first purpose, the chapter concludes that an integrative approach explains the adoption of Bill C-58 more fully than does either the group or the bureaucratic framework. By focussing on the importance both of Canadian partisan elites, in placing the issue of media spillover on the government agenda, and of domestic opinion, in approving cultural nationalist ideas, the third model provides a more complete explanation of the *Time/Reader's Digest* Bill.

In assessing the broader impact of cultural nationalist ideas, this chapter maintains that their influence was dependent on a fragile combination of societal, bureaucratic (especially in the broadcasting field) and domestic political factors. Canadian public opinion supported both controls on media spillover and expenditures to build alternatives to these foreign sources, and was concerned about the threats to identity posed by Americanization. The ability of nationalist organizations, federal regulatory agencies (notably the Canadian Radio-Television and Telecommunications Commission, or CRTC) and nationalists within the governing party to keep these issues in the forefront and to pursue them effectively helps to explain Bill C-58; at the same time, however, these same factors also foreshadow the subsequent weakening of cultural nationalist ideas in the federal policy process.

Bill C-58

Magazine Publishing

Although its subtitle, 'An Act to Amend the Income Tax Act', seemed innocuous, Bill C-58 was the centre of a major political storm during the mid-1970s. Susan Crean, a writer and activist who supported the legislation, observed at the time: 'Bill C-58 was the subject of an impassioned debate across the country, arousing emotions usually reserved for issues like abortion and capital punishment. Charges of censorship and cultural paranoia . . . were heaped upon the government.'[2]

This heated debate addressed core notions of culture, identity and their defence via communications policy. Publishing and broadcasting had long been considered key centripetal forces in Canada, counteracting the centrifugal impact of vast geography, dispersed population and media spillover from the United States. As a result, according to one observer, 'Canada is the most communications-conscious country in the world.'[3] Bill C-58 dealt with very contentious dimensions of this broader media consciousness involving periodicals and television broadcasting, but most of the domestic debate surrounding the bill concerned its treatment of the tax advantages enjoyed by *Time* and *Reader's Digest*.[4]

With reference to periodicals, arguments in favour of Bill C-58 reflected at least two beliefs dating back to the Canada Firsters. First, cultural nationalists viewed the large circulation of US magazines north of the forty-ninth parallel as an impediment to the development of a healthy, independent Canadian industry. Without readers, advertisers and publishers to support autonomous Canadian magazines, it was argued, American products would increasingly dominate the market.[5]

Second, and as a direct consequence of this first point, cultural nationalists maintained that the absence of independent periodicals meant that Canadian voices would not be heard in the cacophony of foreign media. Not only would indigenous Canadian writers have few domestic outlets for their work, but also an essential avenue for the expression of Canadian values and the discussion of Canadian issues would be blocked. As suggested by the epigraph to this chapter, from the 1970 Report of the Special Senate Committee on Mass Media, chaired by Keith Davey, nationalists argued that 'all the means' necessary should be enlisted to ensure cultural survival.[6]

One way to limit foreign periodicals in Canada and, comcomitantly, to improve the position of domestic magazines was suggested in the earlier 1961 Report of the Royal Commission on Publications, chaired by Grattan O'Leary and known as the O'Leary report. It involved amending Schedule 'C' of the Customs Act in such a way as to prohibit entry into Canada of foreign magazines that contained advertising directed to the Canadian market, and altering section 19 of the Income Tax Act in such a way as to eliminate expense deductions for Canadian advertisers in foreign periodicals—including Canadian editions of US magazines.[7]

These recommendations of the O'Leary Commission resulted from the increasingly dominant market position of foreign periodicals in Canada—notably *Time* and *Reader's Digest*—in the decade following the Second World War.[8] By the mid-1950s, US magazines had obtained 80 per cent of the Canadian market share and, by themselves, the Canadian editions of *Time* and *Reader's Digest* accounted for 37 per cent of the advertising revenues of the nation's 12 leading magazines.[9]

Submissions to the O'Leary Commission from Canadian publishers (notably the Toronto-based firm Maclean-Hunter) and advertising interests argued that foreign publications should be limited in order to ensure cultural survival. By way of contrast, *Time* and *Reader's Digest* emphasized to the same Commission their role in stimulating the development of a dynamic industry in Canada. According to the latter, infringements on foreign-based magazine operations would constitute a threat not only to freedom of the press, but also to the periodical medium as a vehicle for the expression of Canadian identity.[10]

Tariff changes recommended by the O'Leary Commission were endorsed by the Liberal government of Lester Pearson, but the tax revisions then proposed exempted advertisers in existing Canadian editions of foreign periodicals. This provision exempting *Time* and *Reader's Digest* disappointed not only Grattan O'Leary (who termed it a 'fraud')[11] and the Canadian publishers but also Walter Gordon—who, as Minister of Finance, introduced the watered-down terms of the 1965 income tax amendments.[12] Clearly, pressures placed on the federal cabinet during the mid-1960s by the publishers of *Time* and *Reader's Digest*, in part through their Canadian readers and employees, were intense. As well, American government officials including President Lyndon Johnson intervened in the dispute. The US threatened to cancel a purchasing contract with Canadair Ltd of Montreal, to limit Canadian oil exports and to delay Senate ratification of the Auto Pact.[13]

As cultural nationalism began to develop in an organized way during the late 1960s and early 1970s, the 1965 tax exemption granted to *Time* and *Reader's Digest* stood out as a visible irritant. This was not the only tax-related grievance of concern to cultural nationalists, however. The revenues that US border television stations collected from Canadian advertisers constituted a parallel and equally contentious matter.

Border Broadcasting

Much like the debate over tax exemptions for advertisers in Canadian editions of foreign periodicals, the discussion of tax deductibility in border broadcasting followed from larger, well-established grievances over continental media spill-over. The critical provision of Bill C-58 relating to broadcasting concerned tax deductibility 'for an advertisement directed primarily to a market in Canada and broadcast by a foreign broadcast undertaking'.[14] In practice, this provision was meant to discourage the purchase of advertising time on US border television stations by Canadian advertisers seeking to reach a Canadian market.

The popularity of American stations among Canadian viewers and the wide reach of foreign signals, as cable television grew through the 1970s, were viewed as creating a drain on Canadian media outlets.[15] According to a 1971 CRTC document entitled *The Integration of Cable Television in the Canadian Broadcasting System*, 'some $12-million to $15-million a year of Canadian money is spent to buy commercial time on U.S. television stations.'[16] The CRTC saw this loss of revenue as a 'real and immediate' threat to Canadian broadcasting.[17]

The threat identified by the CRTC paralleled, in many respects, the dangers seen by Canadian publishers in a foreign-controlled periodicals industry. According to the terms of the 1968 Broadcasting Act, Canada was to have 'a single system . . . the Canadian broadcasting system', which would not only serve local audiences but would also advance Canadian programming and national identity.[18] The CRTC maintained that lost advertising revenues and the larger problem of 'unlimited penetration by United States stations on a wholesale south to north basis would completely destroy the licensing logic of the Canadian broadcasting system as established by the Broadcasting Act'.[19] In 1971, the Commission recommended a series of policies to regulate cable operations. These included deleting commercial advertising from US signals and amending the Income Tax Act so as to eliminate deductibility for 'advertising purchased by Canadian advertisers on stations not licensed by the Commission'.[20]

Although such tax provisions were not introduced as government policy until 1975, they were preceded in 1972 by a novel CRTC amendment to a Calgary cable licence. This amendment, following from the 1971 CRTC policy recommendations, involved the deletion in Calgary of commercials from a Spokane, Washington signal.[21] Commercial deletion became far more charged as a political issue, however, when Rogers Cable of Toronto began the practice in August 1973. While the original CRTC decision on the Calgary licence was protested by the US State Department,[22] the action by Rogers Cable prompted intervention by Secretary of State Henry Kissinger as well as litigation in the Federal Court of Canada by stations in Buffalo, New York.[23]

It was within this context of a lingering dispute over commercial deletion in border broadcasting that the tax provisions of Bill C-58 were introduced. As Katherine Swinton points out in her very thorough study of the subject, the objectives of commercial deletion and tax non-deductibility were the same: namely, to re-direct advertising revenue back to Canada for 'the development of Canadian programming'.[24]

The Societal Perspective on Bill C-58

In light of this background to the periodicals and broadcasting provisions of Bill C-58, the first framework introduced in Chapter 2 can be considered. According to the societal approach, Bill C-58 is best understood as an outcome of competition among organized groups in Canada; proponents of the legislation would be expected on balance to command greater resources, cohesion, expertise and representativeness than opponents. This proposition is difficult to apply in this case, however, because principal actors in both the periodicals and broadcasting debates, including the parent companies of *Time* and *Reader's Digest* as well as the border broadcasters and many of their allies, were based outside the country. Each of these external actors had important links with a foreign government, that of the US, thus imparting an international dimension that is not captured in the model's focus on domestic societal factors. However, since the group approach requires attention above all to competing organized interests, this section examines the attributes of societal groups based outside as well as inside Canada.

Did organizations that favoured Bill C-58 possess more resources than those that opposed it? Probably not; in fact, the reverse seems more likely. Research on the magazine business indicates that the smaller, 'non-establishment sector of the industry' was initially the most supportive of nationalist proposals.[25] This part of the Canadian cultural community, whose most visible representative during the *Time/Reader's Digest* debate was the Canadian Periodical Publishers' Association, had more limited means than the establishment sector of the industry, which included Maclean-Hunter Ltd. In turn, the latter's resources paled in comparison with those available to *Time* and *Reader's Digest*. In 1975, for example, when Bill C-58 was debated on the floor of the House of Commons and in Canadian society more generally, the net income after taxes of Time Canada was $1.4 million,[26] and the organization employed approximately 150 full- and part-time staff.[27] Even more significant, Reader's Digest Magazines Ltd claimed in 1975 that it directly or indirectly employed 1,800 Canadians, that it contributed $30 million annually to the Canadian economy and that the lobby effort to prevent passage of Bill C-58 cost $1.3 million.[28]

In the broadcasting field, the imbalance of resources in favour of groups opposed to this legislation was even more apparent. NBC, CBS, the Motion Picture Association of America, and the National Association of Broadcasters, as well as individual border station owners, were united in their opposition to both commercial deletion and the tax provisions of Bill C-58.[29] Domestic opponents of this legislation included the Association of Canadian Advertisers and the Advertising Agency Association of British Columbia, which feared 'loss of commissions on advertisements sold for use on U.S. stations'.[30] Among the only organized supporters of this part of the legislation in Canada were the Committee for an Independent Canada and the Association of Canadian Television and Radio Actors (ACTRA), which viewed Bill C-58 as promising more work for

Canadian performers.[31] Clearly, the combined resources of the Committee and ACTRA in 1975 were far less than those of opponents of the legislation.

Were the proponents of Bill C-58 more cohesive than its opponents? Again, this is unlikely. The corporate interests represented by the Time Canada and Reader's Digest organizations, American broadcasters and some Canadian advertising groups shared a fundamental belief that the legislation was unfair, misdirected and profoundly unneighbourly. According to its critics, Bill C-58 would not alter the cultural preferences of Canadian readers and television viewers for foreign as opposed to Canadian materials.[32] Although cultural nationalists presented well-integrated arguments in favour of tax changes as a way of financing greater Canadian programming,[33] it is not clear that they constituted a more cohesive organized interest than their adversaries. Overall, both sides were united in their commitment to tightly argued positions.

If the resources of Bill C-58's opponents exceeded those of its proponents and if the two sides were relatively balanced in terms of cohesion, then what can be said about expertise? By the mid-1970s, the knowledge of the magazine industry and of cultural policy in general possessed by the Canadian affiliates of Time and Reader's Digest was quite vast. Both organizations had participated in an intense lobbying process ten years earlier, and had succeeded in gaining exemption at that time from Canadian tax changes. Furthermore, in the period following 1965, the Reader's Digest organization was instrumental in establishing the Magazine Association of Canada as a major lobbyist for periodical interests.[34] These kinds of activities not only offered the publishers of Time and Reader's Digest an understanding of the way the Canadian industry worked but also imparted policy experience, visibility and some measure of control within the cultural field.

By way of contrast, the organizations opposed to the broadcasting provisions of Bill C-58 had less knowledge and experience of Canadian policy than did Time and Reader's Digest, since the cable dispute was of more recent origin than the debate over periodicals. Yet the border broadcasters and their allies learned quickly; they testified at length before House of Commons and Senate committees and met with CRTC officials during 1975 and 1976.[35] Moreover, the expertise of the border broadcasters neatly dovetailed with their cohesiveness; many questioned how simple tax amendments could be expected to shift Canadian preferences from US to domestic cultural products. In the words of Philip Beuth of Capital Cities Communications:

> Some 45 per cent of the Metro Toronto audience watches the Buffalo stations. Preventing Canadian advertisers from using the Buffalo stations will not increase the audience of the other Toronto stations. Our audience will remain. It will simply cripple television as a medium for reaching the total Toronto market-place.[36]

Supporters of Bill C-58, including Moses Znaimer of CITY-TV in Toronto, calculated the potentially very favourable impact on Canadian television that would follow from repatriating advertising capital.[37] Similar arithmetic was done by advocates of the bill's publishing provisions.[38] Yet these experts could not prove through public debate that advertising dollars drained off by foreign media would necessarily return and produce either Canadian employment or Canadian programming. In short, given the nature of the tax deductibility issue as it was debated during the mid-1970s, expertise seems to have been roughly the same among organized groups on both sides.

Were cultural nationalists more representative in the domain of communications policy than their adversaries? In this case, the answer is clearly affirmative. Within Canada, key players in the field supported the legislation; they included prominent editors, publishers, writers, broadcasters and cultural 'notables'.[39] Yet despite this base, the resources and expertise of Bill C-58's opponents helped to impart some degree of representativeness to that interest as well. For example, Canadian directors, readers and employees of *Time* and *Reader's Digest* were mobilized to oppose restrictions on foreign periodicals, and their intervention was noted in the halls of Parliament.[40]

In conclusion, applying the societal model to Bill C-58 yields a prediction of policy stalemate. Opponents of the legislation seem to have controlled greater resources; the two sides were relatively balanced with respect to cohesion and expertise; and the proponents were more representative within the cultural domain. If this situation were to be played out in policy terms, then stalemate would be expected—meaning inertia, indecision and government inaction. The societal model, in short, does not predict that Bill C-58 would come forward as government legislation and that it would ultimately become part of federal communications policy. Instead, the model as interpreted in Chapter 2 yields a prediction that is at odds with the successful passage in 1976 of Bill C-58.

The Bureaucratic Perspective on Bill C-58

Unlike the societal approach, which conceives of policy outcomes as a product of inter-group competition, the bureaucratic view emphasizes administrative preferences, capacity and autonomy as key factors in government decision-making. Yet, like the societal view, the bureaucratic approach is difficult to apply in the case of Bill C-58. Perhaps the most obvious problem here is the matter of administrative relevance. Bill C-58, An Act to Amend the Income Tax Act, was in formal terms a matter of taxation policy and came within the jurisdiction of the Ministry of National Revenue. Yet in terms of public policy it was anything but a specialized issue of advertising deductibility, of interest only to a narrow range of professional accountants, advertisers and tax bureaucrats. During the mid-1970s, Bill C-58 emerged as a cultural and, specifically, communications issue rather than as a matter of taxation policy. If a bureaucratic approach is applied to this case, it would need to focus on the preferences, capacity and autonomy of public administrators in the communications field rather than in the area of national revenue.

Were bureaucratic preferences in the communications sector of the federal state favourable to the terms of Bill C-58? According to the 1968 Broadcasting Act and the 1973 Green Paper on Communications Policy, government ministries and agencies were charged with the explicit task of fostering Canadian cultural activity.[41] In the heavily regulated field of broadcasting, in particular, the 'independent and nationalistic' approach adopted by CRTC chairmen Pierre Juneau and Harry Boyle during the 1970s reflected a clear preference for this general principle and, within it, for the sort of policies advanced in Bill C-58.[42] Such reforms were viewed as a means of diverting advertising revenues from US to Canadian television outlets, thus enlarging opportunities for Canadian programming and reinforcing the public mandate laid out in the Broadcasting Act and subsequent Green Paper.

In the area of periodicals a parallel bureaucratic preference is difficult to identify. Unlike the broadcasting field, the periodicals industry was directed more by itself than by any single federal agency. Nationalists in the periodicals industry lobbied successive secretaries of state and other members of the federal cabinet on the issue of tax deductibility, since until 1980 the Arts and Culture Branch of the Department of the Secretary of State was nominally responsible for periodicals policy.[43] Yet this branch tended not to provide the assertive leadership offered by the CRTC in the broadcasting sector—a pattern that is likely attributable to the fact that the publishing sector was less regulated than the broadcasting sector during the 1970s.

Bureaucratic preferences, in short, seem relevant to only part of the policy terrain covered by Bill C-58: namely, the broadcasting sector, where such preferences were clearly favourable to the terms of the legislation. Yet on the matter of periodicals regulation—which, after all, constituted the core of the *Time/Reader's Digest* controversy—bureaucratic preferences were less clear and less relevant.

A similar situation obtained with reference to bureaucratic capacity. Under the leadership of chairmen who were unambiguous supporters of tax non-deductibility, the CRTC's human and budgetary resources could be drawn upon to support Bill C-58. Although the agency had other priorities besides the passage of this legislation, much of what it was established to accomplish—including licensing Canadian broadcast outlets and enhancing Canadian programming—fell within the purview of Bill C-58. The ability of the main bureaucratic player in the broadcasting sector, the CRTC, to execute its actions was thus quite high; moreover, its formal mandate and elite preferences coincided in such a way as to permit the exploitation of agency resources in support of Bill C-58.

With reference to periodicals, the absence of visible administrative preferences—parallel to those of the CRTC in the broadcasting field—has been noted. A similar problem emerges in attempting to examine state capacity or resources and, finally, administrative autonomy. Both of the latter seem to have been limited in the case of the Arts and Culture Branch, which did not serve as a vehicle for the periodicals provisions of C-58 to the same extent as the CRTC championed its broadcast provisions.

In the broadcasting field, the CRTC in the mid-1970s seemed to operate as a highly autonomous or independent regulator of cable undertakings. It was able to introduce a broad range of sanctions, both positive and negative, within the television industry, including making cable licences conditional on the deletion of foreign commercials.[44] Because of its regulatory clout within the Canadian television industry, the CRTC must be viewed as a highly autonomous, capable bureaucratic actor. As well, the preferences of the CRTC elite in this period were strongly sympathetic to the broadcasting intentions of Bill C-58, yielding an overall score of (+,+,+). The sections of this legislation that concerned non-deductibility for advertising on border stations can thus be explained quite usefully within a state structures framework.

The core portions of Bill C-58, however, concerned the tax treatment of advertisers in *Time* and *Reader's Digest*. The bureaucratic approach draws a virtual blank in this domain, since no prime administrative mover comparable to the CRTC can be identified. The preferences, capacity and autonomy of the main bureaucratic actor in this domain, the Arts and Culture Branch, were far less relevant to the periodicals provision than the CRTC was to the broadcasting section, making it virtually impossible to apply a bureaucratic framework to the periodicals section of Bill C-58.

This failure to explain the central magazine provisions of Bill C-58 confirms the hypothesis outlined in Chapter 2 regarding the limitations of both societal and bureaucratic models on their own. Neither offers an adequate explanation of why Bill C-58 would have been introduced, and neither captures the ideas and political flavour of this debate. This situation leads towards a third approach, one that would consider the impact of nationalist ideas on political actors.

Bill C-58 in an Integrative Perspective

Much of the existing literature on Bill C-58 suggests that this policy was a quintessentially political deed. Rather than viewing it as an outcome of societal competition between organized proponents and opponents, or as a product of bureaucratic structures within the federal state, analysts such as Christina McCall argue that the legislation reflected a straightforward *quid pro quo* within the governing Liberal party. According to her account, 'The only reward [Senator Keith] Davey sought for successfully managing the 1974 campaign was legislation to abolish the so-called Canadian editions of *Time* and *Reader's Digest* as a move to improve the advertising base for real Canadian magazines.'[45]

Both the societal and bureaucratic approaches to Bill C-58 overlook what

McCall and others view as its crucial political ingredient.[46] Neither the response of the Canadian public, media and key partisan elites to cultural nationalist ideas, nor the resistance of the US government to these arguments, has been captured thus far in this chapter. The integrative framework summarized in Figure 2.4 addresses each of these dimensions; in particular, it considers the international, partisan and attitudinal factors overlooked by the two previous models.

Perhaps the easiest way to employ the integrative model is to begin with an empty version of Figure 2.4, re-labelled as Figure 3.1, and literally fill in the blanks. Using the section on the societal model as a guide, it would seem that the resources of Bill C-58's supporters were more limited than those of its opponents (X1), that the cohesion (X2) and expertise (X3) of the two sides were relatively balanced and moderate, and that the representativeness of C-58's supporters within the cultural policy domain (X4) was high.

As its name indicates, the integrative view draws not only from societal conceptions of policy development but also from the bureaucratic model. Variables X5 through X7 in Figure 3.1, the bureaucratic cluster, indicated very conducive conditions during the mid-1970s with reference to administrative preferences (X5), capacity (X6) and autonomy (X7) in the broadcasting field. By contrast, measures for the periodicals sector were difficult to ascertain and are not entered, since bureaucratic actors were less relevant to policy outcomes in this sector than in the broadcasting field.

Taking the scores from the first two models together, it appears that Bill C-58 had mixed chances of success in the mid-1970s. Although societal supporters of the policy obtain high scores with respect to representativeness in the cultural domain (X4), their standing on the other three group measures is weaker. Moreover, the difficulty of applying a bureacratic model to the periodicals section of the legislation permits only a partial reading of variables X5 through X7—where conditions in the broadcasting administration were very favourable.

The three variables remaining in Figure 3.1, X8 through X10, represent the ideas/politics cluster of factors not considered by the two conventional models. According to the hypothesis in Chapter 2, highly or moderately conducive scores on at least one of the three variables in this cluster are necessary for policy success; in Figure 3.1, 2.5 of 3 scores are in the 'somewhat conducive' category.

Variable X8, international influences, concerns in this case the position of the US government on Bill C-58. Scoring this variable is complicated by the fact that Washington intervened officially and very directly to oppose the broadcast section of C-58, at a time when its public position on the periodical provisions was neutral. In the broadcasting field, the US State Department objected to commercial deletion in February 1973, and later opposed both commercial deletion and the treatment of border broadcasters in 1975 and 1976.[47] At a January 1976 meeting in Ottawa with CRTC, External Affairs and Department of Communications officials, representatives of the US State Department as well as the Federal Communications Commission expressed strong resistance to the

FIGURE 3.1

SCORING INDEPENDENT VARIABLES ON BILL C-58

	SOCIETAL CLUSTER				BUREAUCRATIC CLUSTER			IDEAS/POLITICS CLUSTER			ROW TOTALS
	Group resources X_1	Group cohesion X_2	Group expertise X_3	Group representativeness X_4	Bureaucratic preferences X_5	Bureaucratic capacity X_6	Bureaucratic autonomy X_7	International influences X_8	Partisan actors X_9	Media, public opinion X_{10}	
Very conducive conditions				●	●	●	●				4
Somewhat conducive conditions		●	●					●	●	●	4.5
Minimally conducive conditions	●							●			1.5

broadcast section of Bill C-58 and cited it as a major bilateral irritant. The unwillingness of the Canadian government to compromise on either commercial deletion or Bill C-58 led to a further intervention by US Ambassador Thomas Enders before the Senate Banking Committee in the spring of 1976.[48] After Bill C-58 went into effect in 1977, the State Department as well as a number of US legislators continued to press for withdrawal of its broadcast provisions.[49]

The US government adopted a more neutral position on the periodicals provisions of Bill C-58. After intervening very assertively in support of *Time* and *Reader's Digest* during the 1950s and 1960s, the US government backed off from any further action.[50] According to Roger Swanson's analysis of the period following the 1970 release of the Davey report,

> *Time* was evidently sensitive to the fact that if it got the support of the U.S. government, its attempt to prove that it qualified as a 'Canadian' magazine would be compromised. *Time* therefore fought its battle alone, keeping the State Department informed of developments. Unlike the previous period, the U.S. government did not become actively involved.[51]

A similar preference for no official US intervention was expressed by *Reader's Digest*, whose Canadian president instructed the parent organization to 'stay out. Your help would be counterproductive.'[52]

Given this very interesting juxtaposition of concerted US government intervention *against* the broadcasting section of Bill C-58, on the one hand, and its apparent neutrality on the periodicals provisions, on the other, variable X8 is scored using half-circles. The broadcasting terms of the bill were vigorously opposed by the US; hence a half-circle is placed in Figure 3.1 in the category of minimally conducive conditions. Since the US did not officially pursue the periodicals section, a half-circle is also placed in the category of somewhat conducive conditions.

The integrative model establishes a separate measure of attitudinal support, variable X10, encompassing both media and mass-level opinion. Polls from the mid-1970s, summarized in Table 3.1, reflect consistently strong public support for the ideas that Canadian identity was threatened and that government regulation was required to limit US media spillover; overall, support for both cultural and economic nationalism in public opinion polls peaked during this period.[53] Editorial opinion, however, was divided between support for cultural nationalist arguments and opposition to legislation that was viewed as a threat to freedom of expression.[54] Variable X10 is therefore scored 'moderately conducive'.

The Partisan Politics of Bill C-58

The final and, in many respects, crucial element in the integrative model rests in variable X9, partisan actors. The scoring of this variable is somewhat puzzling

TABLE 3.1   CULTURAL NATIONALIST ATTITUDES, 1966-1979

YEAR	SURVEY ITEM	% SUPPORT
1966	Canadian way of life influenced 'too much' by United States	53
1970	US television influence in Canada 'too much'	48
1974	Canadian way of life influenced 'too much' by United States	57
1975	US television influence in Canada 'too much'	59
1977	'Strongly approve' or 'approve' of media content regulations	72
1977	Favour Canadian- rather than US-made television commercials	75
1979	Government support for broadcasting important or very important	84
1979	Government support for magazines important or very important	50

Sources: Sylvia Bashevkin, 'Does Public Opinion Matter? The Adoption of Federal Royal Commission and Task Force Recommendations on the National Question, 1951-1987', *Canadian Public Adminstration* 31 (1988), Table 3; and Paul Audley, *Canada's Cultural Industries* (Toronto: Lorimer, 1983), xxv-xxvii.

at first glance, since Canada and the Liberal party were led during the mid-1970s by an articulate critic of ethnic nationalism.[55] Pierre Elliott Trudeau's distaste for nationalist politics can be attributed to two main sources: first, on a philosophical level, Trudeau had absorbed the liberal anti-nationalist thinking of Lord Acton; and second, as a political activist in Quebec, he consistently opposed both the traditional French-Canadian nationalism of Premier Maurice Duplessis and the modern Quebec nationalism of the Quiet Revolution and following. Terming the 1960s phenomenon 'la nouvelle trahison des clercs', Trudeau condemned 'this self-deluding passion of a large segment of our thinking population for throwing themselves headlong—intellectually and spiritually—into purely escapist pursuits'.[56]

In terms of pan-Canadian or, as he referred to it in his writings, English-Canadian nationalism, Trudeau was on less familiar ground. He subscribed to the view that English-Canadian nationalism tended to stimulate its French-Canadian counterpart: by appropriating the federal state for their own purposes, he implied, English Canadians provoked 'counter-nationalist movements' in Quebec.[57] Trudeau's views were also coloured by his close friendship with economist Albert Breton, who described pan-Canadian nationalism as a selfish, self-aggrandizing project of the Anglophone middle class.[58]

As an outsider in English Canadian politics, however, Trudeau was more prepared to 'do business' with nationalist activists in that milieu than in Quebec. In 1968, for example, Trudeau recognized the need to gather support for his leadership campaign among progressive Liberals in Ontario and elsewhere in English Canada, and won the endorsement of Walter Gordon.[59] Gordon and his colleagues apparently believed that Trudeau shared their ideas about foreign investment or, at the very least, that he would respond to the concerns of nationalists within the Liberal party.[60]

Although they grew increasingly frustrated with the lack of legislative action by the Trudeau government after 1968, Gordon and most of his protégés remained loyal Liberals.[61] Indeed, some activists recruited by Gordon during the Pearson years obtained major party positions in the 1970s. The best-known and, from the perspective of Bill C-58, most pivotal of these was Keith Davey, a former radio sales manager from Toronto who learned his nationalism from Gordon and the editorial pages of the *Toronto Star*.[62] Davey's commitment to cultural nationalist ideas was reinforced in his role as head of the Special Senate Committee on Mass Media, which in 1970 produced a landmark volume entitled *The Uncertain Mirror*.[63] The Davey report recommended that tax exemptions for *Time* and *Reader's Digest* be repealed and, if necessary, that the editorial content, ownership and control of both publications be 'Canadianized'.[64] As well, *The Uncertain Mirror* endorsed non-deductibility for advertising on border television stations, arguing that 'this will curb the pirating of commercial dollars by stations . . . which accept Canadian money but don't play by Canadian rules.' [65]

Trudeau's chief Quebec lieutenant in this period, Marc Lalonde, was puzzled by Davey's emphasis on this seemingly 'irrelevant' matter of English-Canadian cultural nationalism.[66] Yet even with the bewilderment of Lalonde and the reluctance of Trudeau, Davey's success in engineering the 1974 election victory permitted the *Time/Reader's Digest* Bill to appear on the agenda of the new majority government.

Despite its significant backroom support, the debate over Bill C-58 was prolonged and heated, including within the Liberal cabinet. Initially, the legislation defined a Canadian magazine as one that had '75 per cent Canadian equity control and a 'substantially' different content from foreign periodicals'.[67] In the spring of 1975, when Time Canada successfully met these ownership criteria and presented plans for an edition that would contain 41 per cent Canadian content, nationalists including Senator Davey pressed for a more stringent definition of 'substantially different'. The result was a revised bill, presented by Revenue Minister Bud Cullen in October 1975, specifying that not more than 20 per cent of magazine content could be the same as in a foreign publication.[68] This revision essentially obviated compliance by *Time* [69] but left open the possibility of a political compromise that would permit compliance by *Reader's Digest*. If material from foreign versions could be edited and condensed in

Canada and counted as Canadian content, then the latter could continue to enjoy advertising deductibility.

This re-definition of Canadian content to suit the needs of *Reader's Digest* resulted from efforts within the Quebec Liberal caucus to reach a private accommodation with that organization.[70] The Canadian offices of the *Digest* were located in a Montreal riding held by Minister of Public Works C.M. (Bud) Drury, the brother-in-law of Walter Gordon, who had long been associated with the conservative or business wing of the Liberal party.[71] Drury had little sympathy for the nationalist interventionism of either Gordon or Davey, and apparently persuaded the Revenue Minister to create a loophole in Bill C-58 that would be suitable for *Reader's Digest*.[72]

The partisan circumstances surrounding Bill C-58 can thus be described as moderately conducive. Elements of the Liberal caucus in the House of Commons and Senate—notably the progressive Ontario wing, which endorsed the nationalist principles of Gordon and Davey—were strongly supportive of the entire legislative package to limit foreign media spillover, as was the NDP caucus.[73] Party elites including Trudeau and Lalonde had difficulty understanding the importance of the issue to this first group and tended to defer to Davey and others in the honeymoon period following their majority victory. The least supportive segment within the House of Commons, which shared fundamental sympathies with the societal critics of Bill C-58, was comprised of the Conservative Opposition and business Liberals. Given the creation in cabinet of the *Reader's Digest* loophole and the decision of six Liberal MPs to vote against the bill on third reading,[74] it seems that some elites in the governing party worked to prevent and, if necessary, circumvent the conversion of cultural nationalist ideas into federal policies.

Assessing Bill C-58

Counting up the scores in Figure 3.1, we find that very conducive conditions obtained in 4 of the 10 independent variables, somewhat conducive conditions in 4.5, and minimally conducive conditions in 1.5. Following the terms of the propositions in Chapter 2, it would seem that the probability of governmental action favourable to nationalist interests was moderate, about 40 per cent; that the likelihood of policy failure was low, about 15 per cent; and that the probability of a saw-off was moderate, about 45 per cent. This clustering of scores in the middle category seems to be consistent with actual outcomes; that is, the Liberals watered down or 'sawed off' part of the nationalist proposal having to do with the treatment of *Reader's Digest*, while at the same time claiming to have strengthened the provisions affecting *Time*.

The second proposition in Chapter 2 involved the necessity for conducive conditions on at least one of the three variables in the ideas/politics cluster. In Figure 3.1, moderately conducive conditions obtained on one dimension of variable X8 (US government position regarding the periodical section of C-58) as well as on variables X9 and X10. In other words, the receptivity to cultural nationalist ideas among three important political sectors in Canada and the US was moderately conducive, suggesting that favourable political circumstances for converting these ideas into policies were present.

Why was Bill C-58 introduced and ultimately passed as government legislation? Given the views regarding nationalism held by Pierre Trudeau, and the looming threat of Quebec separatism, it is at first glance surprising that the federal government would 'take the heat' both within its own caucus and from official US as well as societal opponents of Bill C-58. Much of that willingness seems attributable to a basic political reality; namely, the nationalist preferences and capacities of key Liberal partisans during the mid-1970s, whose influence within the parliamentary wing of the party created more conducive conditions for the introduction of nationalist ideas and the eventual passage of Bill C-58 than would otherwise have existed.[75] A political and specifically partisan element thus seems crucial in explaining why the government would be willing to pursue the legislation. Moreover, the ability of committed nationalists within the Liberal party to point to poll data on public support for their cultural ideas was also likely relevant.

Does the integrative model offer a better account of Bill C-58 than the other two approaches? To be fair, the bureaucratic view is useful in explaining the broadcast provisions of this bill, even though it overlooks considerable opposition and pressure from the US administration. Compared with the societal perspective, both the bureaucratic and integrative views are preferable in this case although, as noted above, the bureaucratic approach is of little use in explaining the core periodicals provisions of Bill C-58. The only model that seems to capture the bureaucratic dynamic of the border broadcast provisions of Bill C-58 as well as the societal and political dimensions of its publishing provisions is the integrative view—which also acknowledges the role of US government actors. The latter were significant because even though the Liberal government faced more domestic criticism for its treatment of *Time* and *Reader's Digest* than for its handling of the border broadcasters, the costs that it incurred vis-à-vis the US in the broadcast field were far from minor.[76]

To the extent that the integrative model admits politics both in a partisan, parliamentary sense and in an international sense, and to the extent that it explicitly considers the attitudinal environment within which policy action occurs, this third approach is far more useful in understanding Bill C-58 than either of the other two views. Integrative thinking focusses attention on the conversion of nationalist ideas into policy action, and acknowledges that political elites and public attitudes shape that conversion in a very crucial way. It should be emphasized, however, that 7 of the 10 variables in the third model are drawn from conventional approaches; the latter clearly contribute to the explanatory strength of an integrative perspective.

Conclusions

This chapter has employed three approaches identified in Chapter 2 to analyse government action on Bill C-58. Societal and bureaucratic explanations of the core periodicals provisions of the legislation were of limited use; the bureaucratic view was helpful, however, in understanding the broadcasting section of the bill. Merging societal, bureaucratic and political variables in an integrative model predicted that the probabilities of both government action and policy saw-off were moderate; more important, the third model drew out political responses to cultural nationalist ideas that were neglected by the first two approaches.

The fact that the third framework yielded a moderate probability of nationalist success on Bill C-58 (4 out of a possible 10 'very conducive' scores) sheds light on larger questions of pan-Canadian influence. Even during the mid-1970s, when cultural activists held key positions in the Liberal party that allowed them to press for relatively minor tax changes, proponents of Bill C-58 had a difficult time obtaining legislative results. In short, the controversy over C-58 was lengthy and divisive, and its outcome remained in doubt for much of the time that the bill was debated. What conclusions can be drawn from this scenario?

First, with reference to societal actors, cultural nationalists faced an uphill battle in their efforts to marshal expertise, cohesion and, especially, resources. Although organized nationalism was arguably at its peak during the mid-1970s, the groups that endorsed C-58 were not dominant in societal terms over those that opposed the legislation. The financial clout of foreign broadcasters and publishers, combined with their shared sense of a major policy threat and their commitment to respond to that threat, made for a formidable societal opposition. And while these critics did not prevail in the *Time/Reader's Digest* case, their ability to put nationalists on the defensive when the latter were at their crest suggests the fragility of cultural policies like Bill C-58.

Second, applying a bureaucratic perspective to this case indicates the importance of regulatory elites in the broadcasting field. Without the nationalist preferences, high capacity and clear autonomy of the CRTC leadership, Bill C-58's broadcasting provisions would probably not have emerged as they did. The willingness of CRTC decision-makers to argue for the financial, programmatic and national identity benefits of the broadcasting legislation meant that cultural nationalist ideas became part of a sustained regulatory ethos.

Yet this very achievement suggested once again the fragility of the nationalist victory on Bill C-58. If bureaucratic preferences shifted in a direction that was more sympathetic to Canadian private or foreign broadcasting interests, or if the CRTC's preferences remained nationalist but the agency's capacity or autonomy were reduced, then the likelihood of additional policies like Bill C-58 would be vastly reduced. Judging by subsequent developments, the preferences of agency elites have become less assertively nationalist, while bureaucratic autonomy has been reduced in the face of increased political control.[77] These kinds of patterns do not bode well for the future of either Bill C-58 or similar measures.

Third, we can consider the integrative model's focus on political response to nationalist ideas. The position of the US government on the border broadcasting question was unambiguously negative and, as expected, Washington continued to oppose the legislation long after its formal enactment. Yet had the US *not* maintained a neutral position on the publishing section of Bill C-58, Ottawa's willingness to proceed would have been far more doubtful, since it was the fate of *Time* and *Reader's Digest* that controlled centre stage in the domestic debate.

Cultural nationalists might argue that their cause is generally strengthened within Canada by forceful and direct US opposition. Developments subsequent to Bill C-58, however, notably those surrounding a proposed film distribution policy during the mid-1980s, indicate that this is not the case.[78] We would conclude that the official reticence of the US on the domestically contentious terms of Bill C-58 was probably fortunate and, in historical terms, constituted an aberration that worked to the advantage of nationalist interests.

The fate of cultural nationalist ideas in attitudinal and partisan environments suggests that the prospects for success were similarly fragile. Even as members of the general public and prominent federal Liberals endorsed cultural arguments, many other influential media and party actors held explicitly anti-nationalist beliefs, which were incompatible with the terms of Bill C-58. The substantial cabinet concessions that were made to *Reader's Digest* indicate the depth of political division over this policy; they reflect not only the vulnerable position of cultural nationalist ideas in the mid-1970s, but also the tortuous path from world view to policy even during this period.

Notes

[1] Special Senate Committee on Mass Media, *Report*, vol. 1: *The Uncertain Mirror* (Davey Report; Ottawa: Information Canada, 1970), 194.

[2] S.M. Crean, *Who's Afraid of Canadian Culture* (Don Mills, Ont.: General Publishing, 1976), 224.

[3] Arthur Siegel, *Politics and the Media in Canada* (Toronto: McGraw-Hill Ryerson, 1983), 1.

[4] Theodore Hagelin and Hudson Janisch, 'The Border Broadcasting Dispute in Context', in Canadian-U.S. Conference on Communications Policy, *Cultures in Collision: The Interaction of Canadian and U.S. Television Broadcast Policies* (New York: Praeger, 1984), 48.

[5] For a review of cultural nationalist arguments regarding periodical publishing, see Isaiah Litvak and Christopher Maule, *Cultural Sovereignty: The Time and Reader's Digest Case in Canada* (New York: Praeger, 1974), chap. 2.

[6] Special Senate Committee on the Mass Media, *Report*, 194. The Davey committee linked cultural issues with the problem of foreign ownership, arguing that 'creeping continentalism has proceeded far enough in this country. We believe the present situation of the magazine industry is a perfect example of the dangers of an unexamined acceptance of foreign investment' (Davey Report, as quoted in Litvak and Maule, *Cultural Sovereignty*, 93).

[7] Royal Commission on Publications, *Report* (O'Leary Report; Ottawa: Queen's Printer, 1961), 74. A

similar approach had been endorsed in a 1922 telegram from Canadian publishers to the federal government. See Litvak and Maule, *Cultural Sovereignty*, 18. Subsequent proposals for duties on foreign periodicals were included in the 1931 Conservative and 1956 Liberal federal budgets, only to be repealed following changes of government. See John R. LoGalbo, 'The Time and Reader's Digest Bill: C-58 and Canadian Cultural Nationalism', *New York University Journal of International Law and Politics* 9 (1976), 239-40. On US government opposition to these initiatives, see Roger Frank Swanson, 'Canadian Cultural Nationalism and the U.S. Public Interest', in Janice L. Murray (ed.), *Canadian Cultural Nationalism* (New York: New York University Press, 1977), 65-6.

[8]Reader's Digest was incorporated in Canada in 1943, the same year as Time began printing its Canadian edition in Chicago. See Litvak and Maule, *Cultural Sovereignty*, 28.

[9]Ibid., 30-1.

[10]Ibid., 51-3.

[11]Ibid., 73.

[12]According to Gordon, the 1965 initiative was likely as far as the Canadian government could go and still ensure congressional passage of the Auto Pact. See Walter L. Gordon, *A Choice for Canada: Independence or Colonial Status* (Toronto: McClelland and Stewart, 1966), 97; and Gordon's 1969 statement confirming this view, quoted in LoGalbo, 'The Time and Reader's Digest Bill', note 31, 243.

[13]See Swanson, 'Canadian Cultural Nationalism and the U.S. Public Interest', 65-6; Isaiah A. Litvak and Christopher J. Maule, 'Interest-Group Tactics and the Politics of Foreign Investment: The Time-Reader's Digest Case Study', *Canadian Journal of Political Science* 7 (1974), 621-3; and LoGalbo, 'The Time and Reader's Digest Bill', 243.

[14]Bill C-58, *An Act to Amend the Income Tax Act*, September 1976.

[15]See Special Senate Committee on Mass Media, *Report*, vol. 1, 256; and Paul Audley, *Canada's Cultural Industries* (Toronto: Lorimer, 1983), chap. 7.

[16]*The Integration of Cable Television in the Canadian Broadcasting System* (Ottawa: Canadian Radio Television Commission, 1971), 5.

[17]Ibid., 6.

[18]*The Broadcasting Act, An Act to Implement a Broadcasting Policy for Canada*, R.S.C. 1970, section 3.

[19]*The Integration of Cable Television in the Canadian Broadcasting System*, 6.

[20]*Cable Television: Canadian Broadcasting 'A Single System'* (Ottawa: Canadian Radio Television Commission, 1971), 29.

[21]See Hagelin and Janisch, 'The Border Broadcasting Dispute in Context', 47; and Katherine Swinton, 'Advertising and Canadian Cable Television—A Problem in International Communications Law', *Osgoode Hall Law Journal* 15 (1977), 544, 569.

[22]See Swinton, 'Advertising and Canadian Cable Television', 544; Hagelin and Janisch, 'The Border Broadcasting Dispute in Context', 51; and Swanson, 'Canadian Cultural Nationalism and the U.S. Public Interest', 69.

[23]Swanson, 'Canadian Cultural Nationalism and the U.S. Public Interest', 70; Hagelin and Janisch, 'The Border Broadcasting Dispute in Context', 48, 52.

[24]Swinton, 'Advertising and Canadian Cable Television', 558.

[25]Litvak and Maule, *Cultural Sovereignty*, 86.

[26]Isaiah A. Litvak and Christopher J. Maule, 'Bill C-58 and the Regulation of Periodicals', *International Journal* 36 (1980-81), Table 3, 76.

[27]LoGalbo, 'The Time and Reader's Digest Bill', 256.

[28]Marianne Ackerman, 'Happily Ever After', *Saturday Night* (August 1982), 32.

[29]See Swinton, 'Advertising and Canadian Cable Television', note 77, 561; Swanson, 'Canadian Cultural Nationalism and the U.S. Public Interest', 68-9; and Hagelin and Janisch, 'The Border Broadcasting Dispute in Context', 51.

[30]Swinton, 'Advertising and Canadian Cable Television', 563.

[31]Ibid.

[32]See Hagelin and Janisch, 'The Border Broadcasting Dispute in Context', 51.

[33]See, for example, Moses Znaimer, 'Why Let US Stations Dump Programs Here?' Globe and Mail (5 Nov. 1975), 7.

[34]This association also did extensive research on the periodicals industry. See LoGalbo, 'The Time and Reader's Digest Bill', 247; Litvak and Maule, Cultural Sovereignty, 110-14; and Litvak and Maule, 'Interest-Group Tactics and the Politics of Foreign Investment', 625.

[35]See Hagelin and Janisch, 'The Border Broadcasting Dispute in Context', 51.

[36]Beuth as quoted in ibid.

[37]See Znaimer, 'Why Let US Stations Dump Programs Here?' For figures on the revenue effects of Bill C-58, see Richard Collins, Culture, Communication and National Identity: The Case of Canadian Television (Toronto: University of Toronto Press, 1990), 73.

[38]See Audley, Canada's Cultural Industries, chap. 2.

[39]See Crean, Who's Afraid of Canadian Culture; and Swinton, 'Advertising and Canadian Cable Television'. The strong support among most members of the cultural community for Bill C-58 was also described in interviews with Paul Audley, 7 June 1990; Susan Crean, 23 May 1990; Michael de Pencier, 26 June 1990; and Alexander Ross, 17 July 1990.

[40]See LoGalbo, 'The Time and Reader's Digest Bill', 256; Ackerman, 'Happily Ever After', 32; and Murray G. Ross, 'Opting Out of Global Village?' in Globe and Mail (22 Dec. 1975), 7. Ross at the time was a director of Time Canada.

[41]See Swinton, 'Advertising and Canadian Cable Television', 556-7.

[42]Ibid., 558.

[43]According to Audley, Canada's Cultural Industries, this responsibility shifted in 1980 to the federal Department of Communications (253).

[44]See, for example, Swinton, 'Advertising and Canadian Cable Television', 544, 569.

[45]Christina McCall-Newman, Grits: An Intimate Portrait of the Liberal Party (Toronto: Macmillan, 1982), 161.

[46]The view that partisan politics, and especially Senator Davey, played a crucial role was also argued by Isaiah Litvak in a conversation with the author, 17 Jan. 1990.

[47]See Swanson, 'Canadian Cultural Nationalism and the U.S. Public Interest', 69-70, 73; and Hagelin and Janisch, 'The Border Broadcasting Dispute in Context', 52.

[48]See Swinton, 'Advertising and Canadian Cable Television', 580-2.

[49]The US threatened to pass parallel (or mirror) legislation in Congress, and 15 border stations filed a formal complaint under Section 301 of the US Trade Act of 1974. See Leslie G. Arries, Jr, 'The Position of the Border Broadcasters', in Canadian-U.S. Conference on Communications Policy, Cultures in Collision: The Interaction of Canadian and U.S. Television Broadcast Policies (New York: Praeger, 1984), 141-51; Hagelin and Janisch, 'The Border Broadcasting Dispute in Context', 52-5; and Thelma McCormack, 'Revolution, Communication and the Sense of History', in Elihu Katz and Tamas Szecsko (eds), Mass Media and Social Change (London: Sage), 178.

[50]On US actions during the 1950s and 1960s, see Swanson, 'Canadian Cultural Nationalism and the U.S. Public Interest', 65-6.

[51]Ibid., 66. A similar account is offered in Edelgard E. Mahant and Graeme S. Mount, An Introduction to Canadian-American Relations (Toronto: Methuen, 1984): 'The Ford administration in Washington made no special effort to help the two American magazines' (229).

[52]E. Paul Zimmerman, president of Canadian Reader's Digest, quoted in Ackerman, 'Happily Ever After', 33.

[53]See Sylvia Bashevkin, 'Does Public Opinion Matter? The Adoption of Federal Royal Commission

and Task Force Recommendations on the National Question, 1951-1987', *Canadian Public Administration* 31 (1988), 390-407.

[54]Some editorials clearly opposed Bill C-58—especially its broadcasting provisions—during the period when the US was threatening retaliation. See, for example, *Globe and Mail* (24 July 1980) and *Hamilton Spectator* (15 July 1980). On the negative editorial response to its periodicals provisions, see McCormack, 'Revolution, Communication and the Sense of History', 177.

[55]It is frequently argued that although Pierre Trudeau opposed ethnic nationalism, he was quite prepared to pursue a form of state nationalism in order to weaken its ethnic manifestations. See David Milne, *Tug of War: Ottawa and the Provinces Under Trudeau and Mulroney* (Toronto: Lorimer, 1986), 31-2. For a more general treatment of Trudeau's views on nationalism, see Stephen Clarkson and Christina McCall, *Trudeau and Our Times*, vol. I: *The Magnificent Obsession* (Toronto: McClelland and Stewart, 1990), 82-4.

[56]Pierre Elliott Trudeau, 'New Treason of the Intellectuals', in *Federalism and the French Canadians* (Toronto: Macmillan, 1968), 168.

[57]Pierre Elliott Trudeau, 'Federalism, Nationalism, and Reason', in ibid., 200.

[58]Breton's views are presented in Albert Breton, 'The Economics of Nationalism', *Journal of Political Economy* 72 (1964), 376-86. According to Stephen Clarkson, Trudeau adopted Breton's argument in a 1977 talk at the University of Toronto. See Stephen Clarkson, 'Anti-Nationalism in Canada: The Ideology of Mainstream Economics', *Canadian Review of Studies in Nationalism* 5 (1978), 61.

[59]Walter L. Gordon, *A Political Memoir* (Toronto: McClelland and Stewart, 1977), 300.

[60]According to one observer, 'Trudeau was briefly more nationalist than Walter Gordon during the 1950s. He wrote a very positive essay on the Gordon report in *Cité libre* which showed that.' Interview with Stephen Clarkson, 8 Aug. 1990. Gordon quoted approvingly from this *Cité libre* piece in his memoirs, questioning why Trudeau as prime minister had failed to respond to nationalist pressures. See Gordon, *A Political Memoir*, 320.

[61]On Gordon's response to the terms of foreign investment legislation, for example, see *A Political Memoir*, 317-20.

[62]According to McCall-Newman, *Grits*, Davey's father worked at the *Star* for 55 years (48).

[63]See Special Senate Committee on Mass Media, *Report*. The report was published in 3 volumes; *The Uncertain Mirror* was the title of vol. 1.

[64]Ibid., vol. 1, 165-6. The Senate committee proposal regarding Canadianization stated that if removing the 1965 tax exemption did not assist Canadianization, then both the Time and Reader's Digest organizations 'should be required to sell 75 per cent of the stock of their Canadian subsidiaries to Canadian residents, and to have Canadian residents make up at least 75 per cent of their officers and directors' (Litvak and Maule, 'Interest-Group Tactics and the Politics of Foreign Investment', 626).

[65]Special Senate Committee on Mass Media, *Report*, vol. 1, 256.

[66]McCall-Newman, *Grits*, 127.

[67]Swanson, 'Canadian Cultural Nationalism and the U.S. Public Interest', 66.

[68]'Reader's Digest Reprieved', *Canadian News Facts* 10:3 (19 Feb. 1976), 1521. On the so-called 'Cullen Rule' affecting digests, see LoGalbo, 'The Time and Reader's Digest Bill', 261-6.

[69]Ibid., 261; and Swanson, 'Canadian Cultural Nationalism and the U.S. Public Interest', 67.

[70]Swanson, 'Canadian Cultural Nationalism and the U.S. Public Interest', 66; LoGalbo, 'The Time and Reader's Digest Bill', 265; and Ackerman, 'Happily Ever After', 33.

[71]McCall-Newman, *Grits*, 44.

[72]This loophole was viewed as a 'hatchet job' by some cultural nationalists. See Crean, *Who's Afraid of Canadian Culture*, 225; and Ackerman, 'Happily Ever After'.

[73]The role of the Ontario Liberal caucus was cited in a 1982 speech by Trudeau. See James Rusk, 'FIRA to be Revised, U.S. Executives Told', *Globe and Mail* (21 Oct. 1982).

[74]See 'Parliament Passes *Time* Bill', *Canadian New Facts* 10:4 (4 March 1976), 1530-1.

[75]The effects of Bill C-58 included the establishment of *Maclean's* as a weekly magazine and the termination of *Time's* Canadian edition. See Litvak and Maule, 'Bill C-58 and the Regulation of Periodicals'; LoGalbo, 'The Time and Reader's Digest Bill', 269-72; and Arthur Donner and Fred Lazar, *An Examination of the Financial Impacts of Canada's 1976 Amendment to Section 19.1 of the Income Tax Act (Bill C-58) on U.S. and Canadian TV Broadcasting* (Ottawa: Department of Communications, 1979).

[76]See Swanson, 'Canadian Cultural Nationalism and the U.S. Public Interest'; and Swinton, 'Advertising and Canadian Cable Television'.

[77]On changes in the climate of cultural policy and, especially, communications regulation in the Mulroney years, see Mary Vipond, *The Mass Media in Canada* (Toronto: Lorimer, 1989), chap. 7; and Collins, *Culture, Communication and National Identity*, chap. 3.

[78]See Vipond, *The Mass Media in Canada*, chap. 7.

4 | Investment Nationalism: The Case of the National Energy Program

By ignoring the problem of foreign ownership in the past, Canadians have lost a significant share of the benefits of having a strong resource base. If we fail to act now, Canadians will lose once again.[1]

Introduction

This chapter considers a second instance of government action that was relatively favourable to nationalist interests: the adoption of the National Energy Program (NEP) as a vehicle for investment nationalism. The chapter compares the ability of societal, bureaucratic and integrative frameworks to explain the conversion of nationalist ideas into public policy, and evaluates the more general impact of investment arguments. Chapter 5 will consider the well-known and, in nationalist terms, less successful story of Canada-US free trade.

Like Bill C-58 in the cultural field, the National Energy Program is most logically and fully explained using an integrative approach. Integrative thinking draws in partisan factors in particular, which are crucial to explaining the timing of the NEP's introduction in 1980. As well, this framework evaluates the response to investment nationalist ideas in US government and Canadian attitudinal environments, considerations that are neglected by both of the traditional approaches.

The conclusions drawn in this chapter point towards the extremely vulnerable status of investment nationalism during the early 1980s. Societal opponents of the NEP waged a vigorous and ultimately successful campaign to dismantle the legislation, building on the anti-nationalist positions of the US government, several provincial governments and much of the Canadian media. Their victory obviated the favourable circumstances that obtained in the Liberal party, the federal bureaucracy and public opinion in 1980. In short, the case of the NEP reflects a temporary or short-term success story for investment nationalists. Many of their ideas were converted into federal government action in 1980 through the vehicle of the NEP—only to be rolled back systematically in subsequent policies.

The NEP: Background

The National Energy Program was introduced on the floor of the House of Commons on 28 October 1980. As part of the first budget of the restored majority government of Pierre Trudeau, following a brief hiatus of Conservative minority rule under Joe Clark, the NEP responded not only to circumstances in the energy field but also to developments in the area of federal-provincial relations.

At the time of the 1973 world oil crisis, Canada had a minority government, with the New Democrats holding the balance of power between 1972 and 1974. The governing Liberals needed to build an electoral base toward a future majority government and, like the NDP, were pressed by nationalist interests—particularly in Ontario—to develop an independent rather than continentalist energy strategy. Three federal policies adopted in response to the OPEC crisis reflected these pressures: first, domestic oil prices were frozen below the world price; second, a tax on oil exports to the US was imposed to subsidize imports in eastern Canada; and third, Petro-Canada was created as 'a national oil company . . . to help the Canadian state combat the uncertainties over energy supplies in the national interest'.[2]

Liberal resource policy during the early and mid-1970s thus attempted to satisfy a number of overlapping constituencies, including the NDP, central Canadian voters, nationalist interests and energy consumers. Not surprisingly, federal decisions in this period were generally opposed both by the energy industry—largely comprised of US-based multinational corporations—and by provincial governments in western Canada, which viewed such policies as detrimental to the economic and political interests of the oil-producing regions.

The NEP expanded the main lines of Liberal energy policy that had developed since 1973, frequently alienating many of these same constituencies. With reference to intergovernmental relations, the 1980 policy represented a conscious effort by the Trudeau government to re-centralize what was viewed as an increasingly imbalanced, overly decentralized federal system. The NEP was linked to parallel legislative action on constitutional reform and health care, and in other areas where the jurisdiction of the central government was ostensibly being eroded. This 'federal state-building program' of the Liberals attempted to reverse what Pierre Trudeau and the party leadership perceived as a movement towards 'shopping-plaza federalism'.[3]

Early indications that the Liberals planned to introduce a major initiative in the energy field appeared during the 1980 election campaign. Speaking in Halifax on 25 January, for example, Trudeau condemned the Clark government's proposal of an excise tax of 18 cents per litre on gasoline and argued instead for a 'made-in-Canada' oil price, a strengthened Petro-Canada and a goal of 50 per cent Canadianization of the energy sector.[4] Recognizing the extent to which voters in consuming regions feared increased prices and greater vulnerability to world conditions—particularly in the wake of the Iranian revolution—the Liberals developed a series of policy statements that formed the framework for what would become the National Energy Program.[5]

As announced in the fall of 1980, the NEP had three principal objectives: first, to ensure energy security through a combination of greater domestic development and reduced reliance on foreign supply, with a goal of self-sufficiency in oil by 1990; second, to increase Canadian opportunity in the energy industry by requiring 50 per cent domestic ownership and control of the petroleum sector by 1990; and third, to establish a 'made-in-Canada' oil price and to channel a higher share of energy revenues to the federal government—in the government's words, to put in place 'a petroleum pricing and revenue-sharing regime that recognizes the requirement of *fairness*'.[6] Together, these three provisions were viewed as a means of re-capturing federal fiscal and jurisdictional control in the energy field, limiting the role of multinational resource corporations and restricting the growth of provincial energy empires—particularly in Alberta.

Not incidentally, the NEP was also conceived with an eye towards enhancing Liberal fortunes in central Canada.[7] The policy responded to well-established ideas within the investment nationalist stream regarding foreign control of the oil and gas industries; these arguments dated back to the Gordon, Watkins and Gray reports as well as to the writings of activists in the Waffle and the Committee for an Independent Canada.[8] In conceiving the NEP, the Liberals blended this investment nationalist pursuit of 'Canadianization' and a reduced role for multinational firms with an equally pressing concern that federal primacy be restored in the energy field.

Two of the most controversial provisions of the NEP followed from the twin emphases on Canadianization and federal primacy. First, the program would increase domestic ownership and control by altering incentives in such a way as to benefit firms with high rates of Canadian ownership and control, and by imposing a consumption tax to fund Petro-Canada's acquisition of foreign companies. As well, the NEP included a 'Canada Benefits' provision to ensure that oil companies procured the goods and services they required in Canada.[9] Second, the NEP contained a Crown interest or 'back-in' provision, which established a 25 per cent federal interest in all present and future energy development on Canada Lands.[10]

These Canadianization and Crown interest provisions were opposed by many of the same interests that had criticized Liberal policy after the OPEC embargo. For example, the Alberta government rejected the purposes and terms of the NEP, and threatened to reduce the flow of oil from that province to the rest of the country by 180,000 barrels per day. Opposition by Alberta and the oil industry led to a September 1981 federal-provincial agreement known as the Energy Pricing and Taxation Arrangement. This agreement, along with subsequent changes to the NEP embodied in *NEP Update: 1982*, suggested a general backing-off from the policy by the federal government.[11]

The Societal View

Research in the group tradition highlights the importance of intervention by organized interests, hypothesizing that the combined resources, cohesion, expertise and representativeness of policy 'winners' will generally exceed those of policy 'losers'. In the case of the NEP, it is difficult to identify organized societal proponents, since most of the investment nationalist groups that had formed during the late 1960s and early 1970s were organizationally defunct by 1980. The Waffle no longer existed as a cohesive group; it had been purged from the federal and Ontario New Democratic parties in the early 1970s and did not function as an organized unit in 1980-81.[12] Similarly, the Committee for an Independent Canada (CIC) was on the verge of disbanding when the October 1980 budget was announced; its August 1981 endorsement of the NEP as a major step toward fulfilling the goals of investment nationalism was one of the group's final statements.[13] Although Petro-Canada and the Alberta provincial government played important roles in the debates over the NEP, neither meets the group definition of a societal—as opposed to state—actor.

Among the only active societal groups to endorse the NEP was the Public Petroleum Association of Canada. Shortly after its establishment in the mid-1970s, this organization sponsored two conferences that examined critically the influence of major private-sector energy firms, notably Imperial Oil. Association activists were drawn from the Waffle and the Committee for an Independent Canada, as well as from labour and environmental groups including Pollution Probe and the Canadian Arctic Resources Committee.[14] Overall, the Public Petroleum Association articulated a pro-NEP position that reflected both investment nationalist ideas and the emergent environmental and aboriginal critiques of energy policy in the Canadian north. In this sense, the association foreshadowed the broadening of the nationalist coalition that was to take place during the 1985-88 free trade debate.

Two basic sets of players are considered below: the many organized opponents of the NEP in the energy and broader business community, on the one hand, and the more sympathetic nationalist groups (including the CIC and Public Petroleum Association) and a few private Canadian energy firms, on the other. Although it seems obvious that the societal framework would not have predicted the adoption of the NEP as government policy, it is nevertheless useful to evaluate each variable in this approach, beginning with the question of tangible assets.

The imbalance of resources in favour of the NEP's opponents is reflected in the well-financed tactics of leading multinational energy firms (particularly Imperial Oil, Texaco and Gulf) as well as their umbrella organization, the Canadian Petroleum Association (CPA). CPA members 'condemned virtually all aspects of the NEP' but focussed especially on the goal of 50 per cent domestic ownership by 1990.[15] In pressing the federal government to withdraw or at least alter the policy, the CPA and its dominant multinational members were hindered by a negative public image, which they sought to improve through major advertising campaigns. According to Bruce Doern and Glen Toner, 'the CPA developed a $3 million advocacy advertising campaign to help improve the overall image of the industry.'[16] A number of individual foreign firms also organized their own expensive advertising campaigns.

In addition to these efforts to change government policy by altering public attitudes toward the industry, multinational firms devoted considerable time, money and personnel to direct political advocacy. The CPA, for example, hired a former federal bureaucrat as its executive director in order to improve the lobbying clout of the multinationals in Ottawa.[17] This well-financed strategy on the part of foreign oil companies produced 'relentless pressure to alter the NEP'; it was reinforced by parallel demands from other business interest groups including the Canadian Manufacturers' Association and the Business Council on National Issues.[18]

Another resource employed by the multinationals to oppose the NEP was a well-publicized economic sanction—most notably cuts in Canadian operating budgets. Gulf Canada, for example, announced in December 1980 that it would reduce its projected spending for a five-year period by 15 per cent, or $900 million,[19] while Imperial Oil, Shell and Gulf threatened to cancel major frontier exploration projects.[20] The extent of the resources available to these firms through their international parent companies is also relevant. According to Doern and Toner, the home offices of 'the larger foreign-owned firms . . . exerted pressure on the US, British and Dutch governments to pressure Canada to change aspects of the NEP'.[21]

Although the framers of the NEP expected multinational firms to object to the legislation, they were less prepared for a storm of criticism from a number of the policy's intended beneficiaries: the smaller Canadian energy companies.[22] The second and third tiers of the domestic industry reacted negatively to the program, criticizing it in a collective voice through the Independent Petroleum Association of Canada (IPAC).[23] Some of this opposition, which included a national newspaper campaign directed against the policy, followed from an ideological commitment to free market, non-interventionist government policy.[24] Part of it can also be attributed to a belief that the tax and incentive provisions of the NEP were so administratively complicated as to hinder the operations of smaller Canadian firms.[25]

While the resources available to this domestic segment of the industry were clearly less than those that could be mobilized by the multinationals, they were not inconsiderable. Both IPAC and individual Canadian firms lobbied the federal government to alter the taxation and pricing provisions of the NEP.[26] These lobbying efforts, which did have some effect, were complemented by negative sanctions similar to those imposed by the multinationals; most of the Canadian-owned junior firms 'cut back their exploration programs and a number shifted a percentage of their exploration activity to the United States'.[27]

The combined ability of the multinationals and smaller Canadian firms to devote resources to advertising and lobbying, and to withhold the expenditure of funds in Canada, must be viewed in light of the far more limited resources available to NEP supporters. First of all, except for the Committee for an Independent Canada and the Public Petroleum Association, organized supporters of the NEP tended to offer only conditional endorsement. Two major Canadian energy firms, Dome Petroleum and Nova Corporation, agreed with the basic ideas of Canadianization and Crown interest but took issue with their specific terms and procedures. Bob Blair of Nova, for example, argued that the ownership rating procedures were 'inefficient' and 'insulting', and recommended that the back-in provision be withdrawn 'and some other tax technique substituted'.[28] Dome Petroleum expressed similar reservations.

Second, and even more damaging from the perspective of resources, Dome was drawn into an increasingly vulnerable financial situation through the early 1980s.[29] The Canadianization provisions of the NEP, which were intended to benefit the domestic oil sector at the expense of the multinationals, encouraged firms like Dome to borrow heavily to finance expansion and acquisitions. In acquiring Hudson Bay Oil and Gas and in creating Dome Canada, Dome Petroleum incurred a massive debt load just as interest rates rose, energy demand declined and the North American economy entered a severe recession.[30] As a result, the Canadian majors were unable to challenge the well-financed campaigns of the multinationals—who found increasingly ingenious ways to ensure continued profitability despite the NEP.[31]

Third, the resources of the NEP's leading unconditional supporter, the Committee for an Independent Canada, were limited. As Abraham Rotstein, one of its founders, reflected on the CIC's financial status:

> Money was a problem. Very little financial support came in even from protected sectors in the business community, like the banks. We were essentially a populist organization, a movement that didn't have a formal bureaucracy . . . We never had a large budget, and only two or three paid staff people at maximum worked in the Toronto office at any one time.[32]

Moreover, the Committee folded its tent early in the course of the NEP debate. The resources of the policy's final ally, the Public Petroleum Association, were also limited by the relatively weak financial standing of its sponsoring groups and individual members.[33] By way of contrast, the CPA, IPAC and their individual members who opposed the NEP had extensive resources, including not only advertising budgets and lobbying experts but also the threat and actual imposition of spending cut-backs. Thus their resources clearly exceeded those available to societal supporters of the NEP.

In terms of cohesion, opponents once again had an edge. Multinational energy firms were united in their complete disapproval of the NEP; although firms articulated this criticism in various ways, the overall position of the CPA and its members was unambiguously negative. Second- and third-tier Canadian firms tended to oppose the legislation in somewhat different terms than the multinationals, but their position was nevertheless solid, unified and, because it came from the NEP's ostensible beneficiaries, highly visible.

By way of comparison, the signals that emanated from the Canadian majors presented a far less cohesive picture. Dome and Nova conditionally endorsed the concept of Canadianization, but their opposition to its specific procedures tended to undermine the coherence of arguments in favour of the NEP. Because Dome and Nova gave only mixed blessings to the policy, they presented a less compelling position than did the NEP's opponents. Moreover, public statements in favour of the NEP by nationalist interests were largely drowned out in the chorus of energy industry commentary on the policy, in part because the Committee for an Independent Canada was disbanding in this period. Unconditional support from the CIC and Public Petroleum Association thus contrasted with the more critical responses of Dome and Nova, leaving the impression that the opponents of the NEP were more cohesive than its proponents.

The third variable in the societal framework concerns expertise; once again, organized opponents of the NEP seem to have been better equipped than supporters. Doern and Toner argue that both independently and through the CPA, critics of the NEP had access to expert research and advocacy assistance. In their words, 'the large oil companies . . . have extensive analytical and lobbying resources.'[34] This knowledge of the energy sector and experience within the Canadian regulatory environment was reinforced by the industry background of the junior domestic firms that opposed the NEP. By comparison, the combined expertise of Dome, Nova and the nationalist groups was limited; the latter had less money with which to buy outside expertise, and they had fewer in-house staff people whose time could be devoted to defending the NEP.

Finally, in terms of representativeness, societal proponents of the NEP were in this case at some advantage. Although critics of the policy likely outspent supporters, the latter were perceived to constitute a more *legitimate* voice of the Canadian oil industry and a more representative reflection of Canadian energy interests. Jack Gallagher of Dome and Bob Blair of Nova were popular figures who symbolized a positive image of Canada as an aggressive, independent petroleum producer; both seemed to represent the industry's stake in federal energy policy in a more comprehensive manner than did the leadership of the multinational firms. Supported by the various organized groups that endorsed the NEP, nationalist views that the public interest rested in an interventionist energy policy seemed to command fairly broad credibility.

This review of the societal framework suggests that opponents of the NEP controlled greater resources, cohesion and expertise, while supporters were more representative within the domestic policy sphere. The fact that the Liberal government pursued the NEP, defending it through a long and turbulent public debate, is difficult to explain in light of this pattern. Although it might be argued that a focus on organized groups would have predicted the eventual dismantling of the NEP after 1984, this conceptual approach is less useful in explaining how the policy emerged and why the Liberals continued to defend it during the early 1980s.

The Bureaucratic View

At least one analyst has portrayed the NEP as a classic case of bureaucratic dominance in the federal policy process. Peter Foster, a business journalist who wrote *The Sorcerer's Apprentices: Canada's Super-Bureaucrats and the Energy Mess*, maintains that officials in the Department of Energy, Mines and Resources (EMR), under the leadership of deputy minister Marshall (Mickey) Cohen, essentially 'hatched' the idea of the NEP and imposed it on an unwitting political elite. In his view, with the assistance of Edmund Clark and George Tough in EMR, Michael Pitfield and Robert Rabinovitch in the Privy Council Office (PCO), and Ian Stewart, deputy minister of Finance, EMR bureaucrats created the main lines of the policy that came to be known as the National Energy Program.[35]

Foster's bureaucratic argument does not systematically address state preferences, capacity or autonomy; nor does it consider the possibility of alternative explanations. Foster and other writers do suggest, however, that key actors in the federal bureaucracy inclined towards a nationalist and centralist energy policy. Edmund Clark, senior policy advisor in EMR, has been described as a particularly strong interventionist who favoured the kinds of incentive and regulatory instruments employed in the NEP.[36] Other members of the key ENFIN (Energy and Finance) group that helped to develop the NEP were reputed to be less radical than Clark; deputy minister Cohen, for example, was 'generally considered to lean to the right in his political views'.[37] Overall, however, the preferences of senior federal bureaucrats in the period prior to the announcement of the NEP have been portrayed as favourable to such a policy; Petro-Canada executives like Wilbert Hopper and Joel Bell, who worked closely with the ENFIN group, are also described as very sympathetic.[38]

With reference to capacity, administrative actors in the energy field during the late 1970s and early 1980s were generally in a good position to concentrate, co-ordinate and exploit state resources. The external shocks of OPEC and the Iranian revolution offered a strong impetus towards the development of a capable energy bureaucracy; internal tensions associated with federal-provincial pricing and royalty arrangements provided an additional push.[39] Perhaps the clearest indication of growing capacity was the 1976 publication of *An Energy Policy for Canada: Policies for Self-Reliance*. Released by the Department of Energy, Mines and Resources, this document reflected efforts within the federal bureaucracy to establish coherent principles governing energy policy. The paper proposed an assertion of federal interest in the energy field, centred in and around EMR administrators, and devoted considerable attention to problems of foreign control in this sector.[40] By 1976, therefore, energy questions were visible, important policy matters that held the attention of the nation's senior administrative elite. The importance of these questions was reflected not only in the growth in the size of ENR and the creation of ENFIN during this period, but also in the movement of well-respected and highly motivated bureaucrats to EMR and in the broadening of Petro-Canada's budgetary and bureaucratic clout.[41]

If the preferences and capacity of state actors provided favourable conditions for the development of the NEP, what can be said about autonomy? In this case, similarly positive conditions seem to have prevailed. ENFIN constituted an unusually independent bureaucratic group, since it drew on senior officials from EMR, Finance and the PCO, and was not dependent on input from societal groups. In coordination with Hopper and Bell at Petro-Canada, energy decision-makers managed to operate in a fairly self-directed policy stream that percolated with ideas and resources as well as power.

Using the shorthand formulation outlined in Chapter 2, bureaucratic state variables with reference to the NEP can be summarized as (+,+,+). EMR was a highly capable agency by the late 1970s, staffed with senior bureaucrats whose preferences tended to parallel investment nationalist ideas and whose scope for independent action was considerable. As one academic analyst, James Desveaux, summarized these circumstances: 'The potential was created for EMR to short-circuit other agencies and departments in effecting critical decisions: its domain had expanded considerably at the expense of other parts of the bureaucracy. It was becoming hegemonic.'[42]

If these various state factors were neatly in place by the late 1970s and, more specifically, by the fateful evening in December 1979 when a budget vote defeated the Clark government, then one obvious question comes to mind. Why wasn't the NEP introduced earlier? According to Foster, EMR bureaucrats had prepared the same briefing documents for their Conservative ministers as they did for the Liberals who were elected in 1980.[43] If virtually identical conditions prevailed in the state bureaucracy in 1979 and one year later, after the Liberals had returned to power, then the crucial missing ingredient in 1979 would appear to have been partisan and political rather than simply administrative.[44] As demonstrated in Chapter 2, the bureaucratic framework neglects questions of political response to nationalist ideas, focussing instead on administrative determinants of policy action.

In short, neither the societal nor the bureaucratic approach on its own adequately explains the adoption of the NEP as government policy in 1980.

The Integrative View

In contrast to Foster's bureaucratic view, other writers have portrayed the NEP as a fundamentally political effort to enhance federal powers and to limit the fiscal and jurisdictional growth of energy-producing provinces. For example, in *Tug of War: Ottawa and the Provinces Under Trudeau and Mulroney*, David Milne describes the NEP's purpose as 'the strengthening of the federal state', and suggests that such a policy would have been unlikely under either previous or subsequent governments.[45] Without the policy commitment of a series of Liberal ministers of Energy, Mines and Resources, it is argued, few federal regimes would have risked the combined censure of most of the energy industry, the producing provinces, the US government and Canadian business interests. In particular, the roles of Alastair Gillespie in the period 1974-79 and, especially, of Marc Lalonde after the 1980 election are viewed as central: Gillespie was reputed to hold nationalist views and oversaw the expansion of EMR's size and capacity,[46] while Lalonde was 'iron-willed' in his determination to employ energy policy as an instrument for protecting federal powers.[47]

This political line of argument suggests that the credibility and stature of energy ministers within the federal cabinet would be crucial to pursuing a policy as contentious as the NEP. When Lalonde was minister, he enjoyed direct access to and support from a prime minister and a partisan staff who were strongly committed to the jurisdictional purposes of the NEP. Unlike Joe Clark and many of his senior aides, Pierre Trudeau and his advisors following 1980 preferred to confront provincial governments, and were not hesitant to employ the varied instruments of federal power (including Petro-Canada and the Foreign Investment Review Agency, or FIRA) in the process. Rejecting Clark's ideas of privatizing Petro-Canada and co-operating with the producing provinces, the restored Liberal elite believed that energy policy had already progressed too far down the road of foreign control, jurisdictional decentralization and federal capitulation.[48]

How useful is an integrative framework in explaining the emergence of the NEP? As summarized in Chapter 2, a focus on ideas and political responses to them implies that very or moderately conducive conditions on at least one of variables X8, X9 or X10 is necessary to achieve policy success. Without international, partisan or attitudinal support, the conversion of investment nationalist ideas into tangible federal policies would probably not occur. As shown in Figure 4.1, in the case of the NEP conducive conditions did obtain on variables X9 and X10.

This policy's prospects can be examined using Figure 4.1, beginning with the first four societal variables. Resources (X1), cohesion (X2) and expertise (X3) appeared minimally conducive to the emergence of the NEP while conditions of representativeness (X4) seemed highly favourable. As summarized above, the societal groups that opposed the NEP had extensive resources, cohesion and expertise but only limited representativeness. Variables X5 through X7, from the bureaucratic literature, are all coded as very conducive, since the preferences, capacity and autonomy of the administrative actors involved in energy policy were highly favourable to the development of the NEP.

The integrative model introduces an ideas/politics cluster that is absent in the societal and bureaucratic approaches. These variables concern international and specifically US government (X8), partisan (X9) and attitudinal (X10) responses to investment nationalist ideas. Stephen Clarkson's *Canada and the Reagan Challenge* addresses the US response to these arguments, showing the extent to

FIGURE 4.1 SCORING INDEPENDENT VARIABLES ON NATIONAL ENERGY PROGRAM

	SOCIETAL CLUSTER				BUREAUCRATIC CLUSTER			IDEAS/POLITICS CLUSTER			ROW TOTALS
	Group resources X_1	Group cohesion X_2	Group expertise X_3	Group representativeness X_4	Bureaucratic preferences X_5	Bureaucratic capacity X_6	Bureaucratic autonomy X_7	International influences X_8	Partisan actors X_9	Media, public opinion X_{10}	
Very conducive conditions				●	●	●	●		●		5
Somewhat conducive conditions										●	1
Minimally conducive conditions	●	●	●					●			4

which Washington attempted to block the NEP and other nationalist initiatives.[49] Clearly, the official American response to the NEP (variable X8) was obstructionist and minimally conducive; following the defeat of President Jimmy Carter, the new administration of Ronald Reagan aggressively opposed the 25 per cent Crown interest provision, viewing it as unfair confiscation of foreign-owned assets.[50] After Reagan raised the NEP and the issue of Canadian acquisitions in the US at a 1981 meeting with Pierre Trudeau, a senior State Department official suggested that bilateral 'relationships are sliding dangerously towards a crisis'.[51] Beginning in the spring of 1981, as a partial response to this US pressure, the federal government announced a series of amendments to the NEP, including compensation for the Crown interest provision and limits on Canadian bank financing for business takeovers.[52]

This willingness to compromise on key provisions of the NEP also followed from domestic pressure in the oil industry, the producing provinces and the business press. In the face of collapsing energy prices, reduced foreign and domestic demand, rising interest rates and a weakened financial condition among major Canadian oil firms, some specific terms of the NEP were altered. American threats, however, to employ the US Mineral Lands Leasing Act to limit Canadian operations south of the border and to challenge FIRA's legality before a panel of the General Agreement on Tariffs and Trade were likely influential in Canada's decision to roll back NEP provisions.[53]

Variable X10 draws out the attitudinal response to investment nationalist ideas, which ranged from strong support in some quarters to extreme hostility in others. As reported in Table 4.1, poll data from the period of the NEP debate indicate solid public endorsement for the concept of Canadianization. As well, figures in Table 4.2 on attitudes towards foreign investment suggest that approximately two-thirds of the Canadian public during the late 1970s and early 1980s believed that enough US capital was already invested in Canada. Similarly, entries in Table 4.3 indicate that investment policies offering support for Canadian business were also relatively popular in this period. As Marc Lalonde reflected in his own account of the NEP, Canadianization of the energy industry 'had such broad national support that the subsequent Conservative government had to endorse it, even though its pursuit of [Canadianization] seems to have been lackadaisical'.[54]

By way of comparison, leading editorials in the domestic and international business press tended to criticize in harsh terms both the concepts of investment nationalism and the specific terms of the NEP. Some Canadian dailies, especially the *Toronto Star*, were very supportive of nationalist ideas and the NEP, continuing to endorse the original policy even after efforts were made to dilute many of its more controversial provisions.[55] Overall, the attitudinal measure in variable X10 is scored as 'moderately conducive', with the strong support of public opinion and some editorial writers balanced by vigorous opposition in the business press.

The Partisan Politics of the NEP

Variable X9 addresses the positions of partisan actors vis-à-vis investment nationalism and the NEP. Within the House of Commons, Conservative Opposition members criticized the omnibus approach adopted in this legislation and echoed many points raised by the energy industry, the producing provinces and the US government.[56] New Democrats from Ontario tended to welcome the policy, viewing it as an innovative re-working of Waffle nationalism.[57] NDP MPs from the west, however, were more suspicious both of nationalist ideas and of the regional and federal/provincial implications of the NEP.[58]

Among the key political actors in the NEP debate, leading Liberal cabinet ministers in the majority government as well as principal advisors in the Prime Minister's Office (PMO) believed in the need for an aggressively centralist energy policy. As individuals, Marc Lalonde and Pierre Trudeau were probably no more attached to the nationalist world view in 1980 than they had been during the mid-1970s debate over Bill C-58; both, however, remained committed to federal

TABLE 4.1   CANADIAN ATTITUDES TOWARDS ENERGY POLICY, 1980-1983

YEAR	SURVEY ITEM	% SUPPORT
1980	Favour government measures to increase Canadian ownership of oil and gas industry to 50 per cent	70
1981	Favour 75 per cent Canadian ownership of oil industry by 1985	64
1981	Support at least 50 per cent Canadian ownership of oil and gas industry	84
1981	Favour purchase by Petro-Canada of major foreign oil company	55
1981	Oil and gas companies get more than their fair share of energy revenues	47
1981	National Energy Program will increase jobs and aid economic growth	70
1981	National Energy Program will decrease chances of running out of oil and gas in the near future	52
1982	Favour government measures to increase Canadian ownership of oil and gas industry to 50 per cent	61
1983	Favour government measures to increase Canadian ownership of oil and gas industry to 50 per cent	55

Sources: G. Bruce Doern and Glen Toner, *The Politics of Energy: The Development and Implementation of the NEP* (Toronto: Methuen, 1985), 107-8; Peter Foster, *The Sorcerer's Apprentices: Canada's Super-Bureaucrats and the Energy Mess* (Toronto: Collins, 1982), 32; Richard Johnston, *Public Opinion and Public Policy in Canada: Questions of Confidence* (Toronto: University of Toronto Press for Supply and Services Canada, 1986), 176.

TABLE 4.2 CANADIAN ATTITUDES TOWARDS EXTENT OF US INVESTMENT, 1961-1987 (%)

YEAR	1961	1963	1967	1970	1972	1975	1977	1978	1980	1981	1982	1983	1984	1985	1986	1987
Enough now	52	46	60	62	67	71	69	69	64	67	56	57	50	51	53	55
Want more	32	33	24	25	22	16	20	23	20	21	36	35	35	36	34	30
Don't know	16	21	16	13	11	13	12	9	17	12	8	8	14	13	14	15

Note: Respondents were asked, 'Now thinking about US capital invested in Canada, do you think there is enough now or would you like to see more US capital invested in this country?'

Sources: CIPO data reported in F.J. Fletcher and R.J. Drummond, *Canadian Attitude Trends, 1960-1978* (Ottawa: Institute for Research on Public Policy, 1979), Table 12; and *The Gallup Report* (Toronto: CIPO, July 2, 1987).

fiscal and jurisdictional primacy. If such primacy could be advanced using nationalist concepts of Canadianization—as Edmund Clark in EMR and Tom Axworthy in the PMO suggested—then Trudeau and Lalonde were prepared to listen.[59]

From this perspective, the genesis of the NEP rested in a grafting of the ideas of investment nationalism onto the sturdy and not inconsistent tree of federal primacy. In searching for a way to ensure support for its energy policy, particularly in central Canada, the Liberal parliamentary elite merged constitutional centralism with moderate investment nationalism. Its willingness to pursue this approach provided fertile political conditions for the emergence of the NEP; variable X9 is therefore scored as highly conducive.

Overall, then, very conducive conditions for the development of the NEP obtained on a total of 5 out of 10 independent variables in Figure 4.1. Somewhat conducive conditions existed in 1 case and minimally conducive circumstances in 4. Within the ideas/politics cluster, very or somewhat conducive conditions obtained on 2 out of 3 variables. Using the propositions presented in Chapter 2 as a guide, it follows that the political conditions necessary for the policy's introduction were present and that the probability of government action favourable to nationalist positions was moderate, about 50 per cent; that the likelihood of policy saw-off was low, about 10 per cent; and that the probability of policy inaction was moderate, about 40 per cent. This assessment predicts the adoption of the NEP even though it indicates a substantial number of unfavourable circumstances militating against the policy. The 40 per cent likelihood of an outcome *unfavourable* to nationalist interests seems to foreshadow the subsequent rollback of NEP provisions by the Liberals and, more dramatically, by the Conservative government elected in 1984.[60]

Conclusions

This chapter has considered three approaches to government action on the National Energy Program. The NEP was difficult to explain using a group model and, although the bureaucratic approach produced a more useful explanation, neither view could address questions of policy timing. Both frameworks neglected crucial political and, specifically, partisan considerations surrounding the NEP, as well as public, media and official US responses. The integrative model helped to reveal the array of actors for and against the policy, both in Canada and in the US, and explained the NEP more fully than did either of the other two perspectives.[61] It yielded a prediction of moderate, or about 50 per cent, probability of nationalist policy success, as well as a moderate, or 40 per cent likelihood of failure.

Above all, integrative thinking suggests the use of nationalist arguments by some partisan actors whose fundamental purposes were jurisdictional and fiscal. This pattern sheds light on larger questions of pan-Canadian influence; that is,

TABLE 4.3	CANADIAN ATTITUDES TOWARDS PROPOSED POLICIES ON FOREIGN INVESTMENT, 1974-1986 (%)								
YEAR	1974	1975	1976	1979	1980	1982	1984	1986
Government to regulate investment (FIRA)	32	31	31	24	26	29	27	26
More support for Canadian business	33	34	34	35	32	30	33	28
Canada Development Corporation	22	17	17	18	20	15	14	11
Encourage investment from many countries	7	7	7	9	7	7	10	10
Other/Don't know	2	4	4	4	5	7	5	7
(N)	(2 050)	(1 517)	(2 300)	(2 354)	(1 874)	(1 782)	(1 552)	(1 399)

Note: Cell entries are calculated on the basis of respondents who viewed foreign investment as a present or future problem. Column percentages may exceed 100 because of multiple responses.

Sources: Elliott data reported in Terence A. Keenleyside et al., 'Public Opinion and Canada-United States Economic Relations', *Behind the Headlines* 35 (1976), Table 4; Lawrence LeDuc and J. Alex Murray, 'A Resurgence of Canadian Nationalism', in Allan Kornberg and Harold D. Clarke, eds, *Political Support in Canada* (Durham: Duke University Press, 1983), Table 10.4; and LeDuc and Murray, 'Open for Business?' paper presented at Canadian Political Economy conference, Blacksburg, Virginia, 1986, Table 5.

demands for greater domestic control of the energy industry—which emanated from the investment nationalist stream—were pursued in the NEP as part of a broader centralist agenda during the last Trudeau administration, only to be withdrawn later under concerted pressure from powerful and varied opponents. The vigorous and sustained opposition of the Alberta government is understandable from this perspective, as is the wedging of nationalist ideas within larger jurisdictional and regional conflicts.

Comparing this case with the analysis in Chapter 3, one could argue that the political risks and economic costs associated with Bill C-58 were far less than those that followed from the NEP. The former, therefore, was less likely to be clothed in other ideological garments by its sponsors or cast aside by subsequent governments. As indicated by a comparison of the 'minimally favourable' conditions in Figures 3.1 and 4.1, the NEP faced far greater societal opposition than did Bill C-58, even though elements of both policies were strongly opposed by the US administration. Nevertheless, the moderate (40 to 50 per cent) probability of nationalist success that was identified in the cases of both C-58 and the NEP suggests that pan-Canadianism faced mixed policy prospects before 1984, when a majority Conservative government committed to free-market economics and an end to interventionism in the energy sector was elected.

Much of the willingness of the Conservatives to dismantle the NEP followed from societal pressures discussed earlier in this chapter. Prominent business groups, notably the Canadian Petroleum Association and the Business Council on National Issues, had established their own task forces on energy policy by 1983. These industry representatives consulted at length with the Conservative energy critic at the time, Pat Carney, and helped to shape an Opposition policy that directly reflected private sector thinking.[62] With Carney's appointment as Minister of Energy, Mines and Resources following the Conservative victory in September 1984, the stage was set for a major change in federal policy on pricing and incentives in particular. According to most accounts, the Conservatives effectively gutted the NEP within their first year of office.[63]

Yet this societal pressure to dismantle the NEP cannot be divorced from political and bureaucratic factors. Just as key partisan elites in the last Trudeau government were crucial to the introduction of investment nationalist ideas in 1980, so new Conservative decision-makers were instrumental in replacing nationalist, centralist and interventionist arguments with continentalist, decentralist and market-oriented ones. The position of Pat Carney offers a useful counterpoise to that of Marc Lalonde: both were knowledgeable in the energy field, committed to firmly entrenched positions on energy policy, able to command cabinet and prime ministerial support when it mattered, and unlikely to harbour ambitions for federal party leadership. While the two led Canadian energy policy in distinctly different directions, their ability to convert ideas into policy action was remarkably similar.

The integrative model as applied to the NEP also suggests important linkages between political and administrative actors. One could argue that without the well-articulated preferences and extensive capacity and autonomy of bureaucratic elites, Liberal decision-makers in 1980 would have had a difficult time introducing the NEP.[64] This line of thinking helps to explain Conservative concern after 1984 with removing pro-NEP bureaucrats (notably Ed Clark) from the federal government, and with harnessing administrative preferences and capacities to those of their new political masters.

Much of this fundamental shift away from the NEP under the Conservatives can also be attributed to the international and attitudinal influence of the policy's opponents. The US government was harshly critical of the Canadianization provisions of the policy, and continued to press for their withdrawal through the mid-1980s. Aided by a domestic opposition that had its own interest in continued criticism from Washington, the chorus of energy industry, business, provincial and international voices against the NEP—reinforced by sustained opposition in much of the international and domestic press—helped to ensure a dismantling after 1984.

The eventual success of these interests points to the temporary and very vulnerable status of investment nationalist ideas in 1980. Although the Conservative government did not publicly commit itself to a roll-back of the Canadianization provisions, implicitly acknowledging the public support that this idea commanded, it did announce that 'the final nails have been driven into the coffin of the [Liberals'] National Energy Program'.[65] Accords were signed with provincial governments in the producing regions, and questions of Canadian ownership and control were largely removed from the policy agenda; yet, as Marc Lalonde observes in his reflections on the fate of the NEP, energy prices and drilling at the wellhead continued to decline through the late 1980s.[66]

What may have been unclear to investment nationalists in 1984 and 1985 was the linkage between gutting the NEP and moving in the direction of comprehensive Canada-US free trade. Once this connection became obvious, and once Conservative interest in continental energy arrangements within a free trade agreement was revealed, a revival of older debates about investment nationalism and energy policy was not far behind. Chapter 5 examines the question of Canada-US free trade, an issue that drew trade, investment and cultural nationalist ideas onto the public stage once again.

Notes

[1] Canada, Department of Energy, Mines and Resources, *The National Energy Program* (Ottawa: Supply and Services Canada, 1980), 18.

[2] David Milne, *Tug of War: Ottawa and the Provinces under Trudeau and Mulroney* (Toronto: Lorimer, 1986), 76. On the background to federal energy policy, see John N. McDougall, *Fuels and the National*

Policy (Toronto: Butterworths, 1982); G. Bruce Doern and Glen Toner, *The Politics of Energy: The Development and Implementation of the* NEP (Toronto: Methuen, 1985), chaps 3-5; and, from the perspective of a policy-maker, Marc Lalonde, 'Riding the Storm: Energy Policy, 1968-1984', in Thomas S. Axworthy and Pierre Elliott Trudeau (eds), *Towards a Just Society: The Trudeau Years* (Markham, Ont.: Penguin, 1990), 49-62.

[3]Milne, *Tug of War*, 2, 7. On the background to Trudeau's constitutional ideas, see Stephen Clarkson and Christina McCall, *Trudeau and Our Times*, vol. 1: *The Magnificent Obsession* (Toronto: McClelland and Stewart, 1990).

[4]See 'Notes for Remarks by The Right Honourable P.E. Trudeau', Halifax Board of Trade, Halifax, NS, 25 Jan. 1980; and Peter Foster, *The Sorcerer's Apprentices: Canada's Super-Bureaucrats and the Energy Mess* (Toronto: Collins, 1982), 138.

[5]See Doern and Toner, *The Politics of Energy*, 40.

[6]Department of Energy, Mines and Resources, *The National Energy Program*, 2. Emphasis in original.

[7]See Charles F. Doran, *Forgotten Partnership: U.S.-Canada Relations Today* (Baltimore: Johns Hopkins University Press, 1984), 221.

[8]See Royal Commission on Canada's Economic Prospects, *Report* (Gordon Report; Ottawa: Queen's Printer, 1957); *Foreign Ownership and the Structure of Canadian Industry: Report of the Task Force on the Structure of Canadian Industry* (Watkins Report; Ottawa: Queen's Printer, 1968); and *Foreign Direct Investment in Canada* (Gray Report; Ottawa: Information Canada, 1972). James Laxer published a number of books on the energy industry, including *The Energy Poker Game: The Politics of the Continental Resources Deal* (Toronto: New Press, 1970); *Canada's Energy Crisis* (Toronto: Lorimer, 1975); and *Oil and Gas: Ottawa, the Provinces and the Petroleum Industry* (Toronto: Lorimer, 1983). On the ideas of CIC activists, see Abraham Rotstein and Gary Lax (eds), *Independence: The Canadian Challenge* (Toronto: Committee for an Independent Canada, 1972); and Rotstein and Lax (eds), *Getting It Back: A Program for Canadian Independence* (Toronto: Clarke, Irwin, 1974).

[9]Department of Energy, Mines and Resources, *The National Energy Program*, 47.

[10]See Doern and Toner, *The Politics of Energy*, 50-1; and Lalonde, Riding the Storm', 64-6. Among the better-known Canadianization instruments was the Petroleum Incentives Program (PIP), which provided proportionately larger grants to Canadian firms.

[11]See Canada, Department of Energy, Mines and Resources, *The National Energy Program: Update 1982* (Ottawa: Supply and Services, 1982); Lalonde, 'Riding the Storm', 67-9; and James Alexander Desveaux, 'Strategy, Structure and Government Intervention: An Organizational Analysis of Canada's National Energy Program' (Ph.D. dissertation, University of California at Berkeley, 1987).'

[12]It should be noted, however, that many Waffle veterans offered strong support as individuals for the NEP. See Milne, *Tug of War*, 71, 83; and Mel Watkins, 'In Defence of the National Energy Program', *Canadian Forum* (June-July 1981).

[13]McDougall, *Fuels and the National Policy*, note 48, 186; and 'Rusty Nationalist Group Disbanded After Eleven Years', *Globe and Mail* (6 Aug. 1981), 4. For a somewhat different attempt to analyse the NEP using societal perspectives, see Patrick James and Robert Michelin, 'The Canadian National Energy Program and its Aftermath: Perspectives on an Era of Confrontation', *American Review of Canadian Studies* 19 (1989), 64-7.

[14]See James Laxer and Anne Martin (eds), *The Big, Tough, Expensive Job: Imperial Oil and the Canadian Economy* (Toronto: Press Porcepic, 1976); and E.A. Lindquist, 'Behind the Myth of Think Tanks: The Organization and Relevance of Canadian Policy Institutes' (Ph.D. dissertation, University of California at Berkeley, 1989), 120.

[15]Doern and Toner, *The Politics of Energy*, 459.

[16]Ibid., 206. In response to damaging allegations made in a federal report entitled 'State of Competition in the Canadian Petroleum Industry', Imperial Oil placed full-page advertisements in 37 Canadian dailies. See ibid., 209.

[17]Foster, *The Sorcerer's Apprentices*, 145. The CPA appointed Ian Smythe as executive director.

[18]Doern and Toner, *The Politics of Energy*, 467. On the formation of a domestic business alliance against the NEP, see Barbara Jenkins, 'Reexamining the "Obsolescing Bargain": A Study of Canada's National Energy Program', *International Organization* 40 (1986), 156; Stephen Clarkson, *Canada and the Reagan Challenge* (Toronto: Lorimer, 1982), 81; and David Crane, *Controlling Interest: The Canadian Gas and Oil Stakes* (Toronto: McClelland and Stewart, 1982), 23-30.

[19]Doern and Toner, *The Politics of Energy*, 216.

[20]Ibid., 207; and Crane, *Controlling Interest*, chap. 1.

[21]Doern and Toner, *The Politics of Energy*, 107.

[22]Jenkins, 'Reexamining the "Obsolescing Bargain"', 155.

[23]It should be noted that IPAC also included the major Canadian private firms, which were less critical of the NEP, and, until its resignation as a member, Petro-Canada. See Doern and Toner, *The Politics of Energy*, 235.

[24]Foster, *The Sorcerer's Apprentices*, 155.

[25]See Lalonde, 'Riding the Storm', 70-2; and Doern and Toner, *The Politics of Energy*, 246-8.

[26]Doern and Toner, *The Politics of Energy*, 252.

[27]Ibid.

[28]Ibid., 225.

[29]On Dome's response to the NEP, see ibid., 230-1; and Clarkson, *Canada and the Reagan Challenge*, 72. The financial crisis within Dome is addressed in Foster, *The Sorcerer's Apprentices*, chap. 24; and Jim Lyon, *Dome: The Rise and Fall of the House that Jack Built* (Toronto: Macmillan, 1983).

[30]Doern and Toner, *The Politics of Energy*, 228.

[31]See ibid., 207; and Jenkins, 'Reexaming the "Obsolescing Bargain"', 150-2.

[32]Interview with Abraham Rotstein, 28 June 1989.

[33]These individual members included academics and activists of a left-nationalist persuasion, including Jim Laxer and Larry Pratt, whose work during this period focussed on Canadian energy policy.

[34]Doern and Toner, *The Politics of Energy*, 467.

[35]Foster, *The Sorcerer's Apprentices*. For a more systematic application of theories of bureaucratic autonomy to the case of the NEP, see James and Michelin, 'The Canadian National Energy Program and its Aftermath', 67-72.

[36]Ibid., 74-7; and Doern and Toner, *The Politics of Energy*, 41.

[37]Foster, *The Sorcerer's Apprentices*, 76. On the diversity of opinion among federal bureaucrats, see Doern and Toner, *The Politics of Energy*, 38.

[38]Doern and Toner, *The Politics of Energy*, 43.

[39]See ibid., chaps 3, 5; and Desveaux, 'Strategy, Structure and Government Intervention', chaps 3, 4.

[40]See Canada, Department of Energy, Mines and Resources, *An Energy Strategy for Canada: Policies for Self-Reliance* (Ottawa: Supply and Services Canada, 1976); and Desveaux, 'Strategy, Structure and Government Intervention', 101, 130. According to Desveaux, Ian Stewart was the principal author of *An Energy Strategy for Canada* when he served as assistant deputy minister for energy at EMR.

[41]Doern and Toner, *The Politics of Energy*, chap. 3; and Desveaux, 'Strategy, Structure and Government Intervention', chaps 3, 4.

[42]Desveaux, 'Strategy, Structure and Government Intervention', 110.

[43]See Foster, *The Sorcerer's Apprentices*, chap. 9, 10.

[44]Doern and Toner, *The Politics of Energy*, argue that the NEP can best be understood as an outcome of both administrative and political factors (chap. 2). Foster advances a bureaucratic explanation but admits the importance of politics in his text. See *The Sorcerer's Apprentices*, 142.

[45]Milne, *Tug of War*, 70. For a similar perspective, see Desveaux, 'Strategy, Structure and Government Intervention', chap. 4, which argues that a combination of bureaucratic and political preferences and capacities made the NEP possible.

[46]See Desveaux, 'Strategy, Structure and Government Intervention', chap. 3.

[47]Foster, *The Sorcerer's Apprentices*, 132. For Lalonde's own view of the policy, see 'Riding the Storm'.

[48]See Milne, *Tug of War*, chap. 3.

[49]Clarkson, *Canada and the Reagan Challenge*.

[50]According to Doran, *Forgotten Partnership*, the Liberal party in Canada, along with most other analysts, expected Carter to be reelected, and thus 'discounted U.S. opposition' to the NEP (221). On the Reagan administration response to the back-in provision, see Clarkson, *Canada and the Reagan Challenge*, 24-44, 71-4; and Jenkins, 'Reexamining the "Obsolescing Bargain"', 161-63.

[51]Myer Rashish, as quoted in Foster, *The Sorcerer's Apprentices*, 160.

[52]On the weakening of NEP provisions, see Jenkins, 'Reexamining the "Obsolescing Bargain"', 149-53; and Clarkson, *Canada and the Reagan Challenge*, chaps 2, 3.

[53]Jenkins, 'Reexamining the "Obsolescing Bargain"', 163.

[54]Lalonde, 'Riding the Storm', 73.

[55]See Doern and Toner, *The Politics of Energy*, 24; Crane, *Controlling Interest*, 23, 29; and Foster, *The Sorcerer's Apprentices*, 156-7.

[56]See Jenkins, 'Reexamining the "Obsolescing Bargain"', 155; Doern and Toner, *The Politics of Energy*, 24; and Desveaux, 'Strategy, Structure and Government Intervention', 169.

[57]See Doran, *Forgotten Partnership*, 229. It should be noted that the NDP finance and energy critic in this period was Bob Rae, who represented a Toronto constituency and subsequently became Ontario provincial party leader and premier.

[58]Doern and Toner, *The Politics of Energy*, 24.

[59]See Foster, *The Sorcerer's Apprentices*, 50, 77.

[60]See Jenkins, 'Reexamining the "Obsolescing Bargain"', 157; and Clarkson, *Canada and the Reagan Challenge*, chap. 14.

[61]If one criticism can be levelled against an integrative view of the NEP, it is that the perspective gives relatively little attention to provincial governments which opposed the policy—particularly the Alberta government.

[62]See Lindquist, 'Behind the Myth of Think Tanks', 124.

[63]See Milne, *Tug of War*, 111, as well as Lalonde, 'Riding the Storm'; and Clarkson, *Canada and the Reagan Challenge*.

[64]This argument is developed in Desveaux, 'Strategy, Structure and Government Intervention', chap. 4.

[65]See *Globe and Mail* (31 Oct. 1985), B1.

[66]Lalonde, 'Riding the Storm', 74-6.

5 The Adoption of Canada-US Free Trade

The free trade agreement is necessary to secure access to our most vital market and is consistent with policies which are already strengthening our economy and improving the well-being of Canadians. We on this side of the House support the free trade agreement because we believe it will bring prosperity and economic benefits to Canadians from coast to coast.[1]

[In Canada] there is the benefit of living in a relatively peaceful, non-aggressive, and non-violent society where the poor and the sick and the elderly and other disadvantaged are better cared for. And where freedom to develop the way we wish is not constrained by a so-called 'trade' deal that, in reality, is a contract for economic integration that will turn Canada into a de-industrialized warehouse economy and little more than a resource colony of the United States.[2]

Introduction

Recommended by a federal royal commission in 1985[3] and implemented on a timetable beginning in January 1989, continental free trade was one of the major subjects of Canadian policy debate during the late 1980s. As noted in Chapter 1, free trade, or reciprocity, had been a controversial issue in the late nineteenth and early twentieth centuries, particularly in the period of the 1911 federal election. It was later eclipsed by questions of culture and investment except briefly, during the late 1940s, when Prime Minister William Lyon Mackenzie King entertained the idea of a continental agreement.[4] Starting in 1975, however, with the appearance of two studies by the Economic Council of Canada and subsequent reports by the Senate Standing Committee on Foreign Affairs and the Department of External Affairs, interest in Canada-US free trade was renewed.[5]

The decision of the federal government to pursue open bilateral trade reflected a particular understanding of economic and political developments in the 1970s and 1980s, just as opposition to this plan reflected a contradictory reading of many of the same patterns. This chapter begins by reviewing arguments for and against free trade that were advanced during the various stages of debate over the idea and, eventually, over the formal terms of the bilateral agreement, particularly during the years 1985 through 1988. This discussion sets the stage for evaluating the federal government's decision to pursue a comprehensive bilateral trade policy, a decision that led to the signing and implementation of the Canada-United States Free Trade Agreement (FTA) despite nationalist protests.

Before examining arguments for and against free trade, a few comments about focus are in order. First, the purpose of this chapter is to explain on a general level the pursuit of comprehensive free trade by the government of Canada, rather than to explore the specific terms of the FTA. The latter subject would require a lengthy book of its own.

Second, in examining the Canadian government's pursuit of comprehensive free trade, this discussion considers the obverse of the cases examined in Chapters 3 and 4. Unlike Bill C-58 and the National Energy Program, both of which were basically favourable to nationalist interests, bilateral free trade had been defined since the late nineteenth century as a continentalist or anti-nationalist policy. Thus when nationalists and their allies organized to oppose free trade in the late 1980s, they fought tooth and nail against not only the idea, the negotiating process and the terms of the final agreement, but also against the broader processes of continental integration, which threatened all they had achieved with Bill C-58, the NEP and other policies. In short, this chapter addresses the relative inability of organized nationalists to influence federal public policy during the late 1980s.

Finally, in considering the free trade issue, this chapter focusses on fairly recent developments. As noted in Chapter 2, far less secondary literature is available on free trade than on Bill C-58 and the NEP; as a result, much of this discussion relies on primary data drawn from media accounts, direct observation of the trade debate and subsequent interviews with nationalist activists. The narrative is necessarily speculative and impressionistic, buttressed less by references to academic studies than by a more intuitive reading of 'what happened' in the struggle over free trade.

Why Free Trade?

According to the various publications cited in Table 5.1, many compelling reasons existed for Canada to pursue a more open trade policy with the United States. Above all, Canadian firms and the Canadian economy generally could prosper through greater access and greater security of access to the huge American market. Trade between the two countries had grown to the point that more than 75 per cent of Canadian exports were destined for the US; moreover, tariffs in Canada had declined by almost 40 per cent after 1965, so that by the late 1980s approximately 90 per cent of US products were expected to enter with duty rates of 5 per cent or less.[6] Moreover, the Standing Committee on Foreign Affairs projected that by 1987, 80 per cent of Canadian exports to the US would be subject to these same minimal tariffs.[7]

TABLE 5.1   PUBLISHED REPORTS FAVOURABLE TO SECTORAL OR
COMPREHENSIVE FREE TRADE, 1975-1988

YEAR	REPORT
1975	Economic Council Of Canada, *Looking Outward: A New Trade Strategy for Canada* (Ottawa: Supply and Services Canada)
1975	Peyton V. Lyon, *Canada-United States Free Trade and Canadian Independence,* Economic Council Research Study (Ottawa: Information Canada)
1978	Roma Dauphin, *The Impact of Free Trade on Canada,* Economic Council Research Study (Ottawa: Supply and Services Canada)
1978	Senate Standing Committee on Foreign Affairs, *Canada-United States Relations:* Volume 2, *Canada's Trade Relations with the United States* (Ottawa: Supply and Services Canada)
1982	Senate Standing Committee on Foreign Affairs, *Canada-United States Relations:* Volume 3, *Canada's Trade Relations with the United States* (Ottawa: Supply and Services Canada)
1983	Department of External Affairs, *Canadian Trade Policy for the 1980s : A Discussion Paper* (Ottawa: Supply and Services Canada)
1983	Department of External Affairs, *A Review of Canadian Trade Policy: A Background Document to Canadian Trade Policy for the 1980s* (Ottawa: Supply and Services Canada)
1984	Richard G. Harris and David Cox, *Trade, Industrial Policy and Canadian Manufacturing* (Toronto: Ontario Economic Council)
1985	*Report* of the Royal Commission on the Economic Union and Development Prospects for Canada (Macdonald Commission; Ottawa: Supply and Services Canada)
1985	Richard G. Lipsey and Murray G. Smith, *Taking the Initiative: Canada's Trade Options in a Turbulent World* (Toronto: C.D. Howe Institute)
1985	Department of External Affairs, *Canadian Trade Negotiations: Introduction, Selected Documents, Further Reading* (Ottawa: Supply and Services Canada)
1988	Economic Council of Canada, *Venturing Forth: An Assessment of the Canada - U.S. Trade Agreement* (Ottawa: Supply and Services Canada)

The belief that existing continental patterns constituted *de facto* free trade, and that Canada's interests rested in broadening and formalizing this trend, was reflected in the text of a 1983 External Affairs discussion paper. *Canadian Trade Policy for the 1980s* examined potential threats and possibilities facing Canadian decision-makers; one section devoted to trade with the US concluded that a sectoral approach was preferable to a comprehensive bilateral one, and, beginning in 1984, the federal Liberal government entered into sectoral discussions with the US.[8]

This early initiative can be attributed not only to the momentum created by the various studies cited in Table 5.1, but also to the increasingly pro-free trade positions of Canadian business groups and of the Reagan administration in Washington. During his tenure in Ottawa, US Ambassador Paul Robinson held a series of private lunches with leaders of the Canadian Chamber of Commerce, the Business Council on National Issues and the Canadian Manufacturers' Association. Robinson used these meetings as a forum in which to voice his country's opposition to proposed federal and Quebec legislation in the area of film distribution, and to stimulate Canadian interest in bilateral free trade.[9] By 1984, the Manufacturers' Association had reversed its historic opposition to free trade and the Chamber of Commerce had established a permanent task force on the subject; both sought federal government support for a more open bilateral trade policy.[10]

Canada's willingness to consider a new round of trade negotiations in this period also followed from the relative success of the Auto Pact. As J.L. Granatstein suggests, the experience of managed trade under the Auto Pact encouraged Canadian decision-makers to pursue other similar arrangements. The existence of a nearly $20 billion deficit in manufactured goods during the early 1980s, together with concerns that the rise of East Asia's economic strength and a prolonged domestic recession would limit growth in Canada, encouraged federal decision-makers to focus on bilateral opportunities for exporting more petrochemicals, textiles and other products.[11]

A particular set of perceptions concerning global trade also shaped Canadian policy during the 1980s. Believing that the emergence of a world trading system necessitated industrial competitiveness and a restructuring or rationalization of the domestic economy, some Canadian elites endorsed free trade in order to open the large American market to businesses operating in the smaller and less competitive Canadian setting.[12] Given what they viewed as a growing protectionist hostility to trade liberalization in the global marketplace and, more important, in the US Congress, Canadian proponents of what was then termed 'freer trade' believed that the time had come to pursue a bilateral initiative.[13]

In early sectoral discussions, as in the subsequent negotiations towards a comprehensive trade deal, Canada proved to be the more anxious and motivated suitor. The failure of the sectoral approach can be linked to many factors, including the impossibility of trade-offs between sectors within such a strategy, the unwillingness of the US to model new agreements on the bilateral Auto Pact and general hostility towards trade liberalization in the US.[14]

In 1984, Canadians elected a majority Progressive Conservative government that promised jobs, prosperity and more cordial federal-provincial as well as

Canadian-American relations. Believing that the federal state under a series of Liberal governments had been confrontational and interventionist to a fault, the Conservatives set out to dismantle those products of Liberal policy that most offended them and their supporters. Not surprisingly, major provisions of the National Energy Program were eliminated and the Foreign Investment Review Agency (FIRA) was quickly transformed into Investment Canada.[15] In the area of federal-provincial relations, the Mulroney government set out to secure Quebec's participation in the process of constitutional renewal, an initiative that culminated in the 1987 signing of the Meech Lake Accord. Jurisdictional decentralization was thus wedded to market-oriented economics in the first Conservative government—a combination in direct contrast to the centralism and interventionism of the nationalist world view.

Ironically, many of the market-oriented policies that were endorsed in the 1985 report of the Macdonald Royal Commission (including comprehensive free trade) likely earned a more sympathetic hearing from the Conservatives than they would have received from the Liberal government that had appointed the Commission.[16] Although Prime Minister Mulroney and other prominent cabinet ministers had opposed the idea of free trade as recently as 1984,[17] they were increasingly drawn towards three main arguments in favour of an overall bilateral agreement. First, free trade would enable Canadian industry to specialize in those goods and services that it produced most cheaply, a doctrine known as comparative advantage; second, a continental deal would enhance and secure access to a larger market with those specialized products, thus creating economies of scale; and third, free trade would ensure a wider range of product choices in Canada at lower prices, or consumer sovereignty.[18]

These arguments were accompanied by assertions to the effect that free trade would create more jobs, increase economic growth and, above all, protect Canadian producers from the negative effects of US protectionism, notably countervailing duties and other non-tariff barriers.[19] Supported by organized business interests, by most provincial premiers and by the recommendations of the Macdonald Commission, Mulroney announced in September 1985 his government's intention to negotiate 'the broadest possible package of mutually beneficial reductions in tariff and non-tariff barriers' with the US.[20] By expanding bilateral trade and removing obstacles to its future growth, Canadians would reap the benefits of lower consumer prices, higher GNP and—in general—economic and social prosperity.

Under the leadership of chief negotiator Simon Reisman, appointed by Mulroney in November 1985, a 100-member Trade Negotiations Office was created, along with an International Trade Advisory Committee and 14 individual SAGITs (Sectoral Advisory Groups on International Trade).[21] Charged with the task of advising Reisman and his staff, who began meeting with chief US negotiator Peter Murphy in May 1986, the Advisory Committee and SAGITs communicated the views of an overwhelmingly business constituency to the Canadian trade team.[22] Supporting their efforts were well-financed public relations campaigns by the federal government and other sympathetic interests, most notably the pro-trade business coalition formed in March 1987 and known as the Canadian Alliance for Trade and Job Opportunities.[23]

Why Not Free Trade?

Standing in opposition to these governmental, advisory and interest groups was a different network of activists who challenged virtually every argument in support of comprehensive bilateral talks. Instead of viewing the Conservative initiative as a policy designed to create prosperity, critics maintained that the federal government was negotiating the sale of Canada, the end to Canadian autonomy in virtually every sector of its economy, culture and way of life. In the words of Mel Hurtig and Duncan Cameron, two leading opponents whose position is quoted at the beginning of this chapter, the 'so-called "trade" deal . . . is a contract for economic integration that will turn Canada into a de-industrialized warehouse economy and little more than a resource colony of the United States'.[24]

Because opponents believed that a full bilateral agreement threatened Canadian sovereignty in the crucial areas of culture (including communications policy) and investment (especially control over domestic energy resources) as well as trade, the debates that began in 1985 and continued through 1988 were heated, emotional and at times near-apocalyptic. Not surprisingly, continentalists defended with near-religious fervour the virtues of economic growth, larger markets, lower prices and international competitiveness. Their opponents employed equally visceral arguments concerning the loss of identity and threats to sovereignty implied by free trade, building on many older themes from the cultural, investment and trade streams of pan-Canadianism.

From this perspective, much of the opposition to free trade in the late 1980s can be linked to a world view that was fundamentally different from that of the supporters of bilateral talks. Like nationalist activists in earlier periods, these critics of comprehensive free trade distrusted both *laissez-faire* economics in general and the more specific idea that open bilateral competition was in Canada's best interests. While agreeing with free trade supporters on a number of background points—that the economic recession of the early 1980s had been damaging, that the rise of East Asia constituted a significant economic challenge, that US trade actions had a negative impact on Canada, and that the global economy was becoming increasingly integrated and competitive—opponents weaved these considerations into a very different cloth.

Many critics of free trade began with a basic belief that Canada was fundamentally different from the United States. In their view, Canada had rejected pure *laissez-faire* economics; it relied instead on a mixture of public and private initiatives, and was willing to use state intervention to achieve desired social or economic objectives. In the words of James Laxer, a Waffle veteran and political economist who actively opposed free trade,

> Canada's economic history over the past two centuries amounts to a protracted defiance of accepted economic theory. Instead of letting the free play of the market determine everything, a policy which would have drawn us into economic union with the United States long ago, Canadians have opted for the alternative course of tying a nation together on the northern half of North America.[25]

By drawing the country into an ever more dependent relationship with its larger southern neighbour, the Mulroney government was threatening the essence of economic sovereignty and Canadian distinctiveness.

Moreover, critics argued, Prime Minister Mulroney was discarding more than a century of Conservative tradition in his decision to pursue market-oriented strategies like free trade. Sir John A. Macdonald had insisted on the primacy of national over continental economic policies, thus fostering east-west economic cohesion and a tradition of tempering private initiative with public vision. Instead of building on this experience, it was argued, Mulroney was using lower bilateral tariffs and threats of US protectionism as a pretext to introduce neo-conservatism and deregulation in Canada, much as Ronald Reagan and Margaret Thatcher were attempting to do elsewhere. Opponents thus maintained that the free trade initiative was part of a larger plan to weaken the Canadian welfare state, limit government intervention in the economy and, with the passage of time, make the Canadian way of life virtually indistinguishable from that of the United States.[26] In the words of one critic, 'free trade is a codeword for privatization and liberalization; it's Thatcherism through the back door.'[27]

These arguments against free trade were voiced by a broad coalition of interests. Building on the kind of environmental, aboriginal and nationalist coalition that had helped to create the Public Petroleum Association of Canada during the 1970s, many trade union, environmental, church, feminist, social welfare, aboriginal, cultural and farm groups staked out firm positions against comprehensive free trade in the 1980s.[28] In some cases, these interests had made their views known even before the formal recommendations of the Macdonald Royal Commission were released.[29] Together with economic nationalists who had pursued foreign investment and energy issues during the 1970s—most notably Edmonton publisher Mel Hurtig, who was instrumental in establishing the Council of Canadians as a national anti-trade organization based on individual memberships in January 1985—and with cultural nationalists who had supported Bill C-58 and other measures, a broad range of anti-trade interests formed the Pro-Canada Network (PCN) in April 1987. The Network had an organizational base of about 35 member groups, including the Council of Canadians, with a combined membership of several million.[30]

At least three major arguments against free trade were voiced by Network activists during the late 1980s. First, instead of creating jobs and ensuring prosperity, a comprehensive bilateral approach would threaten both employment opportunities and progressive social policies. According to this view, private sector firms that compared relatively expansive (and hence expensive) Canadian with more limited American social welfare provisions would prefer to locate in the US. Employers who remained in Canada would tend to press for policy 'harmonization', meaning a weakening of Canadian health, child care, unemployment insurance and pension standards, as well as a shift away from government intervention in the areas of regional development, agricultural policy, workplace safety and equal pay.[31] According to empirical studies of the 1988 election period, this 'social programmes challenge' was the most effective argument in the anti-trade campaign.[32]

Second, particularly during the federal election campaign in the fall of 1988—when the trade debate reached its crescendo—opponents used a powerful identity argument parallel to that employed in the election of 1911. Typified by Liberal leader John Turner in his challenge to Prime Minister Mulroney during their television debate, critics questioned how and indeed *if* Canada could continue to exist as a sovereign country once east/west trade and transportation ties were replaced by continental north/south integration.[33] Would Canada not be drawn towards the lean, mean American-style system of ruthless competition that had already reduced many US cities to burned-out centres of violence, poverty and drug abuse? How could the traditional Canadian emphasis on collective and not simply individual rights be maintained in the face of a thoroughly asymmetric integration of mouse with elephant? Why should Canadians tie their nation's fate to that of a declining and, in many respects, unattractive American empire?[34]

Much of this second line of criticism returned to core questions of national identity or 'Canadianness'. Instead of agreeing with free trade supporters that culture was a specific economic sector that could be defined outside the terms of bilateral discussions, many artists and writers maintained that culture was a way of life, a system of values, that was directly jeopardized by free trade.[35] Ultimately, because cultural industries were not exempted from the tariff (s. 401), investment (s. 1607) and trade remedy (s. 2005.2) provisions of the final agreement, critics claimed that the being known as Canada was under far greater threat *with* free trade than without it.[36]

Finally, opponents rejected specific provisions of the 1988 agreement that they believed were most damaging to Canadian sovereignty and identity. In addition to section 2005.2, which permitted US commercial retaliation in any sector against Canadian cultural policy, critics devoted particular attention to the treatment of energy resources, foreign investment and dispute settlement mechanisms. Maintaining that free trade as negotiated would forfeit Canadian control of domestic energy reserves and eliminate the possibility of any future initiative like the National Energy Program, that it virtually wiped out federal controls on foreign investment and, finally, that it failed to protect Canada from US trade remedy legislation, opponents focussed on what they took to be a systematic sell-out of Canadian interests.[37] Given the long-standing commitment of Canadian nationalists to federal intervention in the energy and investment fields, combined with the Conservative government's earlier claim that free trade would protect Canadian industry from the negative effects of US trade practices, it is not surprising that this debate over the terms of the agreement was particularly heated.

In this same vein, critics argued that the bilateral agreement dramatically weakened those provisions of the Auto Pact which had assisted the Canadian automotive industry, that it jeopardized the Canadian service sector by permitting free trade in services and that it failed to develop a promised and very necessary subsidy code. Frequently, these specific points were merged with a broader critique of policy harmonization and the cultural threat implied by free trade, in effect portraying both Canada and free trade in a light that was unrecognizable to proponents of the policy.[38]

Among government negotiators and supporters of the trade initiative, such criticisms were dismissed as nationalist cant or, in the words of International Trade minister John Crosbie, the ravings of 'CBC-type snivellers, the Toronto literati, the alarm-spreaders and the encyclopedia-peddlars'.[39] A number of difficulties did arise during the trade negotiations; at one point Simon Reisman suspended formal talks and, at other junctures, US duties on Canadian shingle and softwood lumber exports threatened to jeopardize the process.[40] But when the eleventh hour had almost passed, at 11:40 PM on 3 October 1987, formal agreement on the Canada-US Free Trade Agreement was finally reached.

Alternatives to Free Trade

If organized opponents of free trade were harshly critical of the government's decision to pursue a comprehensive bilateral deal, then what was their alternative? Or was there an alternative? These questions are particularly important to understanding the nationalist/continentalist conflict over free trade. If continentalists were able to frame a positive story about the benefits of free trade, if they were able to develop a narrative that spoke to the *advantages* of such a policy, then they would likely command the same 'good news' position that nationalists had held in debates over the NEP and Bill C-58. By way of contrast, if nationalists were forced to rely on what Emery Roe terms an 'anti-story', a negative narrative constituting little more than a defensive rebuttal to the tale of benefits advanced by the other side, then *they* would be strategically disadvantaged—much like the opponents of Bill C-58 and the NEP.[41]

The literature produced by trade critics, together with interview materials, suggests that nationalists generally agreed on four broad points.[42] First, most believed that Canada's interests could be pursued more effectively through reduced interprovincial trade barriers within the country and expanded multilateral—as opposed to bilateral—trade initiatives as part of the General Agreement on Tariffs and Trade (GATT).[43] However, proponents of a bilateral deal countered this argument with claims that Canada-US talks complemented rather than undermined the multilateral route; moreover, they saw the GATT process as relatively slow, cumbersome and unlikely to respond in the near future to crucial problems facing the Canadian economy.[44]

Second, critics called for a long-term as opposed to 'quick fix' approach to economic policy. Instead of using an external source of trade competition to restructure the Canadian economy, anti-trade activists emphasized internal sources of economic weakness. And whereas supporters of free trade identified these problems as low competitiveness, limited rationalization and other market imperfections, analysts who opposed the bilateral approach offered an updated version of Harold Innis's staples thesis. In their view, Canada was a resource-dependent state whose key extractive and manufacturing sectors were controlled either by foreign- (frequently US-) based multinational corporations, or by Canadian firms holding distinctly continentalist and comprador outlooks.[45] Because of the dominant role of foreign direct investment, Canada did not autonomously determine its own economic development, and would be even less likely to move in the direction of economic independence once bilateral free trade became a reality.[46]

In light of this position, critics argued for reduced Canadian reliance on foreign investment and greater emphasis on indigenous research, development and technological training.[47] In turn, proponents claimed that internal improvements to the Canadian economy would not occur unless international sources of competition were brought to bear; furthermore, they maintained that the performance of capital investments in Canada was far more important than their country of origin.[48]

Third, opponents of free trade believed that Canada should continue to fight US countervail and other trade remedy actions on a case-by-case basis rather than through a comprehensive bilateral deal.[49] Although their position was reinforced by the inability of Canadian negotiators to gain protection from US legislation in the text of the final agreement, it was challenged by trade advocates who claimed that the traditional Canadian approach was no longer viable.[50]

Last and most important, critics argued in favour of an active, interventionist federal state that could plan as well as manage the domestic economy. Frequently captured in the phrase 'industrial strategy', this position laid out an option by which the Canadian federal state would assert a national presence in the economy, rather than retreating from interference in the marketplace. In the words of Mel Watkins, a Waffle veteran who was active in the Pro-Canada Network: 'I spoke very widely across Canada against free trade and based on my experience, most Canadians still believe in a positive role for government in the economy.'[51]

More than any other argument posed by critics of free trade, this one in favour of government involvement acted as a lightning-rod to trade advocates. Business groups and regional interests that had long opposed what they saw as the centralist, interventionist and central Canadian biases of the Foreign Investment Review Agency and the National Energy Program viewed the ideas of state planning, economic management and 'positive government' as synonymous with more FIRAs and yet another disastrous NEP.

In attempting to articulate their alternative, opponents of free trade thus faced two very significant problems. First, they relied for the most part on ideas drawn from the late 1960s and following, when investment nationalists had articulated what was then an innovative critique of foreign control and a demand for interventionist state responses. Twenty years later, this position seemed less compelling; unlike the period of the Waffle and the Committee for an Independent Canada, the late 1980s were characterized by neither new social movement formation nor wide-eyed trust in the managerial abilities of the federal government. Instead, the opponents of free trade had to direct their arguments to an increasingly cynical and alienated public, for whom prosperity sounded preferable to yet another attempt at state interventionism. As the experiences of Watkins and others suggested, by the late 1980s the economic views of the business community were often considered to be more legitimate than those advanced by critics of free trade.[52]

Second, free trade opponents were cast in the role of narrators of an 'anti-story'.[53] Instead of establishing the terms of the debate and painting a positive picture of jobs and prosperity, they were increasingly tied to an oppositional discourse, seeking only to discredit the continentalist scenario. By 1990, nationalists could claim that many of their worst-case predictions about free trade had come to pass;[54] in the context of the mid-1980s, however, these warnings sounded merely reactive and essentially negative.

Nationalist arguments faced a somewhat different problem in their treatment of culture—an area where critics might have been expected to be at least as vocal as in the economic field. If, from a nationalist point of view, free trade threatened Canadian identity at least as dramatically as it jeopardized economic sovereignty, then where was the cultural content of the alternative? Although opponents argued that free trade would further limit domestic control of the media industry, a curious disjuncture remained between the identity-based priorities of cultural activists and the primarily investment- and trade-driven alternatives posed by economic nationalists.

The next section considers the societal approach as a framework for explaining the pursuit of comprehensive free trade; nationalist alternatives are explored in Chapters 6 and 8.

The Societal Perspective

From a distance, group theories appear to explain easily the basic question of 'who won' on free trade. Pitting Goliath against David, the well-organized and well-financed business lobby in favour of comprehensive free trade against the disparate, less affluent coalition that opposed it, societal analysis points unmistakably towards the victory of the former. As well, in this case the societal approach has the advantage of vocal, identifiable and reasonably cohesive interests on both sides, making for a clear contest between two sets of highly motivated players.

Resources

In terms of tangible assets, organized supporters of free trade controlled far more than did their adversaries. Estimates differ on the amount of money spent to convince the Canadian public of the benefits of comprehensive free trade, depending in part on whether the pro-trade campaigns of the federal government, various provincial governments and the federal Conservative party are included in the calculations. To make the comparison of resources more manageable, however, one can begin with the societal interests that either endorsed or opposed free trade, and consider other expenditures as adjuncts.

Accounts of the activities of the leading national pro-trade group, the Canadian Alliance for Trade and Job Opportunities, report that the approximately 35 business associations represented in the Alliance contributed about $5,250,000 between April 1987 and March 1989. During the period prior to the fall 1988 elections, the Alliance is estimated to have spent approximately $2.9 million, of which more than $2.3 million was devoted to advertising and consultants.[55] According to Thomas d'Aquino, president of the Business Council on National Issues and a leading participant in the Alliance, another $2 million of this $5.25 million was devoted to promoting free trade during the seven-week federal election campaign in the fall of 1988.[56] Other accounts have estimated that the Alliance spent as much as $4 million during this campaign period, primarily on full-page advertisements in major daily newspapers, and that it had earlier spent about $3 million on newspaper and television advertisements during the spring of 1987.[57]

Aside from the Business Council on National Issues, which represented 150 major private sector corporations, the Alliance had the support of the Canadian Manufacturers' Association, the Canadian Chamber of Commerce, the Canadian Federation of Independent Business and the Pharmaceutical Manufacturers' Association. Its joint chairmen were Peter C. Lougheed, former Conservative premier of Alberta, and Donald S. Macdonald, who served as a federal Liberal cabinet minister before heading the Royal Commission on the Economic Union and Development Prospects for Canada. In addition to these prominent individuals and groups, other supporters of free trade included the National Citizens' Coalition (a right-wing lobby group that spent about $720,000 on pro-trade activities), the National Association of Manufacturers, the Canadian Exporters Association and the Council of Forest Industries of British Columbia.[58]

On the other side of the debate, the resources available were relatively modest.[59] Most accounts estimate the amount of money spent by the Council of Canadians and the Pro-Canada Network at less than $1 million, usually in the range of $750,000.[60] About $650,000 of this was spent on producing 2.2 million copies of a 24-page pamphlet by *Montreal Star* cartoonist Aislin (Terry Mosher) and Toronto writer Rick Salutin, entitled 'What's the Big Deal?'[61] Inserted in about 20 daily newspapers during the 1988 election campaign, the pamphlet sought to raise public interest in the trade issue and, at the same time, focus attention on what were viewed as crucial weaknesses both in the concept and in the negotiated terms of free trade. Like the Canadian Alliance for Trade and Job Opportunities, the Pro-Canada Network was also supported by about 35 constituent groups.

Not only was the $2 million figure cited by the Canadian Alliance more than double the $750,000 spending level of the Pro-Canada Network, but also the pro-trade effort was reinforced by a federal government advocacy campaign that cost approximately $24 million.[62] Designed to promote free trade through a series of advertisements, glossy information pamphlets and a toll-free national telephone hotline, this government publicity campaign presented many of the same arguments—and certainly the same overall policy position—as the Canadian Alliance for Trade and Job Opportunities. Moreover, arguments advanced by the federal government and its allies in the Alliance were amplified by the federal Conservative party organization and by some provincial governments, including those of Quebec and Alberta. In Alberta, for example, an eight-page pamphlet in support of free trade was sent to 836,000 households during the federal election campaign.[63] As well, many Canadian firms sent letters to their employees, inserted literature in pay envelopes, held 'information sessions' in the workplace and sponsored newspaper advertisements urging support for free trade.[64]

The ancillary resources available to anti-trade organizations were comparatively limited. In addition to the Pro-Canada Network, the provincial governments of Ontario, Manitoba and Prince Edward Island formally opposed free trade, as did the federal Liberal party and the federal NDP, but even so the opponents of free trade did not have the 'deep pockets' available to the other side. According to one account, for example, the combined anti-trade expenditures by the Canadian Labour Congress, Ontario Federation of Labour, Canadian Auto Workers and United Steelworkers were less than $3 million, or about half of the total funds raised by the Canadian Alliance to endorse free trade.[65] Although many prominent individuals endorsed the anti-trade position, including Margaret Atwood, Pierre Berton, Eric Kierans and David Suzuki, their presence was not sufficient to counter the array of political and economic elites and the financial assets available to free trade supporters. Even after the Pro-Canada Network was established as an organized coalition to draw together opponents in labour (notably the Canadian Labour Congress, Canadian Automobile Workers and Canadian Union of Public Employees), feminist (National Action Committee on the Status of Women), environmental (Pollution Probe), church

(United Church of Canada and Canadian Conference of Catholic Bishops), agricultural (National Farmers Union), aboriginal (Assembly of First Nations), cultural (Canadian Conference of the Arts and ACTRA) and other organizations, and even after regional and provincial affiliates of the PCN emerged, this resource imbalance persisted.

Group Cohesion

Was one side in the free trade debate more cohesive than the other? Although both groups were internally united by the end of 1988 and even though very few defections occurred from the ranks of either side, supporters seemed to enjoy some advantage. Linked by a shared perception that bilateral talks would lead to prosperity and business expansion, supporters wasted little time determining if and why they would endorse free trade. Clearly, the prospect of larger continental markets and reduced government intervention in the Canadian economy appealed directly to most business interests, which were prepared to campaign forcefully and with a single voice in favour of free trade.

By way of contrast, opponents faced a more difficult task both in developing and in articulating their positions. Veterans of the cultural and investment nationalisms of the 1970s—many of whom assumed leadership positions in the Council of Canadians and, later, the Pro-Canada Network— possessed a well-integrated world view in which free trade was seen as threatening national identity, reinforcing resource dependence and ensuring a truncated pattern of industrial development.[66] Other voices in the Pro-Canada Network, however, had diverse origins in the environmental, native rights, feminist and labour movements; many of these interests shared little common history either with each other or with English Canadian nationalism. Unlike the business advocates of free trade, then, who were linked by a basic market ethos, the opponents of this policy possessed a less identifiable core belief system.[67]

One leading figure in the fight against free trade, Mel Hurtig, had been involved in the nationalist activities of the Committee for an Independent Canada during the 1970s . But other prominent opponents, such as Tony Clarke and Maude Barlow, had come to oppose free trade through other social movements. Clarke was active in the Canadian Conference of Catholic Bishops, an organization that had spoken out in response to the human costs of the 1981-82 recession. For Barlow, the women's movement provided a critical impetus towards political activism, which eventually propelled her towards leadership roles in both the Council of Canadians and the Pro-Canada Network.[68]

In such cases, the pattern of recruitment from outside established nationalist channels had the advantage of providing new faces in the leadership of the anti-trade coalition. Moreover, by establishing the Pro-Canada Network, anti-trade forces gained a broader grass-roots base than had been developed by either the Waffle or the Committee for an Independent Canada. Bringing together diverse interests under a single Network umbrella posed considerable problems, however. Could organizations that were themselves umbrella coalitions, like the National Action Committee on the Status of Women, speak with a unified voice inside a larger coalition? How would labour and environmental groups, or feminist and Catholic interests, set aside their differences on other issues in order to co-operate on defeating free trade? Could a coherent critique of this policy emerge from such different starting points?

The various policy statements and publications produced between 1985 and 1988 by the Council of Canadians, the Pro-Canada Network and other coalitions and groups opposed to free trade indicate that a basic common ground did emerge. Critics zeroed in on what they viewed as the regressive, market-driven ideology of the federal Conservatives—what John Warnock referred to as 'the new right agenda'.[69] In their willingness to weaken Canadian social provisions, risk job losses and sell off precious natural resources—in the hope of pleasing not only domestic business interests but also the Reagan administration—Conservatives and, in particular, Prime Minister Mulroney were castigated for negotiating the end of Canada.

Although this position constituted a sweeping indictment of free trade and the government that signed a continental agreement, it remained a more nuanced, complex and less straightforward line of argument than that advanced by societal advocates of free trade. In short, it was likely easier for the latter to unite as a business alliance and 'sell' prosperity to the public than it was for a more diverse group of opponents to organize—and then to make the case for their 'anti-story' about policy harmonization, the new right agenda and threats to national identity.[70]

A somewhat different problem related to cohesion also plagued anti-trade activists. Because they were courted politically by both federal opposition parties and because many had a history of either NDP or Liberal involvement, free trade opponents at times divided internally along party lines.[71] For example, concern was expressed by some participants in the Council of Canadians and the Pro-Canada Network that Mel Hurtig and Maude Barlow were too closely associated with the Liberal party; in fact, Barlow actively sought a federal Liberal nomination in an Ottawa constituency prior to the 1988 elections. At the same time, other moderate or centrist activists worried that the rhetoric of the anti-trade campaign was too radical and left-of-centre, captured in their view by New Democrats, ex-Wafflers and their allies in the trade union movement.

One way out of this bind, and one method of avoiding a split of the anti-FTA vote in the 1988 elections, involved strategic voting. By studying previous election returns from individual ridings and identifying which opposition party candidate was more likely to defeat the Conservative nominee, nationalists hoped to ensure the defeat of free trade at the polls. Other activists in the Pro-Canada Network and Council of Canadians endorsed a Liberal-NDP alliance to circumvent partisan differences for a single watershed election. Like strategic voting, however, the idea of a temporary alliance ran straight into partisan concerns about the viability of the Liberals and the NDP after 1988.[72]

Finally, critics of free trade faced a problem of cohesion within specific parts of their support base, notably the arts and agricultural sectors. Although Canadian business with few exceptions endorsed comprehensive free trade, important cultural and farm interests broke ranks with the anti-trade side. For example, novelist Mordecai Richler and painter Christopher Pratt were among the more than sixty signatories to 'Artists and Writers for Free Trade', while many western Canadian grain and meat producers participated enthusiastically in pro-trade efforts.[73]

Whether real or simply perceived, these divisions among anti-trade interests tended to weaken internal cohesion, and likely aided the pro-trade side.

Policy Expertise

If proponents of free trade had more resources and greater internal cohesion than their adversaries, then what can be said about expertise? A comparison of the two sides suggests that although both had a wealth of experts and expertise, the supporters again enjoyed some advantage. The importance of this factor should not be underestimated: indeed, for much of the 1980s the trade issue unfolded primarily as a debate among experts. Members of the general public served as more or less passive consumers of technical judgements on the numbers of jobs that free trade would either create or threaten, and the extent to which a bilateral agreement would protect or undermine Canadian sovereignty.

One advantage that seemed to accrue to the pro-trade side was a more authoritative base of expertise. In addition to the numerous governmental and Economic Council of Canada studies cited in Table 5.1, free trade received the endorsement of many research organizations (including the Economic Council of Canada and the C.D. Howe Institute), most academic economists, leading business organizations and, of course, the Macdonald Royal Commission.[74] Each of these bases of support was capable of generating large amounts of expert knowledge favourable to comprehensive bilateral trade, and each contributed to an outpouring of pro-trade literature, speeches and position papers in the years 1985-88.

Those on the other side of the debate also had access to an experienced—if somewhat less authoritative—group of experts. Research organizations including the Science Council of Canada and the Canadian Centre for Policy Alternatives opposed free trade.[75] Many Canadian academics were publicly critical of the policy and participated in the Pro-Canada Network research team and other similar efforts; these analysts, however, constituted a minority among the professional ranks of Canadian economists in the late 1980s and were at a clear disadvantage vis-à-vis pro-trade experts.[76] As Stephen Brooks argues in his account of this issue:

> The state, important business organizations, and establishment think tanks are generally presumed to be credible sources of expert information. This presumption

and the sheer capacity of these organizations to generate data, analysis, and expert-backed arguments, usually enable what we might call 'establishment expertise' to dominate the marketplace for policy-relevant ideas/information.[77]

Prominent critics from feminist, social welfare, environmental, aboriginal and cultural groups spoke with considerable policy knowledge of their respective sectors, and in these fields seemed to possess greater legitimacy than did the mainstream economists who defended free trade. Yet even in areas outside the traditional domain of neo-classical economics, anti-trade experts had a difficult time controlling the terms of discourse. In the crucial area of health care policy, for example, where opponents argued that pressures towards continental harmonization would eventually threaten Canadian standards, pro-FTA forces enlisted the crucial support of Mr Justice Emmett Hall. Widely credited with the creation of medicare in Saskatchewan, Hall rebutted the harmonization argument, undermining one of the most powerful claims in the opposition's arsenal.[78]

As in the case of group cohesion, then, the proponents of free trade likely controlled more expertise than did its opponents, although this advantage was less marked than with respect to cohesion and, above all, resources, where the imbalance was quite lopsided in favour of pro-trade interests.

Representativeness

Of the four criteria specified in the societal model, only the last would seem to have favoured anti-trade interests. Proponents were in a weaker position with respect to representation because of their overwhelmingly business constituency—a base that seemed relatively narrow when compared with the more socially diverse constituency of opponents.

The Canadian Alliance for Trade and Job Opportunities stated in its published advertisements that 'Our Alliance consists of the vast majority of Canadian exporters, importers, Chambers of Commerce, manufacturers, and small business groups.'[79] This assertion sounded hollow, however, when compared with the opposition's base among a broad range of trade union, cultural, social welfare, feminist, aboriginal, agricultural and environmental groups represented in the Pro-Canada Network, and the minority business groups opposed to the FTA in the food processing, textile and service sectors.[80]

Recognizing this weakness, pro-trade interests attempted to broaden their representational base beyond the business community. Particularly during the 1988 federal election campaign, efforts were made to counter the powerful identity arguments advanced by cultural nationalists, primarily through the formation of 'Artists and Writers for Free Trade'. One prominent newspaper advertisement by this group included more than sixty names, and acknowledged the assistance of the Canadian Alliance for Trade and Job Opportunities.[81] Although such efforts tended to complicate the question of where Canada's cultural community stood on free trade—a problem noted above with respect to cohesion—they alone could not provide the degree of social diversity to the pro-trade side that already existed among its opponents.

In terms of representativeness, then, the organized opposition seemed to command a broader and more diverse policy constituency than did the proponents.

Assessing the Societal Perspective

The failure of nationalists and their allies to block free trade in the late 1980s is thus explained in part by a societal approach. More limited resources, together with less group cohesion and expertise than existed among trade proponents, tended to hinder anti-trade efforts; these three factors were not counter-balanced by the greater representativeness of trade opponents. In short, a societal perspective suggests that comprehensive free trade was adopted as government policy because societal proponents outflanked opponents on three out of four criteria.

Although it yields an empirically correct conclusion, the group approach nevertheless fails to address at least two other important questions. First, if the federal state operates as a more or less impartial umpire among competing organized interests, as the societal model suggests, then why did it not pursue a comprehensive policy before 1985? Explaining the timing of open free trade seems to require consideration of partisan, attitudinal and international factors—all of which are absent from the societal view and await the introduction of an integrative framework.

Second, the societal view begs questions of nationalist influence. If the two sides were as unevenly matched as this approach suggests, then how did nationalist arguments receive any public or governmental attention during the late 1980s? For example, why would pro-trade interests have worked to enlist the support of Emmett Hall or 'Artists and Writers for Free Trade', if their opponents were as weak as the group model suggests? In other words, nationalists and their allies may have seemed more threatening to trade supporters than this view indicates, perhaps because of media and public opinion factors that are neglected in the societal perspective.

The Bureaucratic View

Are bureaucratic explanations more helpful than the societal approach? The answer to this question seems to be negative, since statist arguments on their own would not have predicted Canada's adoption of comprehensive free trade.

Studies in the bureaucratic tradition emphasize the role of administrative preferences, capacity and autonomy in shaping policy decisions. With reference to free trade, the main federal agency responsible for international trade was the Department of External Affairs (DEA). As reported in Table 5.1, DEA produced two major trade studies in 1983, primarily in response to an identified crisis in this policy area, and published an interim report on formal negotiations in 1985.

Were bureaucratic preferences at External Affairs consistent with the adoption of a comprehensive bilateral policy? According to a 1983 paper entitled *Canadian Trade Policy for the 1980s*, DEA endorsed a sectoral rather than a comprehensive approach. Thus the trade strategy preferred by this key administrative actor in 1983 differed from that undertaken by the federal government only two years later; the expressed preferences of DEA were not congruent with those pursued shortly thereafter as government policy.[82]

Parallel conclusions regarding the preferences of senior federal bureaucrats follow from attitudinal data collected later in the 1980s. According to one report, 'most of the deputy ministers in Ottawa were opposed to free trade' in the period before support for a bilateral agreement was adopted as government policy.[83] Findings from this survey reinforce the public record of DEA publications; that is, bureaucratic preferences did *not* tend towards comprehensive free trade.

That these views had little sustained effect on government policy may be attributable to problems of bureaucratic capacity and autonomy. Within the federal state, dispersed responsibilities in the area of international trade made it difficult to co-ordinate resources across departments. As Grace Skogstad observes in her study of federal policy,

> External Affairs is responsible for tariffs and import quotas and within this department, the branch of International Trade is responsible for the negotiation of international trade agreements. The Department of Finance is responsible for the domestic implementation of the GATT, including its Subsidies and Countervailing Duties Code. The decision to conduct an inquiry to determine whether goods entering Canada are unfairly subsidized or being dumped, as well as the inquiry itself, is carried out by the Customs and Excise division of National Revenue. And, of course, line departments are important players, insofar as they possess the substantive expertise regarding the probable political, economic and social impacts of negotiated agreements.[84]

This problem of low capacity as a result of dispersed and unco-ordinated patterns of responsibility was compounded by divergent outlooks in each of the varying departments involved in international trade. For example, Skogstad notes that elites in Agriculture Canada were consistently sympathetic to protectionist domestic interests through the mid-1980s, while other sectors of the federal bureaucracy—notably External Affairs—placed a premium on fostering diplomatic good will, possibly at the expense of these same domestic interests.[85] In short, dispersed resources and authority in the area of international trade hindered administrative action at the federal level, while differing perspectives on trade policy further limited bureaucratic capacity.

If conflicting preferences and low capacity make it difficult to explain comprehensive free trade using a bureaucratic model, then what can be said about autonomy? Once again, it is difficult to argue that administrative elites operated independently of societal actors. At a July 1984 symposium on 'Canada and the Future of the Global Trading System', sponsored by the Macdonald Royal Commission, Anthony Halliday of External Affairs reviewed the federal government's adoption of a sectoral approach and explained that 'the selection of sectors was not based on any economy-wide analysis, but on more immediate trade problems and expressions of interest from the private sector.'[86] Halliday went on to observe that the terms of any new sectoral agreements were largely dictated by the refusal of the US to consider the Auto Pact as an acceptable prototype.[87] The fact that Canadian private sector and US governmental interests narrowly circumscribed bureaucratic action in this period casts doubt on the independence of state actors, and hence on their ability to determine trade policy autonomously. In fact, federal officials seemed to lack the policy independence required for pursuing an aggressive sectoral, let alone comprehensive, trade strategy.

The bureaucratic approach thus yields a not very useful score of (-,-,-) in this case. Administrative preferences in the part of the federal state responsible for international trade, the Department of External Affairs, favoured a sectoral as opposed to comprehensive approach through the early 1980s; furthermore, bureaucratic capacity and autonomy in the area of trade policy were limited. This pattern suggests that the pursuit of any new trade strategy would have required an impetus from *outside* the state bureaucracy and that, once administered, this external 'kick-start' would necessitate a major re-organization of the federal trade machinery.

As well, this review of the societal and bureaucratic approaches once again confirms the hypothesis outlined in Chapter 2: neither model explains adequately the adoption of a comprehensive policy. In the case of the societal framework, the timing of the policy's introduction is difficult to explain, and the apparent threat posed by nationalist interests to pro-trade groups is hard to fathom. With reference to the bureaucratic view, comprehensive free trade seems literally to have come out of nowhere, since it was not congruent with administrative preferences, capacity or autonomy in the period prior to 1985.

The Integrative Approach

In many respects, the preceding discussion of the bureaucratic view foreshadows the ideas/politics cluster of variables introduced below. For example, the importance of US government influences was apparent to officials in External Affairs, who acknowledged American preferences *for* a comprehensive bilateral strategy and *against* sectoral agreements modelled on the Auto Pact. Moreover, the organizational disunity of the federal trade bureaucracy and its relative lack of policy autonomy suggest that partisan factors likely intervened to 'kick-start' a new trade strategy.

Two propositions guide this application of the integrative model. First, as explained in Chapter 2, conducive conditions are expected to obtain on at least one of the three variables in the ideas/politics cluster, in order for policy action to occur. In the case of free trade, as summarized in Figure 5.1, favourable circumstances existed on all three of these factors. Second, the sum of independent variables in the three 'stripes' provides a short-hand summary of the likelihood of government action. Five out of 10 highly conducive conditions are identified in this case, meaning that comprehensive free trade was moderately likely in the period after 1984.

Because the policy under consideration in this chapter is the adoption of open Canada-US free trade, Figure 5.1 is scored with reference to continentalist or anti-nationalist preferences, in contrast to the pro-nationalist scoring of Figures 3.1 and 4.1. As indicated by the entries for the societal and bureaucratic clusters in Figure 5.1, proponents benefitted from very favourable levels of resources (X1), cohesion (X2) and expertise (X3) as compared with opponents, but had minimal representativeness within the policy domain (X4) and confronted relatively unfavourable conditions in the federal bureaucracy (variables X5, X6 and X7).

Turning to the ideas/politics cluster in the integrative approach, it would seem that explanations of Canada's pursuit of comprehensive free trade following 1985 rest on a congruence between US and Canadian political preferences, on the one hand, and those of organized Canadian business, on the other. The Reagan administration was concerned about growing protectionist sentiment during the early 1980s—not only in the US Congress, but also in Canadian federal and provincial policies that threatened to restrict US film distribution activities.[88] Believing that comprehensive free trade could prove beneficial to American private sector interests, in part because it would limit Canada's ability to introduce future nationalist policies modelled on Bill C-58, FIRA and the NEP, US interests saw the election of a Conservative majority government in 1984 as a golden opportunity for pursuing such a strategy. Since President Reagan was in his second and final term of office, officials in Washington were particularly inclined towards a 'fast-track' approach that would limit congressional influence and ensure that a bilateral agreement was in place before a new president took office.[89] Variable X8, US government response to the idea of comprehensive free trade, is thus scored as highly favourable in Figure 5.1.

Yet even with conducive societal conditions and official US support, the Canadian political environment had to shift substantially to permit the introduction of free trade discourse—let alone a free trade policy—in Ottawa. The 1984 elections set the stage for just such a sea change. Gone were many of the centralist, interventionist and moderately nationalist partisans of Liberal rule, and in their stead was a more decentralist, pro-business and pro-US Conservative elite. Although Prime Minister Mulroney and many of his cabinet colleagues (with the exception of John Crosbie) had earlier opposed comprehensive free trade and did not pursue it as an issue in 1984, after the election they were clearly responsive to Canadian business and US government interest in such an agreement.

FIGURE 5.1   SCORING INDEPENDENT VARIABLES ON ADOPTION OF COMPREHENSIVE FREE TRADE POLICY

	SOCIETAL CLUSTER				BUREAUCRATIC CLUSTER			IDEAS/POLITICS CLUSTER			ROW TOTALS
	Group resources X_1	Group cohesion X_2	Group expertise X_3	Group represent-ativeness X_4	Bureaucratic preferences X_5	Bureaucratic capacity X_6	Bureaucratic autonomy X_7	International influences X_8	Partisan actors X_9	Media, public opinion X_{10}	
Very conducive conditions	●	●	●					●	●		5
Somewhat conducive conditions										●	1
Minimally conducive conditions				●	●	●	●				4

Part of this responsiveness can be linked to the warmly pro-American predilections of Brian Mulroney. Raised in the branch-plant setting of Baie-Comeau, Mulroney tended to admire US investors who brought jobs and a reasonable standard of living to the small resource towns of northern Quebec. In the well-worn story of singing as a child for Colonel McCormick of the Chicago *Tribune* was an important lesson for Mulroney's adult experience: cordial relations with Americans could produce tangible rewards. This lesson seemed to bear fruit in Mulroney's subsequent career as president of the Iron Ore Co. of Canada, a subsidiary of the Hanna Mining Co. in Cleveland.[90]

This willingness to respond to business and US preferences for comprehensive free trade, to the *ideas* of continentalism, was also linked to Mulroney's less than sympathetic view of Canadian nationalism. In the same 1984 speech in New York City in which he declared Canada 'open for business,' Mulroney spoke of the need to limit both nationalist and bureaucratic influences on government decision-making. In his words, 'The North Shore was not built by federal civil servants or people preaching economic nationalism from the safety of downtown Toronto.'[91]

Mulroney's profound antipathy towards what he viewed as the interventionist, largely pro-Ontario bias of economic nationalism found a warm reception in Conservative circles. Many westerners in the party were pleased to be part of a government that desired closer continental relations; furthermore, they opposed the kinds of centralist and regionally insensitive policies that were typified, in their view, by the National Energy Program. As noted in Chapter 4, the efforts of the Conservative minister of Energy, Mines and Resources, Pat Carney, to dismantle the NEP were part and parcel of this anti-nationalist, pro-market orientation of the federal Conservatives.

What was the response to continentalist ideas among the opposition parties after 1984? Both the Liberals and the New Democrats opposed the specific terms of free trade as negotiated, but they differed in a number of important respects. Some Liberal MPs, especially those of a business Liberal persuasion, endorsed the *idea* of free trade but not the actual bilateral agreement. Many of these parliamentarians had supported sectoral initiatives pursued by the Liberals prior to 1984. Others, of a nationalist and interventionist persuasion, rejected both the idea and the actual negotiated agreement. Within the NDP, a general consensus existed that neither continentalist ideas nor continentalist agreements were acceptable.[92]

What was ironic about this partisan debate was the extent to which the Liberals, with all their internal divisions, managed to position themselves in 1988 as the leading opponents of free trade. Not surprisingly, the failure of the NDP's parliamentary leadership and backroom advisors to place the issue front and centre within the party's 1988 platform was a subject of enormous controversy *after* the election.[93]

Variable X9 in Figure 5.1 involves the response to continentalist ideas in the governing federal party. After 1984, circumstances seemed very favourable because of the fundamentally anti-nationalist and anti-interventionist predilections of the Mulroney Conservatives; moreover, the Opposition Liberals were internally divided in their position on free trade, making it easier for the governing party to act on its continentalist preferences. Variable X9 is therefore coded as 'very conducive'.

With party and international actors favourable to continentalist ideas, the pursuit of free trade seemed to await only a softening of editorial and public opinion. In 1985, officials in the Prime Minister's Office developed a communications strategy that anticipated harsh public criticism of this initiative.[94] Their plan was to downplay free trade, permitting members of the Macdonald Commission and pro-trade business groups to assume the leadership and take much of the heat for the policy. Although this strategy was not entirely successful—as reported in Table 5.2, public support for free trade tended to decline and opposition to increase after early 1987—opponents of the policy were divided electorally between the Liberals and the New Democrats,[95] and this division would clearly work in the Conservatives' favour. While they could count on most supporters to endorse their party, they also tried to persuade an important swing group that neither opposition party had a credible alternative to free trade, and that Brian Mulroney was more competent than either of the opposition party leaders.[96]

The ability of the Conservatives to soften and in many respects divide public opinion was strengthened by widespread editorial support for free trade.[97] With a few exceptions such as the *Toronto Star*, which vigorously and relentlessly opposed it, most domestic media outlets, especially the business press, tended to endorse free trade.[98] In Quebec in particular, media opinion was virtually unanimous in its support.[99] Variable X10, media and public opinion on the continentalist idea of free trade, is thus coded as somewhat conducive, with those elements of public opinion opposed to the policy counter-balanced by fairly broad media support for it.

The very favourable positions of both the Canadian and the US governments towards comprehensive free trade, combined with moderate support in media and public opinion, pushed it forward as a viable policy option after 1984. The conducive conditions shown in Figure 5.1 for each of the variables in the ideas/politics cluster (X8, X9 and X10) are crucial in explaining the adoption of a policy that could not have been predicted by reference to societal or bureaucratic factors on their own. The total of five very conducive conditions, including all three variables in the ideas/politics cluster, and one somewhat conducive meant that free trade was moderately probable as a policy after 1984.

Nevertheless, four of the variables were minimally conducive, suggesting a moderate (approximately 40 per cent) likelihood of policy failure in this period, primarily because of circumstances in the bureaucratic sector. This pattern sheds light on the actual negotiation of a comprehensive bilateral agreement. It suggests that reorganizing the federal trade bureaucracy was necessary as a prior condition for such an initiative—a reorganization that did occur with the establishment of the Trade Negotiations Office, the International Trade Advisory Committee and the Sectoral Advisory Groups on International Trade after 1985. Moreover, the integrative approach helps to explain why crucial stages of the bilateral negotiations were handled by political operatives in the Prime Minister's Office, who were not subject to the problems of mixed preferences, low capacity and limited autonomy that had long plagued bureaucratic actors in the trade field.

TABLE 5.2	FREE TRADE ATTITUDES IN CANADA, 1984-1988[a]		
DATE	SURVEY	% SUPPORT FREE TRADE	% OPPOSE FREE TRADE
April 1984	Environics	78	17
December 1984	Gallup	54	29
June 1985	Environics	65	30
November 1985	Environics	58	31
February 1986	Environics	54	35
June 1986	Environics	52	36
September 1986	Gallup	42	38
October 1986	Environics	57	33
March 1987	Environics	57	28
June 1987	Environics	56	34
October 1987	Environics	49	34
December 1987	Environics	40	39
October 1988	Canadian Facts	38	40
October 1988[b]	Environics	31	51
October 1988[b]	National Election Study	31	47
November 1988	Gallup	34	41
November 1988	National Election Study	40	44
November 1988	Canadian Facts	36	43
November 1988	Carleton University Journalism	42	44

[a] Cell entries after October 1987 denote attitudes towards Canada-US agreement rather than the idea of free trade
[b] Conducted after televised leaders' debates

Sources: Gallup Report, 6 Nov. 1986; Canadian Facts National Political Surveys for Canadian Broadcasting Corporation; Donna Dasko, 'Canadian Public Opinion' in Duncan Cameron (ed.) *The Free Trade Papers* (Toronto: Lorimer, 1986); Donna Dasko 'The Canadian Public and Free Trade', in Duncan Cameron (ed.), *The Free Trade Deal* (Toronto: Lorimer, 1988); Richard Johnston et al., 'Free Trade in the Canadian Elections', paper presented at American Political Science Association meetings, San Francisco, 1990; and Lawrence LeDuc, 'Voting for Free Trade?' in Paul Fox and Graham White (eds), *Politics: Canada* (7th ed. : Toronto: McGraw-Hill Ryerson, 1991).

Comparing Models and Policies

Although the future prospects of cultural, trade and investment nationalism are discussed at greater length in Chapter 8, some preliminary comparisons of their policy influence can be offered at this point. As well, a few comments are ventured about the merits of the three frameworks that were introduced in Chapter 2.

Examination of how comprehensive free trade came to be pursued as federal policy reveals many of the difficulties that faced nationalists during the 1980s. Confronted with a solid phalanx of well-financed and cohesive business groups together with Conservative government elites and US political interests that endorsed continentalist ideas, the opponents of free trade faced an uphill struggle. Although they enjoyed substantial public and some media support, the attitudinal environment was deeply divided and subject to the manipulative pull of electoral and especially 'leadership' politics in the period of the 1988 federal elections.

Proponents of free trade had sharpened their skills during earlier debates over the National Energy Program, when they mounted a vigorous attack on its Canadianization and Crown interest provisions. Chapters 4 and 5 suggest that both the ultimate success of these anti-NEP efforts and the introduction of a comprehensive free trade policy can be linked with the same political event: namely, the 1984 election of a majority Conservative government. Supported in large part by regional and business interests that had grown tired of the centralist and interventionist impulses of previous Liberal regimes, the Conservatives believed that they held a *carte blanche* of sorts to dismantle the NEP and to embark on a new, more cordial continental relationship. Could trade and investment nationalists have prevailed in this environment? Probably not. As argued in Chapters 3 and 4, the status of nationalist ideas during the mid-1970s debate over Bill C-58 and during the early 1980s controversy over the NEP was fragile and vulnerable at best; even during this presumed peak of nationalist influence, policy success was far from assured.

Yet how could Bill C-58 as a cultural nationalist priority escape unscathed through the 1980s? Was it less regionally divisive, or less of an ideological thorn in the side of the societal groups that championed free trade and struggled against the NEP? As suggested in Chapter 3, cultural as opposed to economic nationalist policies may have survived longer not only because of the strong private sector support they enjoyed among the ranks of Canadian publishers and broadcasters, but also because public and bureaucratic endorsement of these provisions was relatively firm. In addition, the significance of retaining some nationalist provisions outside the trade and investment areas was not lost on federal elites. Conservative politicians, for example, continued to maintain even after 1988 that their government was unwilling to sacrifice Canadian identity and the ideas of cultural nationalism at the altar of free trade.

This point underlines the critical importance of *ideas* to governmental action. By considering the relationship of party elites, public and media attitudes and US government interests to nationalist or, conversely, continentalist ideas, an integrative approach moves policy analysis beyond the narrow and rather facile confines imposed by existing paradigms. Building on the strengths of the societal and bureaucratic frameworks, acknowledging that neither on its own is adequate for any of the three cases examined in this study, an integrative model helps to make better sense of state action. It sheds light on the limits of organized group intervention, in this instance the limits of cultural, investment and trade nationalism in Canada, and on the degree to which bureaucratic action is frequently dependent on political will.

In drawing together societal and administrative considerations with a focus on *political* receptivity to ideas, integrative thinking reveals some very difficult challenges which faced organized nationalists in the 1980s. One of these concerned the creation of a societal alternative to the powerful business coalition that supported free trade. Could the Pro-Canada Network provide such an alternative? What costs and benefits accrued to member groups which did participate? Chapter 6 examines these questions using the National Action Committee on the Status of Women as a case study.

Notes

[1]Prime Minister Brian Mulroney, speech delivered in House of Commons, 30 Aug. 1988, reprinted in Norman Hillmer (ed.), *Partners Nevertheless: Canadian-American Relations in the Twentieth Century* (Toronto: Copp Clark Pitman, 1989), 152.

[2]Mel Hurtig and Duncan Cameron, 'No Longer Will Canada Make Economic Sense', *Globe and Mail* (14 Nov. 1988), A7.

[3]See Royal Commission on the Economic Union and Development Prospects for Canada (Macdonald Commission), *Report* (Ottawa: Supply and Services Canada, 1985).

[4]See J.L. Granatstein, 'Free Trade between Canada and the United States: The Issue that will not Go Away', in Denis Stairs and Gilbert R. Winham (eds), *The Politics of Canada's Economic Relationship with the United States*, Royal Commission Research Studies, vol. 29 (Toronto: University of Toronto Press for Supply and Services Canada, 1985), 36-43; and Michael Hart, 'Almost but not Quite: The 1947-48 Bilateral Canada-U.S. Negotiations', *American Review of Canadian Studies* 19 (1989), 25-58.

[5]See Economic Council of Canada, *Looking Outward: A New Trade Strategy for Canada* (Ottawa: Supply and Services Canada, 1975); Peyton V. Lyon, *Canada-United States Free Trade and Canadian Independence*, Economic Council Research Study (Ottawa: Information Canada, 1975); Senate Standing Committee on Foreign Affairs, *Canada-United States Relations*, vol. 2, *Canada's Trade Relations with the United States* (Ottawa: Supply and Services Canada, 1978); Department of External Affairs, *Canadian Trade Policy for the 1980s: A Discussion Paper* (Ottawa: Supply and Services Canada, 1983); and other sources cited in Table 5.1.

[6]Senate Standing Committee on Foreign Affairs, *Canada-United States Relations*, vol. 3, *Canada's Trade Relations with the United States* (Ottawa: Supply and Services Canada, 1982).

[7]Ibid., 33.

[8]See Department of External Affairs, *Canadian Trade Policy for the 1980s*; David Leyton-Brown, 'The Canada-U.S. Free Trade Agreement', in Andrew B. Gollner and Daniel Salée (eds), *Canada Under*

Mulroney: An End-of-Term Report (Montreal: Véhicule Press, 1988), 104-5; and John Whalley with Roderick Hill (eds), *Canada-United States Free Trade*, Royal Commission Research Studies, vol. 11 (Toronto: University of Toronto Press for Supply and Services Canada, 1985).

[9]See Joyce Nelson, 'Losing it in the Lobby: Entertainment and Free Trade', *This Magazine* 20 (October/November 1986), 14-23; and interview with Paul Audley, 7 June 1990. For a more general statement of Nelson's views, see her book *The Perfect Machine: TV in the Nuclear Age* (Toronto: Between the Lines, 1987).

[10]See Gordon Ritchie, 'The Negotiating Process', in John Crispo (ed.), *Free Trade: The Real Story* (Toronto: Gage, 1988), 18-19; and Alan M. Rugman, 'Why Business Supports Free Trade', in ibid., 95-104.

[11]See Granatstein, 'Free Trade between Canada and the United States', 47.

[12]For example, Canada's ambassador to the US at the time, Alan Gotlieb, subscribed to this view. See ibid.

[13]On the use of this 'freer trade' language, see Duncan Cameron, 'Introduction', to Cameron (ed.), *The Free Trade Papers* (Toronto: Lorimer, 1986), xx; and Robert M. Campbell and Leslie A. Pal, *The Real Worlds of Canadian Politics: Cases in Process and Policy* (Peterborough, Ont.: Broadview Press, 1989), 322.

[14]See Campbell and Pal, *The Real Worlds of Canadian Politics*, 319; Leyton-Brown, 'The Canada-U.S. Free Trade Agreement', 105; Whalley, *Canada-United States Free Trade*, 12ff., 58ff., 88ff., 205ff.; and D.L. McLachlan, *Canada-US Free Trade: The Faltering Impetus for a Historic Reversal* (Calgary: Detselig, 1987), 47.

[15]On these changes, see Stephen Clarkson, *Canada and the Reagan Challenge* (Toronto: Lorimer, 1985), chap. 14; Arpad Abonyi, 'Government Participation in Investment Development', in Gollner and Salée (eds), *Canada Under Mulroney*, 158-85; Elizabeth Smythe, 'From Investment Canada to National Treatment: Canada's Foreign Investment Regime and the Canada-United States Free Trade Agreement', paper presented at Canadian Political Science Association meetings, Laval University, June 1989; and David Milne, *Tug of War: Ottawa and the Provinces Under Trudeau and Mulroney* (Toronto: Lorimer, 1986).

[16]Royal Commission on the Economic Union and Development Prospects for Canada, *Report*. On the adoption of a free trade recommendation by the Commission, see Richard Simeon, 'Inside the Macdonald Commission', *Studies in Political Economy* 22 (1987), 167-79.

[17]See Cameron, 'Introduction', xiv; and Marjorie Cohen, 'Our Social and Economic Programs are in Greater Danger than Ever Before', in Laurier LaPierre (ed.), *If You Love This Country: Facts and Feelings on Free Trade* (Toronto: McClelland and Stewart, 1987), 97.

[18]This position is argued in many publications, including John Crispo, 'Introduction', to Crispo (ed.), *Free Trade*, 1-5; and Richard G. Lipsey, 'The Free Trade Agreement in Context', in Marc Gold and David Leyton-Brown (eds), *Trade-offs on Free Trade: The Canada-U.S. Free Trade Agreement* (Toronto: Carswell, 1988), 67-78.

[19]Much of this part of the debate was carried on using the language of economic modelling. See Richard G. Harris and David Cox, *Trade, Industrial Policy and Canadian Manufacturing* (Toronto: Ontario Economic Council, 1984); and Whalley, *Canada-United States Free Trade*, esp. appendices to 'Introduction', 17-41.

[20]Mulroney as quoted in *Globe and Mail* (27 Sept. 1985).

[21]See Campbell and Pal, *The Real Worlds of Canadian Politics*, 390-1.

[22]Ritchie, 'The Negotiating Process', 19.

[23]About 35 business associations were members of the Alliance, but it should be noted that not all businesses in Canada supported free trade. The Business Council for Fair Trade was established to represent firms in the service and manufacturing sectors that opposed free trade. See Nick Fillmore, 'The Big Oink: How Business Won the Free Trade Battle', *This Magazine* 22 (March-April 1989), 20.

[24]Hurtig and Cameron, 'No Longer will Canada Make Economic Sense'.

[25]James Laxer, *Leap of Faith: Free Trade and the Future of Canada* (Edmonton: Hurtig, 1986), 2.

[26]For a detailed statement of this position, see John W. Warnock, *Free Trade and the New Right Agenda* (Vancouver: New Star Books, 1988).

[27]Interview with David Wolfe, 18 June 1990. A similar position is argued in Reg Whitaker, 'No Laments for the Nation: Free Trade and the Election of 1988', *Canadian Forum* (March 1989), 13.

[28]On the Public Petroleum Association, see Chapter 4 above as well as Evert A. Lindquist, 'Behind the Myth of Think Tanks: The Organization and Relevance of Canadian Policy Institutes' (Ph.D. dissertation, University of California at Berkeley, 1989).

[29]See Daniel Drache and Duncan Cameron (eds), *The Other Macdonald Report* (Toronto: Lorimer, 1985). As noted in Chapter 6, the National Action Committee on the Status of Women was one of the groups that made known its opposition to free trade early in the course of the debate.

[30]The Pro-Canada Network was founded at the 'Maple Leaf Summit' of the Council of Canadians. Interview with Maude Barlow, 14 Oct. 1989.

[31]This position is argued in many sources, including Denis Stairs, 'Canada will be a less Relaxed, a less Gentle, a less Tolerant Place in which to Live', in LaPierre (ed.), *If You Love this Country*, 212-16. It was also rebutted in many articles, including Thomas J. Courchene, 'Social Policy and Regional Development', in Crispo (ed.), *Free Trade*, 135-47.

[32]Richard Johnston, André Blais, Henry E. Brady and Jean Crête, 'Free Trade in the Canadian Elections: Issue Evolution in the Long and the Short Run', paper presented at American Political Science Association meetings, San Francisco, 1990, 12.

[33]On 25 Oct., Turner argued in his debate with Mulroney: 'I happen to believe that you've sold us out. With one signature of a pen. You have thrown us into the North-South influence of the United States. And, will reduce us, I am sure, to a colony of the United States, because when the economic levers go, the political independence is sure to follow.' For accounts of the 1988 campaign, see Rick Salutin, *Waiting for Democracy: A Citizen's Journal* (Markham, Ont.: Penguin, 1989); Graham Fraser, *Playing for Keeps: The Making of the Prime Minister, 1988* (Toronto: McClelland and Stewart, 1989); and Robert Mason Lee, *One Hundred Monkeys: The Triumph of Popular Wisdom in Canadian Politics* (Toronto: Macfarlane, Walter and Ross, 1989).

[34]This general line of argument can be found throughout LaPierre (ed.), *If You Love this Country*.

[35]According to pro-trade sources, section 2005.1 of the final agreement formally exempted culture. On the cultural implications of the FTA, see Gold and Leyton-Brown (eds), *Trade-offs on Free Trade*, chap. 11.

[36]See ibid. as well as Rick Salutin, 'Keep Canadian Culture off the Table—Who's Kidding Who?' in LaPierre (ed.), *If You Love This Country*, 205-10.

[37]Arguments about specific provisions of the legislation were raised by many authors, far too numerous to list individually. For a sampling of some of them, see LaPierre (ed.), *If You Love This Country*; Duncan Cameron (ed.), *The Free Trade Deal* (Toronto: Lorimer, 1988); Gold and Leyton-Brown (eds), *Trade-Offs on Free Trade*; Marjorie Montgomery Bowker, *On Guard for Thee: An Independent Review of the Free Trade Agreement* (Hull: Voyageur Publishing, 1988); David Orchard and Citizens Concerned About Free Trade, *Free Trade: The Full Story* (Saskatoon: Patriots' Press, 1988); and Ed Finn (ed.), *The Facts on Free Trade* (Toronto: Lorimer, 1988).

[38]See Daniel P. Drache, 'The Mulroney-Reagan Accord: The Economics of Continental Power', in Gold and Leyton-Brown (eds.), *Trade-offs on Free Trade*, 79-88. A leading proponent of free trade, Richard Lipsey, commented: 'Drache seems to live in a different country from the one I live in, a country that has negotiated with a different foreign power, and that produced a different FTA from the one I have read. Readers who also live in Drache's country will not be convinced by anything that I say.' Lipsey, 'The Free Trade Agreement in Context', in Gold and Leyton-Brown, 68.

[39]Crosbie as quoted in Campbell and Pal, *The Real Worlds of Canadian Politics*, 341. Mulroney made similar statements, referring to anti-trade activists as 'neo-reactionaries' who were 'timorous, insecure

and fretful'. See *Toronto Star*, 9 March 1986.

[40]See Campbell and Pal, *The Real Worlds of Canadian Politics*, 329, 332.

[41]See Emery M. Roe, 'Narrative Analysis for the Policy Analyst: A Case Study of the 1980-1982 Medfly Controversy in California', *Journal of Policy Analysis and Management* 8 (1989), 251-73.

[42]For the broad lines of this alternative, see Abraham Rotstein, *Rebuilding from Within: Remedies for Canada's Ailing Economy* (Toronto: Lorimer, 1984); and Warnock, *Free Trade and the New Right Agenda*, part III.

[43]This argument was often captured in the phrase 'diversified trade'. See Warnock, *Free Trade and the New Right Agenda*, chap. 17; David Crane, 'We Should Rededicate Ourselves to Finding our own Solutions to a Better Economic Future', in LaPierre (ed.), *If You Love This Country*, 98-102; Robert A. Young, 'The Canada-U.S. Agreement and its International Context', in Gold and Leyton-Brown (eds), *Trade-offs on Free Trade*, 20-8; and Bruce W. Wilkinson, 'Canada-United States Free Trade: Setting the Dimensions', in Allan M. Maslove and Stanley L. Winer (eds), *Knocking on the Back Door: Canadian Perspectives on the Political Economy of Freer Trade with the United States* (Halifax: Institute for Research on Public Policy, 1987), 7-26.

[44]See Thomas J. Courchene, 'The Canada-U.S Free Trade Agreement: Selected Political and Economic Perspectives', in Gold and Leyton-Brown (eds), *Trade-offs on Free Trade*, 36-44.

[45]See Mel Watkins, 'The Case Against United States-Canada Free Trade', *Canada-United States Law Journal* 10 (1985), 92.

[46]Ibid., 91-3.

[47]See Crane, 'We Should Rededicate Ourselves to Finding Our Own Solutions to a Better Economic Future'; and Wilkinson, 'Canada-United States Free Trade'.

[48]See Peter Cornell, 'In Support of Trade Liberalization: A Comment on Bruce Wilkinson's Paper', in Maslove and Winer (eds), *Knocking on the Back Door*, 29; and Alan M. Rugman, 'Multinationals and the Free Trade Agreement', in Gold and Leyton-Brown (eds), *Trade-offs on Free Trade*, 10.

[49]See Watkins, 'The Case Against United States-Canada Free Trade'; and Fred Lazar, 'The Trade Agreement: A Dissenting Opinion', in Gold and Leyton-Brown (eds), *Trade-Offs on Free Trade*, 440.

[50]On the anti-trade position, see Drache, 'The Mulroney-Reagan Accord'. For a pro-trade view, see Crispo, 'Introduction' to Crispo (ed.), *Free Trade*.

[51]Interview with Mel Watkins, 19 June 1990.

[52]Interviews with Mel Watkins, 19 June 1990, and Peter C. Newman, 7 Oct. 1989.

[53]See Roe, 'Narrative Analysis for the Policy Analyst'.

[54]See, for example, Maude Barlow, *Parcel of Rogues: How Free Trade is Failing Canada* (Toronto: Key Porter, 1990).

[55]These figures are drawn from G. Bruce Doern and Brian W. Tomlin, *Faith and Fear: The Free Trade Story* (Toronto: Stoddart, 1991), chap. 9.

[56]D'Aquino's figures are summarized in Hugh Winsor, 'Can't Finance National Elections by "Selling Fudge"', *Globe and Mail* (14 March 1990), A4.

[57]See Hugh Winsor, 'Tory MP Decries Large Corporate Donations', *Globe and Mail* (13 March 1990); Nick Fillmore, 'The Big Oink', 13-14; and Janet Hiebert, 'Fair Elections and Freedom of Expression Under the Charter', *Journal of Canadian Studies* 24 (Winter 1989-90), 80.

[58]On the National Citizens' Coalition, see Hiebert, 'Fair Elections and Freedom of Expression Under the Charter', 80; and Fillmore, 'The Big Oink', 15. The Consumers' Association of Canada initially endorsed free trade but later changed its position.

[59]Ibid.

[60]Ibid.

[61]Fillmore, 'The Big Oink', 15; and Salutin, *Waiting for Democracy*, 34.

[62]Bowker, *On Guard for Thee*, 103.

[63]See Salutin, *Waiting for Democracy*, 125; Hiebert, 'Fair Elections and Freedom of Expression Under the Charter', 85; and Fillmore, 'The Big Oink', 15.

[64]See Fillmore, 'The Big Oink', 17-18.

[65]See ibid.

[66]These individuals included Waffle veterans Mel Watkins and James Laxer, CIC activists Abraham Rotstein and Mel Hurtig, trade union nationalists Rick Salutin and Laurell Ritchie (both of whom had worked for the Confederation of Canadian Unions) and cultural activists Margaret Atwood and Pierre Berton.

[67]Members of the cultural community, for example, were divided in their positions on free trade. Some observers believe that this division damaged the cohesion and credibility of anti-trade efforts. Interview with Gerald Caplan, 25 May 1990.

[68]See Tony Clarke, 'Quietly Amassing an Army to do Battle with Free Trade', *Globe and Mail* (6 Oct. 1988); Barlow, *Parcel of Rogues*; and interview with Maude Barlow, 14 Oct. 1989.

[69]See John W. Warnock, *Free Trade and the New Right Agenda* (Vancouver: New Star Books, 1988).

[70]See Roe, 'Narrative Analysis for the Policy Analyst'.

[71]According to Doern and Tomlin, *Faith and Fear*, chap. 9, the membership of the Council of Canadians in 1988 was comprised of 25% Liberal and 15% New Democratic partisans, and more than 50% non-partisans.

[72]For a statement of the strategic voting thesis, see James Laxer, 'This Time Out it's Who Wins, Not How You Play the Game', *Globe and Mail* (20 Oct. 1988), A7. This idea was generally considered too complicated to succeed, and according to Johnston et al., 'Free Trade in the Canadian Elections', did not work.

[73]See 'Artists and Writers for Free Trade', *Globe and Mail* (19 Nov. 1988); and Grace Skogstad, 'The State, Organized Interests and Trade Policy: The Impact of Institutions', paper presented at Canadian Political Science Association meetings, University of Victoria, May 1990.

[74]On the position of academic economists, see Simeon, 'Inside the Macdonald Commission'; William G. Watson, 'Canada-US Free Trade: Why Now?' *Canadian Public Policy* 13 (1987), 337-49; and R.A. Young, 'Political Scientists, Economists, and the Canada-US Free Trade Agreement', *Canadian Public Policy* 15 (1989), 49-56. On the position of policy institutes and the contributions of the Macdonald Commission to this debate, see Stephen Brooks, 'The Market for Social Scientific Knowledge: The Case of Free Trade in Canada', in Brooks and Alain-G. Gagnon (eds), *Social Scientists, Policy, and the State* (New York: Praeger, 1990), 79-94.

[75]See Brooks, 'The Market for Social Scientific Knowledge'.

[76]Prominent academics opposed to free trade included Bruce Wilkinson of the University of Alberta; Stephen Clarkson, Abraham Rotstein and Mel Watkins of the University of Toronto; Daniel Drache and James Laxer of York University; and Duncan Cameron of the University of Ottawa.

[77]Brooks, 'The Market for Social Scientific Knowledge', 92.

[78]On the use of experts to defend free trade, see Lee, *One Hundred Monkeys*, 219.

[79]See *Globe and Mail* (19 Nov. 1988), A7.

[80]Many of these minority business interests were organized in the Business Council for Fair Trade. Opponents of free trade included the Petroleum Marketers Association of Canada, the Canadian Independent Computer Services Association, McCain Foods Ltd and Hunt-Wesson Canada. See Doern and Tomlin, *Faith and Fear*, chap. 9. On other business organizations opposed to free trade, see Warnock, *Free Trade and the New Right Agenda*, 118.

[81]See 'Artists and Writers for Free Trade'.

[82]See Department of External Affairs, *Canadian Trade Policy for the 1980s*.

[83]See *The Compas Forecast: Respondent's Report, Spring/Summer 1989* (Ottawa: Compas Inc., 1989), as summarized in Doern and Tomlin, *Faith and Fear*, chap. 9, 28.

[84]Skogstad, 'The State, Organized Interests and Trade Policy', 8.

[85]Ibid.

[86]Colleen Hamilton and John Whalley, 'U.S. Trade Policies and Canadian Interests: Summary of the Proceedings of a Research Symposium', in Whalley (ed.), *Canada-United States Free Trade*, 206.

[87]Ibid., 207.

[88]See Joyce Nelson 'Losing it in the Lobby: Entertainment and Free Trade'.

[89]See Gilbert Winham, 'Formulating Trade Policy in Canada and the U.S.: The Institutional Framework', in Grace Skogstad and Andrew Fenton Cooper (eds), *Agricultural Trade: Domestic Pressures and International Tensions* (Halifax: Institute for Research on Public Policy, 1990), 29-38.

[90]For biographical material see L. Ian MacDonald, *Mulroney: The Making of the Prime Minister* (Toronto: McClelland and Stewart, 1985); and Rae Murphy, Robert Chodos and Nick Auf der Maur, *Brian Mulroney: The Boy from Baie-Comeau* (Toronto: Lorimer, 1984).

[91]Mulroney as quoted in Ron Graham, *One-Eyed Kings: Promise and Illusion in Canadian Politics* (Toronto: Collins, 1986), 364.

[92]See Fraser, *Playing for Keeps*; Lee, *One Hundred Monkeys*; and Doern and Tomlin, *Faith and Fear*, chap. 10, on opposition party positions.

[93]CAW president Bob White, along with other prominent New Democrats, criticized party strategy on free trade. See excerpts from White's letter to the NDP elite in *Toronto Star* (7 Dec. 1988), A23.

[94]See Prime Minister's Office, 'Communications Strategy for Canada-U.S. Bilateral Trade Initiative', in Cameron (ed.), *The Free Trade Papers*, chap. 1.

[95]See Allan Gregg and Michael Posner, *The Big Picture: What Canadians Think About Almost Everything* (Toronto: Macfarlane, Walter and Ross, 1990), 122.

[96]On Conservative strategy, see Lawrence LeDuc, 'Voting for Free Trade? The Canadian Voter and the 1988 Federal Election', in Paul Fox and Graham White (eds), *Politics: Canada* (7th ed.; Toronto: McGraw-Hill Ryerson, 1991); Johnston et al., 'Free Trade in Canadian Elections', 10, 15; Fraser, *Playing for Keeps*; and Lee, *One Hundred Monkeys*.

[97]One of the most prominent of these divisions was the class one. See Fraser, *Playing for Keeps*, 424.

[98]Other exceptions to this pattern included the *Montreal Gazette* and *Edmonton Journal*. See Alan Frizzell and Anthony Westell, 'The Media and the Campaign', in Frizzell, Jon Pammett and Westell (eds), *The Canadian General Election of 1988* (Ottawa: Carleton University Press, 1989), 75-90.

[99]This problem was particularly troubling for nationalist activists who recognized the importance of the *Toronto Star*'s position in English Canada. See Salutin, *Waiting for Democracy*; and Philip Resnick, *Letters to a Québécois Friend* (Montreal: McGill-Queen's University Press, 1990), 52.

6 | NAC'S Opposition to Free Trade:
The Costs and Benefits

Considering the current structure of the Canadian economy and the industries which will be adversely affected by free trade, women will be the major losers in a bilateral free-trade deal with the United States.[1]

Introduction

The importance of building a societal alternative to pro-trade business interests was clear to nationalists as early as the mid-1970s. The creation of the Public Petroleum Association, a coalition of environmental, aboriginal and investment nationalist groups that supported policies like the National Energy Program, suggested the beginnings of an organized counterpoise to pro-trade efforts.[2] As the Business Council on National Issues, Canadian Chamber of Commerce, Canadian Manufacturers' Association and other groups developed a united front in support of a comprehensive bilateral strategy during the 1980s, critics were faced with the question of how best to oppose free trade.

One of their earliest efforts began in Toronto in December 1985, when Laurell Ritchie called together representatives of labour, women's, agricultural, social service, church, university and cultural groups. Ritchie was active in the Confederation of Canadian Unions, an organization of independent trade unions outside the umbrella of the Canadian Labour Congress, and served as a member of the Employment Committee of the National Action Committee on the Status of Women (NAC). The meeting called by Ritchie was held at the NAC office, and the group that evolved from this event called itself the Coalition Against Free Trade.[3]

From these early beginnings, NAC obtained an unprecedented policy profile as a vocal critic of free trade. This policy intervention by Canada's principal national feminist organization was significant for at least two reasons. First, it reflected an extension in the *substance* of NAC's policy focus beyond conventional 'women's issues',[4] notably legal rights and social policy questions (such as abortion and child care), towards an integration of these issues with the broader national agenda of what became known as the Pro-Canada Network. Second, NAC's *strategy* on the trade question, combined with the shift in substance, represented a change from its earlier emphasis upon co-operative relations with the federal government in order to obtain reforms on women's issues. In the free trade debate of 1985-88, NAC entered into formal coalitions with other groups opposed to this cornerstone of Conservative policy, thereby imparting a more confrontational tenor to its relations with the federal government.

How did these shifts in substance and strategy occur? On what bases did NAC's leadership articulate a feminist critique of the free trade agreement? And, most important, what costs and benefits could follow from NAC's sustained opposition to free trade, not only for that organization and for the larger Canadian women's movement but also for other participants in anti-FTA activities? Each of these questions is explored below, with the first two providing background material for a primary focus on the final, two-part question.

In addressing the question of costs and benefits, this chapter borrows elements of the integrative framework developed in Chapter 2. As a societal group, what resources, cohesion, expertise and representativeness characterized NAC prior to its involvement in the free trade debate? How were existing problems in these areas affected by that engagement? With respect to ideas and politics, what was the partisan response to NAC's linkage of feminism with nationalism? Did such a connection resonate in Canadian public opinion? Discussing these questions points towards larger issues of polarization in Canadian political life, matters that are evaluated below in Chapter 8.

The National Action Committee

Organizational Development
The three initial policy priorities of the National Action Committee in the years following its establishment in 1972 were identified as 'expansion of daycare, insertion of "sex" as a prohibited basis of discrimination under Canadian human rights provisions, and decriminalization of abortion'.[5] Mirroring the emphasis on legal rights and social policy of first-wave feminism earlier in this century, NAC set out quite simply to improve the status of Canadian women.[6]

The organizational origins of NAC can be located in efforts by a group of women known as the Committee for the Equality of Women in Canada (CEW) during the 1960s to establish a federal royal commission on the status of women. Led by Laura Sabia, who served as president of the Canadian Federation of University Women, CEW placed its demands for a commission on the front pages of the national press and eventually won the case in the federal cabinet.[7]

The hearings of the Royal Commission on the Status of Women (RCSW) brought together feminists from very disparate backgrounds, including radical student groups, the nascent women's liberation movement and older middle-class women's groups such as the Federation of University Women.[8] Eventually, 167 recommendations were presented in the final RCSW *Report*; they provided a clear policy agenda for the emerging Canadian women's movement, which Sabia called together in 1971 under the umbrella of the National Ad Hoc Action Committee on the Status of Women.[9] In early 1972, the name was shortened to the National Action Committee on the Status of Women;[10] the group's original purpose as stated in the official summary of its founding convention held in Toronto in 1972 (entitled 'Strategy for Change') was to ensure the implementation of the Royal Commission proposals.[11]

In embarking on this challenging task, NAC faced the obvious question of how to organize. Initially, it operated through a steering committee, composed in 1971 of representatives from 15 member women's groups that ranged from the Catholic Women's League and the YWCA to a group called Women's Liberation Movement (Toronto).[12] The bulk of representatives in early NAC steering committees were from older, established women's organizations, leading one source to describe the group as 'largely a coalition of institutionalized feminist organizations'.[13]

Given this pattern, it is not surprising that NAC developed over the years along the lines of an increasingly mature, institutionalized umbrella interest group.[14] It grew to include approximately 130 member groups by 1977, 280 by 1984, and 586 by 1988; this last figure means that about five million women held membership in NAC's constituent groups by the late 1980s.[15] At the same time, a shift occurred away from informal steering committees and towards a formalized organizational structure that included a volunteer executive board elected at annual general meetings and issue sub-committees, as well as paid staff in Toronto and Ottawa. Like many interest groups in the Canadian federal system, NAC attempted to integrate a regional dimension at the board level through specified provincial and territorial representative positions.[16]

Organizational Tensions within NAC

This organizational development appeared on the surface to be fairly smooth and, with reference to models of interest group formation, fairly 'normal'. Indeed, NAC attracted a series of dynamic, knowledgeable and politically prominent women to serve as president during its first fifteen years of existence; they included Lorna Marsden, Lynn McDonald, Grace Hartman, Doris Anderson and Chaviva Hosek.

This expertise and apparent success, however, obscured at least two major threats to NAC's cohesion, resources and representativeness, and hence to its policy influence. First, NAC faced a potential for internal ideological conflict because of its efforts to represent all varieties of Canadian feminism.[17] Most activists and constituent groups within NAC shared a fundamental belief that issues like abortion, child care and women's legal rights had been neglected and in fact limited by existing political institutions, including political parties, legislatures and government bureaucracies. The numerical under-representation of women within such institutions and the fact that the dominant political discourse seemed to make women's issues and their advocates invisible at all levels of the political process were thus identified as crucial 'access' problems.[18] Believing that established institutions would not otherwise act on women's issues,

NAC attempted to bring about change through press conferences designed to educate the public, meetings with cabinet ministers, submissions to legislative committees and an annual lobby of MPs on Parliament Hill.[19]

Some activists and constituent groups within NAC, however, believed that the organization needed to address not only the treatment of women's issues within the policy process, but also the nature of the policy process itself. These feminists were concerned with more than simply legislative action on NAC's issue priorities; instead, they questioned the very purpose of reforming rather than transforming established political structures and social institutions. In some cases, their critique began with a radical feminist emphasis upon grass-roots consciousness-raising, feminist process and non-hierarchical organization; in others, it employed a class-based analysis characteristic of socialist feminism.[20] Whichever the case, radical and socialist feminism differed quite dramatically from the reform-oriented approach to women's issues that prevailed for the most part in NAC through the mid-1980s, and that came to be termed—sometimes pejoratively—mainstream or liberal feminism.[21]

This internal ideological threat to cohesion was moderated within NAC by a tradition of compromise and consensus-building.[22] However, these strategies were effective tools for maintaining unity only as long as liberal feminists could claim to be obtaining results externally. Through the mid-1980s, this seemed to be the case as issues of abortion reform, child care, women's constitutional rights and equal pay received increased public and governmental attention.[23] The appointment of Maude Barlow as special advisor on women's issues in the Prime Minister's Office during the last Trudeau government seemed to reflect this success. Barlow was an active feminist who had devoted particular attention to issues of pornography and women's representation in the media; in subsequent years, as noted in Chapter 5, Barlow was a leading activist in the struggle against free trade.

Ironically, these apparent achievements of liberal feminism revealed a second set of tensions—both external and internal—that concerned NAC's relationship with the federal government. On one level, the policy changes that NAC had helped to bring about were increasingly criticized by conservative anti-feminist groups, most notably REAL Women;[24] in 1987, the latter challenged the federal government's practice of subsidizing feminist organizations and applied for similar funding through the Secretary of State. The opposition to NAC and feminism represented by REAL Women constituted more than simply a public relations nuisance. Indeed, by targeting NAC's main source of operating funds, such groups were a threat to NAC's resources, representativeness and basic viability, especially after the election in 1984 of a Conservative federal government that included members sympathetic to REAL Women.

Moreover, because they were related to ongoing conflicts within NAC over the group's relationship to government, the emergence of REAL Women and its threat to federal funding exacerbated the ideological differences outlined above.

If NAC were to continue relying primarily upon public subsidies, and receive only token financial support from its member groups, then would it be able to operate independently of government? Was the Canadian state fundamentally supportive of feminism, or was it simply employing women's organizations to advance its own purposes? In the language of interest group theory, was NAC (and, through it, Canadian feminism) becoming a 'captured', fully institution-alized pressure group, thus surrendering its capacity to function as a critical, protest-oriented social movement?[25]

During the mid-1980s, such questions were increasingly raised about the implications of close relations between organized Canadian feminism and the federal government. Perhaps only implicitly, this discussion constituted a re-evaluation of liberal feminism and its strategy for incremental legislative reform. One of the most influential statements of the tension between feminist societal interests and government in this period was Sue Findlay's 'Facing the State', an analysis of the limits to liberal reform as seen through the eyes of a former federal civil servant.[26]

The Free Trade Challenge

In light of this ferment, it is not surprising that relations between NAC and the federal government became less co-operative and increasingly adversarial follow-ing 1984. The political expectations of many liberal feminists had been raised as a result of the 1984 national leaders' debate on women's issues, sponsored by NAC, and at least two key organizers of that debate went on to contest public office.[27] This weakening in the liberal feminist leadership within NAC occurred at the same time as socialist and radical feminists were working both to strengthen their representation and to re-organize NAC along more grass-roots lines.[28] By the fall of 1985, the stage was set for a potentially very significant confrontation between NAC and the policies of the federal Conservative government.

On 4 September 1985, only days before the final Macdonald Commission report[29] was released, NAC presented four main criticisms of free trade at an Ottawa press conference. It should be noted that this critique and virtually all of NAC's subsequent statements on the free trade issue were based on research by Marjorie Cohen, an economist who became active in the Toronto-based Coalition Against Free Trade and the national Pro-Canada Network. In 1985, Cohen was a vice-president of NAC as well as co-chair of its Employment Committee.

First, in general terms, NAC argued that the costs of a free trade agreement 'may be steepest for those who are already most disadvantaged in the labour force—women . . . A bilateral comprehensive trade agreement with the U.S. will have a disproportionately severe impact on women workers.'[30] Cohen later expanded on this argument in the book-length study quoted in the epigraph to this chap-ter.[31] Second, since women who held manufacturing jobs were concentrated in what were identified as the most vulnerable secondary sectors (textiles, clothing, small electrical products, sporting goods, toys and games, and leather products), many were likely to lose their jobs as a direct effect of free trade.

Third, the prospects for re-employment among these women were not promising because a high percentage were immigrants 'who will have little chance of finding other jobs when their manufacturing jobs disappear'.[32] And fourth, while the effects of free trade on the employment of women in the service sector were less clear, NAC predicted that the expansion of large multinational firms in this area would likely 'displace Canadian labour'.[33]

NAC's critique of free trade was further developed and publicized in the fall of 1985, when Cohen represented NAC at the founding meetings of the Coalition Against Free Trade in Toronto and the Council of Canadians in Ottawa, and when the NAC Employment Committee (co-chaired by Cohen and Lynn Kaye, who was elected NAC president in 1988) presented a brief against free trade to the Joint House of Commons-Senate Committee on External Affairs and International Trade.

Cohen's opposition to free trade on behalf of NAC, however, was hardly the only female or feminist voice to be raised in opposition. Margaret Atwood presented a stirring brief to the parliamentary commmittee, part of which appeared in the *Globe and Mail*. In Atwood's words,

> Canada as a separate but dominated country has done about as well under the U.S. as women, worldwide, have done under men; about the only position they've ever adopted toward us, country to country, has been the missionary position, and we were not on the top.[34]

As well, trade union activist Laurell Ritchie spoke and wrote widely against the deal, and was instrumental in calling together the various groups that became the Ontario Coalition Against Free Trade.[35] A retired judge in Edmonton, Marjorie Montgomery Bowker, compiled a straightforward textual critique of the trade agreement that attracted broad public and media attention.[36] Maude Barlow participated in early efforts to establish a national anti-trade organization based on individual memberships, known as the Council of Canadians; she served as a member of its founding board and eventually became chair of the group.[37]

Women's opposition to free trade continued through 1986, when NAC co-sponsored the 'Against Free Trade Revue' in Toronto, and raised the issue in newspaper articles and meetings with government ministers.[38] This criticism intensified in 1987 following unanimous endorsement by the annual general meeting of a resolution opposing the negotiation of a free trade agreement.[39] Also during the spring of 1987, NAC became one of the founding members of the Pro-Canada Network, formed at the Council of Canadians' 'Maple Leaf Summit' in Ottawa, and continued its efforts to build provincial and local coalitions against a free trade deal. Two background papers critical of the initiative were published in 1987, along with Cohen's book on the subject.[40]

The main lines of NAC's critique of free trade, first articulated in its 1985 press statement and refined through these 1987 publications, linked a basic economic argument—to the effect that many women working in the manufacturing and service sectors risked losing their jobs—with broader claims regarding the societal costs that would follow from a weakening of Canadian labour and social legislation through 'harmonization' with less progressive US standards. Canadian provisions in the areas of child care, equal pay and health care were seen to be threatened by a more market-driven, privatized, less interventionist or regulated economy under free trade.[41] This same view concerning the potentially very negative implications of free trade for women was reiterated in a number of publications and speeches by participants in the Pro-Canada Network.[42]

NAC's critique of free trade reached a crescendo of sorts during the 1988 federal election campaign. The organization produced a number of pamphlets outlining its opposition to the deal[43]; as well, it made the issue a priority within the 'Women's Equality Accord', a series of NAC positions on child care, free trade, reproductive rights and violence against women and children.[44] In highlighting the trade issue during the federal election campaign, NAC sought 'to mobilize women to oppose politicians who favour the deal'.[45]

Costs to NAC

This discussion of NAC's organizational development and its opposition to free trade has thus far avoided the crucial question of consequences. To put the matter boldly, what risks were entailed in NAC's participation in various anti-trade coalitions and, on the other hand, what benefits could accrue to the organization? More generally, what were the costs and benefits of building an alternative to the business groups that supported free trade?

One of the only indications that NAC activists considered the question of consequences appears on the first page of a 1987 study by Ann Porter and Barbara Cameron : 'Free trade presents the women's movement in Canada with an important question: should organizations committed to advancing women's right to equality become involved in debates over general economic strategy?'[46] Obviously, Porter and Cameron believed that NAC *should* become involved, and they defended this view on two grounds: first, since governments frequently link feminist demands for equality with broader concerns about fiscal restraint, women's issues and economic policy are inseparable; and second, free trade could hold direct implications for NAC's core priorities: namely, women's jobs and equal employment legislation.

These arguments by Porter and Cameron reflected an apparent consensus among the leadership both of NAC and of other groups in the Pro-Canada Network that involvement in the trade debate was crucial to defending the larger policy concerns of their organizations, whether these groups were representative of labour, agricultural, feminist, environmental, cultural or other interests. Since these groups endeavoured to focus public attention on their specific positions vis-à-vis free trade, NAC cannot be considered unique in its willingness to link established priorities regarding women's rights and social policy with questions about the impact of free trade.

What is noteworthy about the feminist intervention on free trade, however, was the vulnerability of NAC as compared with other interests. At the time, NAC relied upon approximately $680,000 of annual financial support from the federal government, which represented about 65 per cent of its yearly budget.[47] NAC risked a partial or complete cut-off of such resources by any government— notably the Progressive Conservative majority government re-elected in 1988— that might seek to 'punish' the group for its opposition to free trade.[48] As noted above, NAC had been threatened by the Conservatives as recently as 1987, in the conflict with REAL Women, with a loss of financial support in a matter unrelated to the trade debate;[49] its relations with governing party elites became more adversarial and less co-operative through the 1980s. As a former NAC activist reflected in 1989,

> We have to consider years of federal government frustration with NAC's whole approach, its lobbying style, its unwillingness to give credit to government on anything—not to mention the very negative impressions of NAC held by Conservative backbenchers. NAC was and is perceived as in some ways out of control . . . I think that the government had lost patience with being insulted.[50]

Without federal funds to subsidize staff, publications, postage and other expenses, NAC faced the possibility of dependence on contributions from individual women and women's organizations—ironically, the very constituency that it believed faced a direct economic threat as a result of free trade.

This risk to federal funding was compounded by NAC's clear identification with groups opposed to the Conservatives during the 1988 election campaign. By formally entering and, in some cases, sponsoring anti-trade coalitions, NAC linked itself with other groups that were socially and ideologically distant from the dominant federal party.[51] These coalition partners, including NAC, faced the likelihood that they would become even more remote from Conservative elites as a result of their actions and, in turn, less and less able to command the ear of government the way business interests could.[52] The decisions of the federal Conservatives in the spring of 1989 to reduce NAC's funding by more than 50 per cent to approximately $300,000 by 1992, and to refuse to participate in the annual NAC lobby on Parliament Hill, reflected one side of this growing estrangement.[53] A year later, in its February 1990 budget, the government eliminated an additional $1.6 million from the Secretary of State Women's Program, much of which would have gone to women's centres and periodicals, and again refused to participate in the NAC lobby.[54]

On the other side, NAC took a pivotal role in organizing opposition to Conservative fiscal, transportation, unemployment and child care policies during the same period, drawing together many of its partners from the anti-trade coalition, and launched a particularly strong effort to block new abortion legislation during the spring of 1990.[55] In partisan terms, then, NAC's intervention linked the group more closely with opposition party positions in the late 1980s and decreased the likelihood of cordial or co-operative relations with the governing Conservatives.

As well, NAC's opposition to free trade raised problems of internal cohesion. As might have been expected, women's groups affiliated with the federal Progressive Conservative party were among the first to threaten to disaffiliate from NAC at the May 1988 annual meeting.[56] Although this threat did not result solely from the handling of the free trade issue, but rather from a more general criticism of NAC's political orientation, it reflected ongoing ideological strife within the organization. Even though Conservative women's organizations subsequently decided to continue as members of NAC, the 1988 annual meeting did not resolve these tensions, nor did it head off a confrontation between some radical feminists, on the one hand, who argued for a thorough reform of organizational processes within NAC, and liberal and socialist feminists, on the other, who identified policy issues such as free trade and NAC's electoral strategy as priorities. The apparent victory of the latter in May 1988 meant that NAC continued its opposition to free trade through the election period, although not without some internal dissent.

Finally, in its opposition to free trade NAC risked deploying scarce resources for research and publicity on a contest that, in the short term, NAC 'lost'; in the longer term, moreover, this loss could prove to be demoralizing to its activists. Such circumstances threaten any organization that relies heavily on volunteer labour, such as NAC, which needed to develop new policies in light of the reality of free trade and a second Conservative majority government. As well, the impact of free trade both on women in the manufacturing and service industries and on Canadian social policy could prove to be less damaging than NAC argued—possibly even as favourable as the advocates of free trade maintained.[57] Even though the latter seems unlikely, the risk to NAC's credibility and to the organization's expertise in the area of women's employment loomed large during the late 1980s.

Benefits to NAC

The potential costs of NAC's opposition to free trade, however severe, need to be compared with the possible benefits. One such benefit followed from the response to free trade among Canadian women in general. Linkages between feminist and nationalist ideas seemed to resonate in female public opinion; in fact, NAC explicitly linked its opposition to free trade with the existence of a substantial gender gap.[58] As summarized in Table 6.1, Canadian public attitudes were divided in that women showed considerably *less* support than men for both the concept of free trade and the specific bilateral agreement that had been negotiated. Gender differences in support for free trade in 1987 and 1988 averaged 15 per cent, reaching a peak of 20 per cent in the October 1988 Environics poll. Although this gender gap had more complex origins than simply NAC's campaign against free trade (for example, it was likely related to lower support for Prime Minister Mulroney and the Conservatives among women), the pattern permitted NAC to argue that its opposition was representative, that it was grounded in empirically documented reservations among Canadian women about free trade.[59] As a benefit, then, NAC could point to the congruence between its position and female public opinion and, furthermore, it could claim some credit for helping to shape women's attitudes.

Another set of benefits that accrued to NAC involved political visibility and experience. By raising questions about women's jobs, child care and equal pay policy in a debate that would likely have neglected such issues, NAC worked to articulate a feminist perspective on free trade. The fact that free trade advocates, including the federal government, prepared detailed rebuttals to this critique indicates that the 'women's issue' dimension was accepted as a credible part of the debate, even though the two sides continued to view the category of women in different terms. While opponents of the deal argued that women as workers could lose jobs and so on, proponents held to a more traditional discourse in which women were viewed as consumers, whose families would benefit from lower prices, and as mothers, whose children would have greater economic opportunities.[60]

The political visibility that NAC gained externally was accompanied by an important internal pay-off. The free trade debate presented many opportunities for NAC activists to speak publicly and to play a pivotal role in building coalitions

TABLE 6.1	GENDER GAP IN FREE TRADE ATTITUDES(%)[a]					
DATE OF POLL	FAVOUR FREE TRADE			UNDECIDED		
	MEN	WOMEN	DIFFERENCE	MEN	WOMEN	DIFFERENCE
October 1987	55	43	12	12	21	9
December 1987	47	34	13	16	26	10
June 1988	46	31	15	17	27	10
October 1988	53	33	20	11	18	7

[a]The question wording in 1987 was 'Do you strongly agree, somewhat agree, somewhat disagree, or strongly disagree that there should be free trade between Canada and the United States?' In 1988, the question was 'Do you strongly favour, somewhat favour, somewhat oppose or strongly oppose the free trade agreement that has been negotiated between Canada and the United States?' The surveys were conducted by Environics Research Group and were reported in the *Globe and Mail* on 28 Oct. 1987, 30 Dec. 1987, 1 July 1988, and 14 Oct. 1988.

against this policy; such activities demonstrated their expertise on women's issues and further developed their skills as organizers and communicators. The experience gained by NAC activists was valuable, and could not have accrued had the organization avoided the trade issue.

Furthermore, it can be argued that NAC's external profile benefitted through its involvement in issue coalitions. By participating in the Pro-Canada Network and other provincial and local anti-trade groups, NAC established itself as a competent and committed player in the national debate; no longer could it be dismissed as a transitory group concerned only with the rights of women narrowly defined.[61] Working with labour, church, agricultural and other or-ganizations on free trade thus made NAC an integral part of the societal coali-tion.

Implications for the Women's Movement

NAC's efforts to oppose free trade in the years 1985-88 cannot be viewed in isolation from their consequences for the larger Canadian women's movement. As the principal voice of Canadian feminism, NAC in many respects constitutes the main public face of the women's movement; its actions therefore hold direct implications for this larger constituency.

In terms of costs, NAC's actions on free trade carried at least one potential drawback that mirrored alliances earlier in this century between first-wave fem-inism and the progressive movement. By entering coalitions or 'mainstreaming' with non-feminist organizations, NAC faced the very significant threat of co-op-tation. Would its arguments regarding the specific implications of free trade for women be swallowed up and marginalized within broader critiques of the pol-icy? How autonomous and politically visible would feminist issues be in the anti-FTA movement? Apparently, NAC activists anticipated these questions and worked not only in large coalitions with non-feminist groups but also in smaller feminist coalitions and independently, where co-optation was less of an organ-izational threat.[62]

A second set of potential costs to the women's movement concerns relations with the federal government. If NAC constitutes the leading voice of Canadian feminism, and if free trade identified NAC very closely with anti-government positions and coalitions, would the larger Canadian women's movement also be identified as anti-government in orientation, and hence marginal to power and policy influence? If the women's movement were characterized as an out-sider vis-à-vis federal policy, how could it attract liberal feminists who, as argued above, already faced substantial problems within NAC? The growth of other, potentially more effective liberal feminist groups during the 1980s (notably the Women's Legal Education and Action Fund, or LEAF) meant that NAC might no longer draw the same mixture of activists that it had attracted in earlier periods.[63] That is, if liberal feminists were weakened as a faction and only socialist and radical streams remained within the organization, then NAC's ability to represent the broader range of Canadian women would be jeopardized.

Third and probably most important, one cannot dismiss the resource costs to the women's movement of NAC's actions on free trade. Research on Canadian interest groups indicates that resource limitations, including restrictions on staff and volunteer resources, are generally associated with diminished external influence and weakened internal cohesion.[64] Curiously, this very pattern of *decline* in group maturity, or de-institutionalization, may have been actively pursued by some NAC activists who were uncomfortable with the organization's development along the standard lines of a large, hierarchical interest group. However, there is little doubt that the reduction in resources, and the shift away from institutionalization, towards the fluidity more typical of movements, would weaken the public profile of the Canadian women's movement and, by implication, further limit NAC's policy impact.

Again, these potential costs must be weighed against potential benefits, and it is with reference to these that the significance of NAC's intervention on free trade is clearest. Among the broad array of societal interests that opposed free trade, NAC and by extension the Canadian women's movement gained enormous credibility. Although the women's movement had existing ties with some groups in the Pro-Canada Network—in part through shared experiences during the 1960s and 1970s—the free trade debate reinforced and made visible this linkage.[65] In particular, the progressive political credentials of the Canadian women's movement were firmly established as a result of NAC's activities in the years 1985-88.

More important, by focussing on the impact of free trade among women who worked for hourly wages in manufacturing and service sector jobs, NAC blunted older criticisms to the effect that the Canadian women's movement was primarily concerned with the career mobility of a small number of privileged, professional women. The Canadian women's movement, through NAC, thus gave voice to the concerns of immigrants in the textile industry, for example, whose job prospects would otherwise have been left out of the trade debate.[66] NAC tried to influence policy outcomes for these women; in so doing, it helped to establish the Canadian women's movement as a vehicle for more than the aspirations of an affluent minority.

Finally, NAC's actions quite simply put Canadian feminism on the policy map. They identified linkages between free trade as a major federal government policy initiative and the lives of Canadian women, a connection that might have been ignored without NAC's intervention. In itself, this was no small accomplishment on behalf of the Canadian women's movement.

Building a Societal Alternative

What was the importance of NAC's participation to the larger anti-trade cause? First, NAC and more than thirty other societal groups in the Pro-Canada Network and smaller coalitions helped to breathe new life into nationalist efforts. The establishment of the Council of Canadians had given nationalism a fresh start in the 1980s, but this organization based on individual memberships could not begin to command the resources, expertise and representativeness of the constituent groups that later formed the Pro-Canada Network. NAC, the Canadian labour movement and other Network organizations brought their own considerable bases of support to the anti-trade side, along with a degree of policy knowledge and commitment that was essential to fighting free trade on national, provincial and local levels. In short, NAC and other interests offered a new lease on life for Canadian nationalism.

Second, groups like NAC brought new faces and new identities to the nationalist cause. For example, the participation of the labour movement in the anti-FTA cause gave what had been primarily a middle-class phenomenon a more grassroots and representative image. Similarly, NAC brought women's faces to the anti-trade leadership—something that had generally not been seen except in the cultural nationalist stream. Pan-Canadianism began to *look* like modern Canada during the late 1980s, and this resemblance was due in large measure to the participation of groups like NAC in the Pro-Canada Network.

Yet building bridges between these various interests within the Network was a difficult task. At times, feminists struggled to have themselves and their issue priorities recognized; for example, tensions emerged during discussions in the fall of 1988 over the anti-trade cartoon booklet by Terry Mosher (Aislin) and Rick Salutin. An entry that Salutin refers to as the 'hooker cartoon' was withdrawn as a result of pressure from some sponsoring organizations. This pressure led Salutin to consider resigning from the Coalition Against Free Trade because of what he viewed as censorship of the cartoon material.[67]

NAC's opposition to free trade thus highlighted problems that continued to confront feminists in policy coalitions during the late 1980s. At the same time, however, this involvement underlined the importance of creating a more broadly based and contemporary Canadian nationalism. All told, NAC's contributions seemed to more than balance the tensions thus created; in fact, these tensions were probably a necessary part of the coming of age of pan-Canadianism.

Conclusions

Were NAC's activities during the 1985-88 free trade debate appropriate? This chapter has argued that vigorous opposition on the part of an ideologically diverse, financially dependent umbrella organization of Canadian women's groups to *the* major economic initiative of the federal government was fraught with danger. Having ended up on the losing side in the trade debate, NAC activists were faced with the need to develop new policy positions and to cope with internal demands for organizational reform and external threats to funding, credibility and policy influence.

In hindsight, would NAC have been better off to avoid the free trade debate, or perhaps to moderate its opposition to the policy? Avoiding the issue was probably neither possible nor advisable for NAC: if the potential job and social policy consequences of free trade had been drawn out by unions and other opposing groups, then NAC would have needed to intervene at some point to specify the implications for its constituency. In other words, minimizing the costs of intervention by avoiding the trade issue altogether would have amounted to an abdication of NAC's responsibility to evaluate and respond to government policy as it affects Canadian women.

On the other hand, while a milder critique of free trade would not have involved an abdication of responsibility, would it have either minimized the risks or enhanced the benefits outlined above? Perhaps the easier half of this question concerns benefits. NAC's ability to (1) argue that it was responsive to female public opinion on free trade, (2) acquire political visibility and experience and (3) gain credibility among other groups opposed to the deal would probably *not* have increased under conditions of more moderate opposition. In fact, the second and third benefits might not have accrued at all if NAC had pursued a mild, low-key approach in its opposition.

The other side of the coin involving reduced costs is more difficult to assess. The threats to federal funding, internal cohesion and co-operative relations with the governing party might well have been minimized had NAC's opposition been milder. For example, one could argue that the federal Conservatives would have been less likely to link NAC's position on free trade with the organization's annual funding application if it had pursued the trade issue less vigorously, or that internal ideological tensions might have been less severe under such circumstances.

However, arguments to the effect that resources, cohesion and policy influence would not have been as threatened under different conditions are simply speculative matters of degree. Once NAC intervened—which, according to this analysis, was likely under most scenarios—the stakes were already high. And, like the high-stakes risks associated with free trade itself, the costs and benefits of NAC's intervention on this issue will take time to reveal themselves fully.

In the interim, it seems clear that NAC and the other societal groups that participated in anti-trade efforts have been increasingly tied to an oppositional political discourse. With pro-market, continentalist supporters of free trade in the business community pitted against interventionist, anti-free trade interests that sought to build an alternative coalition, a polarization occurred that paralleled the lines of European class politics. As long as a Conservative federal government willing to punish its societal foes and reward its friends remained in power, this clash of interests continued to play itself out in an ever-expanding range of policy areas.

Chapter 8 will return to the consequences of the trade debate, after Chapter 7 examines relations between the nationalisms of Quebec and English Canada.

Notes

[1]Marjorie Griffin Cohen, *Free Trade and the Future of Women's Work: Manufacturing and Service Industries* (Toronto: Garamond Press and the Canadian Centre for Policy Alternatives, 1987), 15.

[2]On the Public Petroleum Association, see Chapter 4, above.

[3]Rick Salutin, *Waiting for Democracy: A Citizen's Journal* (Toronto: Penguin, 1989), 12; and interview with Marjorie Cohen, 26 Aug. 1988.

[4]The term 'women's issues' is used only reluctantly in this discussion. Although it is clear that the policy questions were initally placed on the public agenda through the mobilization of Canadian women's organizations, the phrase has unfortunately created assumptions to the effect that (1) such issues are exclusively or primarily of proper concern to women; and (2) governmental responsibility for them is appropriately vested in the hands of separate, minor and often poorly funded departments. Given that the term has been established in common parlance, it is employed here.

[5]Alison Prentice, Paula Bourne, Gail Cuthbert Brandt, Beth Light, Wendy Mitchinson and Naomi Black, *Canadian Women: A History* (Toronto: Harcourt, Brace Jovanovich, 1988), 350.

[6]On this historical background, see Catherine L. Cleverdon, *The Woman Suffrage Movement in Canada* (Toronto: University of Toronto Press, 1974); and Veronica Strong-Boag, *The New Day Recalled: Lives of Girls and Women in English Canada, 1919-1939* (Toronto: Copp Clark Pitman, 1988).

[7]See Prentice et al., *Canadian Women*, 344-9; and Cerise Morris, '"Determination and Thoroughness": The Movement for a Royal Commission on the Status of Women', *Atlantis* 5 (1980), 1-21.

[8]See Nancy Adamson, Linda Briskin and Margaret McPhail, *Feminist Organizing for Change: The Contemporary Women's Movement in Canada* (Toronto: Oxford University Press, 1988), 51-2.

[9]See Royal Commission on the Status of Women, *Report* (Ottawa: Information Canada, 1970).

[10]According to Prentice et al., *Canadian Women*, the original name was shortened in order for the group to receive federal funds for its inaugural conference in 1972 (350).

[11]See Adamson et al., *Feminist Organizing for Change*, 268-70. For a more complete organizational history, see Jill Vickers, Chris Appelle and Pauline Rankin, *Politics as if Women Mattered: A Political Analysis of the National Action Committee on the Status of Women* (Toronto: University of Toronto Press, forthcoming), chap. 2.

[12]The member groups represented on NAC's first steering committee are listed in Adamson et al., *Feminist Organizing for Change*, 52.

[13]Ibid., 53.

[14]See A. Paul Pross, 'Pressure Groups: Talking Chameleons', in Michael S. Whittington and Glen Williams (eds), *Canadian Politics in the 1980s* (Toronto: Methuen, 1984), 296-300.

[15]See Prentice et al., *Canadian Women*, 364; and Adamson et al., *Feminist Organizing for Change*, 5, 71-2.

[16]According to Vickers et al., *Politics as if Women Mattered*, regional representation was instituted in 1980 (101). On the impact of federalism on interest groups, see William D. Coleman, 'Federalism and Interest Group Organization', in Herman Bakvis and William M. Chandler (eds), *Federalism and the Role of the State* (Toronto: University of Toronto Press, 1987), 173-4.

[17]Prentice et al., *Canadian Women*, 361-4.

[18]See Sylvia B. Bashevkin, *Toeing the Lines: Women and Party Politics in English Canada* (Toronto: University of Toronto Press, 1985), chap. 1.

[19]See Christine Appelle, 'The New Parliament of Women: A Study of the National Action Committee on the Status of Women' (Carleton University MA thesis, 1987).

[20]See Prentice et al., *Canadian Women*, 357-61.

[21]See Adamson et al., *Feminist Organizing for Change*, 175.

[22]Prentice et al., *Canadian Women*, 364.

[23]NAC adopted equal pay as an issue priority in 1975, International Women's Year. See Adamson

et al., *Feminist Organizing for Change*, 63.

[24]REAL was an acronym for Realistic, Equal, Active, for Life. See Prentice et al., *Canadian Women*, 365-6; Karen Dubinsky, *Lament for a 'Patriarchy Lost?' Anti-Feminism, Anti-Abortion* and *REAL Women in Canada* (Ottawa: Canadian Research Institute for the Advancement of Women, 1985); Lorna Erwin, 'REAL Women, Anti-Feminism and the Welfare State', *Resources for Feminist Research* 17 (1988), 147-9; and Danielle Crittenden, 'REAL Women Don't Eat Crow', *Saturday Night* (May 1988), 27-35. REAL Women received approximately $21,000 in federal funds to support a conference held in Ottawa in April 1989.

[25]See Pross, 'Pressure Groups'; A. Paul Pross, *Group Politics and Public Policy* (Toronto: Oxford University Press, 1986); Hugh G. Thorburn, *Interest Groups in the Canadian Federal System*, Royal Commission Research Studies, vol. 69 (Toronto: University of Toronto Press for Supply and Services Canada, 1985); and Paul Wilkinson, *Social Movement* (London: Macmillan, 1971).

[26]Sue Findlay, 'Facing the State: The Politics of the Women's Movement Reconsidered', in Heather Jon Maroney and Meg Luxton (eds), *Feminism and Political Economy* (Toronto: Methuen, 1987), 31-50.

[27]They were Chaviva Hosek, who subsequently won election as a provincial Liberal MPP in Ontario, and Nadine Nowlan, who was later elected to Toronto City Council. On the growing interest of Canadian political parties in actively recruiting women in this period, see Bashevkin, *Toeing the Lines*, chaps 4, 5.

[28]Vickers et al., *Politics as if Women Mattered*, refer to the period after 1979 as one of internal 'trouble and strife' (chap. 2). See Adamson et al., *Feminist Organizing for Change*, chap. 7; and Carolyn Egan, 'Toronto's International Women's Day Committee: Socialist Feminist Politics', in Maroney and Luxton (eds), *Feminism and Political Economy*, 118.

[29]Royal Commission on the Economic Union and Development Prospects for Canada, *Report* (Ottawa: Supply and Services Canada, 1985).

[30]National Action Committee on the Status of Women, 'Free Trade Could Be Costly for Women Workers', *Feminist Action* (October 1985), 2.

[31]Cohen, *Free Trade and the Future of Women's Work*, 15.

[32]National Action Committee, 'Free Trade Could be Costly for Women Workers', 2.

[33]Ibid.

[34]Margaret Atwood, '. . . The Only Position They've ever Adopted Toward Us, Country to Country, has been the Missionary Position', in Laurier LaPierre (ed.), *If You Love this Country: Facts and Feelings on Free Trade* (Toronto: McClelland and Stewart, 1987), 20. Atwood's comments also appeared in the *Globe and Mail*, 5 Nov. 1987.

[35]See Laurell Ritchie, 'A Warning for Workers', *Policy Options* (September 1986), 27-9.

[36]Marjorie Montgomery Bowker, *On Guard for Thee: An Independent Review of the Free Trade Agreement* (Hull: Voyageur Publishing, 1988).

[37]Interview with Maude Barlow, 14 Oct. 1989.

[38]Organized by Rick Salutin, the Revue was held on the first anniversary of the Reagan-Mulroney Shamrock Summit. Speakers included Walter Gordon, Marjorie Cohen and Bob White. See Salutin, *Waiting for Democracy*; Ritchie, 'A Warning for Workers'; and National Action Committee on the Status of Women, 'NAC Hands Agenda to Minister: McDougall Attends Meeting', *Feminist Action* (October 1986), 1.

[39]National Action Committee on the Status of Women, 'AGM Delegates Approve New NAC Policies', *Feminist Action* (July 1987), 5.

[40]See Cohen, *Free Trade and the Future of Women's Work*. Both background papers were published by the Canadian Advisory Council on the Status of Women, a government-funded and government-appointed organization established in 1973. At the same time as it published Marjorie Cohen, *Free Trade in Services: An Issue of Concern to Women* (Ottawa: Canadian Advisory Council on the Status

of Women, 1987) and Ann Porter and Barbara Cameron, *Impact of Free Trade on Women in Manufacturing* (Ottawa: Canadian Advisory Council on the Status of Women, 1987)—both critical of free trade—the Advisory Council also published a background paper favourable to free trade by Katie Macmillan of the C.D. Howe Institute, entitled *Free Trade and Canadian Women: An Opportunity for a Better Future* (Ottawa: Canadian Advisory Council on the Status of Women, 1987). On the Advisory Council's position regarding free trade, see Canadian Advisory Council on the Status of Women, 'Communiqué: Labour Adjustment Programs are Necessary to Help Women Adapt to Changing Work Conditions,' 28 Sept. 1988.

[41]Cohen, *Free Trade and the Future of Women's Work*.

[42]These included Maude Barlow, 'Women and Free Trade: The Sell-Out of Equality', speech delivered to Liberal Party of Canada (Ontario) Women's Commission (26 March 1988); Patricia Lane, 'The Impact of the Free-Trade Deal on Work', in Duncan Cameron (ed.), *The Free Trade Deal* (Toronto: Lorimer, 1988), 215-22; Sue Vohanka, 'How Women Would be Victimized', in Ed Finn (ed.), *The Facts on Free Trade* (Toronto: Lorimer, 1988); and John W. Warnock, *Free Trade and the New Right Agenda* (Vancouver: New Star Books, 1988).

[43]These pamphlets included 'What Every Woman Needs to Know about Free Trade', 10 pages; and 'Free Trade: A Bad Deal for Women', 7 pages. In addition, NAC co-sponsored a Women's Equality Debate in Toronto on 3 Nov. 1988, and successfully pressured for the inclusion of a one-hour 'women's issues' segment in both federal leaders' debates.

[44]National Action Committee on the Status of Women, 'Women's Equality Accord: Priority Issues for Women's Equality', *Feminist Action* (October 1988), 12-13.

[45]Marjorie Cohen, 'Election Priorities', *Feminist Action* (September 1988), 12.

[46]Porter and Cameron, *Impact of Free Trade on Women in Manufacturing*, 1.

[47]Appelle, *The New Parliament of Women*, 55, 64.

[48]This perception was reinforced following the 1988 federal elections, when NAC activists believe they 'paid a hefty price for violating a tacit agreement between the government and advocacy groups'. See Sean Fine, 'Tories Weary of Paying Critics', *Globe and Mail* (16 July 1990).

[49]On the events of 1987, see Stevie Cameron, 'REAL Women Group Declared Ineligible for Federal Money', *Globe and Mail* (16 January 1987). In February 1989, it was rumoured that the federal government would provide funds for REAL Women through the same channel by which it funded NAC, namely the Secretary of State Women's Program; federal funds were subsequently awarded to REAL Women for a conference in April 1989. See Doris Anderson, 'Ottawa Puts Squeeze on Feminists', *Toronto Star* (25 Feb. 1989).

[50]Confidental interview.

[51]On NAC's role in coalitions, see Varda Burstyn and Judy Rebick, 'How "Women Against Free Trade" Came to Write its Manifesto', *Resources for Feminist Research* 17 (1988), 139-42.

[52]See William D. Coleman, *Business and Politics: A Study of Collective Action* (Kingston: McGill-Queen's University Press, 1988).

[53]See Catherine Dunphy, 'Shaky NAC may be Headed for a Fall', *Toronto Star* (11 May 1989).

[54]See Stevie Cameron, 'Women's Centres Across Canada begin to Close as Funding Dries Up', *Globe and Mail* (7 April 1990); and Paula Todd, 'Women Won't be Silenced, Tories Warned', *Toronto Star* (12 May 1990). Aboriginal groups including native women's groups also experienced major funding cuts in the same federal budget.

[55]See Todd, 'Women Won't Be Silenced'; and Ross Howard, 'Budget Foes Organize to Focus on Tory Social Policy Changes', *Globe and Mail* (1 June 1989).

[56]On the events of May 1988, see Ann Rauhala, 'Largest Feminist Association Faces Crisis', *Globe and Mail* (16 May 1988). Alison Edgar of the Ottawa Progressive Conservative Women's Caucus, appearing on CBC's Morningside program on 19 May 1988, stated that free trade and Meech Lake were not properly on the NAC policy agenda and argued that NAC was too conflictual in its relations with the federal government.

[57]See, for example, Macmillan, *Free Trade and Canadian Women*; Katie Macmillan, 'Women as Winners', in John Crispo (ed.), *Free Trade: The Real Story* (Toronto: Gage, 1988), 117-25; and Richard G. Lipsey, 'The Economics of a Canadian-American Free Trade Association', in Michael D. Henderson (ed.), *The Future on the Table* (Toronto: Masterpress, 1987), 48, on the potential benefits of free trade for Canadian women.

[58]This linkage was made in NAC's election pamphlet, 'What Every Woman Needs to Know about Free Trade', 1.

[59]See Michael Adams and Donna Dasko, 'Poll Shows Tories Gaining, Grits Keeping Lead', *Globe and Mail* (29 July 1988).

[60]At each stage of the free trade debate, the federal government advertised widely its publications on the sectoral implications of the policy. Each of these publications series included a pamphlet on women and free trade.

[61]According to Marjorie Cohen, NAC's intervention on the free trade issue 'helped to build bridges to women's groups across Canada and to other interest groups as well'. Interview, 26 Aug. 1988.

[62]See Burstyn and Rebick, 'How "Women Against Free Trade" Came to Write its Manifesto'; and Marjorie Cohen, 'Free Trade Survey: Were Women Active?' *Feminist Action* (April 1989), 3.

[63]See Prentice et al., *Canadian Women*, 404; and Dunphy, 'Shaky NAC May be Headed for a Fall'.

[64]Pross, 'Pressure Groups', 296-300.

[65]See Prentice et al., *Canadian Women*, 350.

[66]See Ritchie, 'A Warning for Workers'; and Charlene Gannage, 'Towards an Alternative Economic Strategy: The Case of Women Garment Workers', in Marc Gold and David Leyton-Brown (eds), *Trade-Offs on Free Trade: The Canada-U.S. Free Trade Agreement* (Toronto: Carswell, 1988), 394-406.

[67]See Salutin, *Waiting for Democracy*, 30-4.

7 Solitudes in Collision? Pan-Canadian and Quebec Nationalisms in Perspective

You cannot wilfully ignore our sentiments on free trade and expect us to blithely allow you to get your way on constitutional reform . . . If we are to live together, we will have to recognize the principle of reciprocity in our relationship. It cannot be all take, take, take on the one side and give, give, give on the other.[1]

Introduction

In some respects, the historical background presented in Chapter 1 makes it difficult to view Anglo-Canadian and Quebec nationalisms as anything other than competing or colliding. Imperial nationalism in English Canada during the late nineteenth and early twentieth centuries, as Carl Berger suggests, 'appeared alien and threatening to French Canadians'—while French Canada was often viewed at a suspicious distance by supporters of imperial unity.[2] To make matters more conflictual, some early Anglo-Canadian nationalists were drawn from the ranks of the Orange Order, a connection that imparted an anti-Catholic and anti-French streak to elements of the imperial movement.[3]

This early development of pan-Canadianism as an essentially Anglophone phenomenon was reinforced in more recent times by a clear division between its political agenda and the goals of Quebec nationalism. As demonstrated in Chapter 1, the pan-Canadian world view begins with a fundamental emphasis on the centrality and primacy of the federal state; Quebec nationalism since the 1960s, by contrast, has turned on a pivot of decentralization and, in some cases, provincial independence. From a pan-Canadian perspective, the basic federal division of powers acts as an obstacle to effective national action, since jurisdictional turf has been increasingly shared with the provinces. From a Quebec nationalist perspective, however, the problem is virtually the reverse; federal and other provincial interests are seen as limiting the ability of the Quebec government to act in a sovereign manner.

Thus the world views of modern Quebec nationalism and pan-Canadian nationalism have developed with reference to two entirely different axes: federal-provincial and French-English tensions, on the one hand, and nationalist-continentalist tensions, on the other.[4] The in-group/out-group dimensions of the two nationalisms are also fundamentally different: while pan-Canadianism has identified a primarily English Canadian in-group and a US out-group, Quebec nationalism has focussed on a Francophone in-group residing in Quebec and an Anglophone out-group residing in parts of Montreal and in the rest of Canada. If pan-Canadian nationalism is characterized as both English Canadian in origin and centralist in orientation, emphasizing the need for a strong federal government to control US economic and cultural influences, then it by definition appears hostile to the interests of Quebec nationalism, and vice versa.

The willingness of Quebec nationalists to embrace the United States as a political and entrepreneurial counterweight to English Canada reflects one aspect of this collision scenario; Anglo-Canadian opposition to continental integration and to Quebec's demands for decentralization reflects the opposite side. From a Québécois perspective, Canadian federal governments have attempted to impose English- or pan-Canadian nationalism (in the guise of 'national unity') at the expense of other Canadian nationalisms. In the words of Michel Brunet, '"National unity" has always been a slogan under which the English-speaking majority has concealed its own nationalistic ends with the hope of compelling the Québécois to renounce their own collective ends.'[5] Conversely, English Canadian nationalists have viewed Quebec's support of decentralization and continental free trade in equally threatening terms. As quoted in the epigraph to this chapter, Philip Resnick sensed Quebec's betrayal of English Canadian nationalism in the wake of the 1988 federal elections and the Meech Lake Accord: 'You cannot wilfully ignore our sentiments on free trade and expect us to blithely allow you to get your way on constitutional reform.'[6]

Alternatives to Collision

If one reading of the relationship between English-Canadian and Quebec nationalisms suggests tension and collision, however, another approach points towards somewhat more common ground. Perhaps the most obvious counterpoise to the collision view follows from theoretical studies of federal states and societies. In 1968, applying William Riker's ideas to the Canadian case, Michael Stein described federalism as a pattern of 'bargains, compromises and balances'.[7] According to Stein, federal political systems by definition

> operate to give autonomous expression to both the national political system and political culture and to regional political subsystems and subcultures . . . The autonomy of each of these systems and subsystems is counterbalanced by a mutual interdependence. This balance maintains the overall union.[8]

Stein's view of federal societies as necessarily consensual and, indeed, tolerant of the internal diversity that provided their original *raison d'être* suggests possibilities for accommodation between Quebec and pan-Canadian nationalisms.

More recent work on the federal-provincial division of powers suggests similar possibilities. By arguing that the concept of 'province-building' has been extended to the point that all provincial governments appear to be an undifferentiated mass of anti-federal actors, Robert Young and his colleagues reject 'the assumption that federalism has become a zero-sum game'.[9] In their view, co-operation is at least as significant to the functioning of Canadian federalism as conflict, since federalism by definition requires a degree of institutional 'tolerance' and, in attitudinal terms, 'dual loyalties' among the mass public.[10]

Empirical research on 'dual loyalties' suggests that Canadians indeed hold multiple attachments, and that most apparently feel comfortable doing so.[11] In the words of Richard Johnston, federal political arrangements have not produced a zero-sum system of loyalties, since

> Canadians tend to like both their province of residence and the country as a whole. Moreover, feeling for one is positively, not negatively, correlated with feeling for the other. The controlling factor is not a we/they one, so much as a general capacity for identification with communities.[12]

If this literature can be said to offer an alternative to the collision thesis, it is that disparate nationalisms could be accommodated in Canada—particularly in areas where their priorities do not directly conflict.

Hypotheses and Data

Since possibilities exist for both collision and accommodation between Quebec and pan-Canadian nationalisms, the analysis in this chapter is framed in parallel terms. To put the first alternative boldly, do the two solitudes 'collide'? Can it be argued that pan-Canadian nationalism is limited by an absence of concern about US cultural and economic control among Francophone Quebeckers or, in more extreme terms, that Quebec nationalists are essentially continentalist? Conversely, is Quebec nationalism constrained by a bias in favour of strong federal government among English Canadians or, in sharper language, are pan-Canadian nationalists basically centralist? In terms of the second thesis, can it be argued that the two nationalisms have achieved an accommodation of sorts? Do their respective proponents reflect an element of tolerance or, possibly, multiple loyalty?

Both sets of questions are examined using two sources of data: first, the views of Anglo-Canadian and Quebec nationalist writers who have explicitly addressed French/English relations; and second, mass-level data from three Social Change in Canada Surveys (1977, 1979, 1981) and a CBC/*Globe and Mail* poll conducted in October 1990.[13] The first set of materials is more speculative and impressionistic than the second, but it points towards conclusions that dovetail with the results of public opinion research.

The chapter is organized as follows: first, the priorities of Anglo-Canadian and

Quebec nationalism are discussed, especially the potential for a tilt towards centralism in the former and towards continentalism in the latter. Second, the attitudes of the proponents of each nationalism towards the priorities of the other during the 1970s and following are considered. Findings from this analysis lead in turn to a discussion of the larger implications of attitudinal collision versus accommodation.

Nationalisms in Canada

Examining the degree to which Anglo-Canadian and Quebec nationalisms may have collided or, alternatively, been accommodated requires a working definition of each concept. This is no easy task, since both are ideologically heterogeneous and therefore difficult to pin down in definitional terms. As André Laurendeau observed with respect to Quebec:

> Having lived almost all my adult life among nationalists, I am still struck by their extraordinary diversity. There are nationalists in language …There are economic nationalists … and there are social nationalists. Besides, there is cultural nationalism, political nationalism, not to mention pure and simple traditionalism when it takes itself for a doctrine.[14]

Modern English Canadian nationalism, as reflected in Chapter 1, is also internally diverse; for example, investment nationalists in the Committee for an Independent Canada differed from others whose ideas followed from the Waffle Manifesto. As Ramsay Cook explains in his comparison with developments in Quebec, 'English Canada has not had a Garneau, a Groulx, or even a Brunet; it has not had a single nationalist doctrine.'[15]

Taking account of this diversity, Chapter 1 defined pan-Canadian nationalism as *the organized pursuit of a more independent and distinctive Canadian in-group on the North American continent, primarily through the introduction by the federal government of specific cultural, trade and investment policies that would limit US out-group influences.* Commitment to this objective will be treated here as evidence of pan- or Anglo-Canadian nationalism, while the obverse commitment to closer continental relations will be viewed as evidence of integrationism. As Kim Nossal explains, integrationism tends 'to stress the benefits of economic integration between Canada and the United States and downplay the political costs'.[16]

Can it be argued that pan-Canadian nationalism is inherently centralist? From the perspective of policy success, restrictions on foreign media spillover and economic control seem to require a strong federal government to enforce consistent national standards. If the threat of US influence is as ominous as Anglo-Canadian nationalists maintain, then a coherent and unified response by Ottawa probably constitutes the best hope for an indigeneous counterweight—since provincial governments would hardly measure up to the American challenge.[17]

This same focus on state control also informs Quebec nationalism. Although the problem of ideological diversity exists here as well, the basic common ground among various Quebec nationalisms rests in *a vigorous defence of Francophone language, cultural and economic rights, primarily through the intervention of an assertive, powerful government based in Quebec City*.[18] Since this regime could be a provincial government with special status within Confederation, a separate independent state, or some compromise between the two (for example, sovereignty-association), Quebec nationalism can be viewed along a political continuum from increased provincial powers to outright national independence. Support for this core objective will be treated as evidence of Quebec nationalism.[19]

Does the latter contain an unavoidable tilt towards continentalism? Robert Gilpin suggests at least two reasons why closer Quebec-US relations, including greater American investment, are pursued by Quebec nationalists. First, the latter desire economic growth in Quebec and oppose further English Canadian investment. From this perspective, US capital provides a convenient and less ideologically troubling source of development.[20] Second, Quebec nationalists resent Ontario's disproportionate share of foreign investment dollars and seek a greater share for Quebec.

A third rationale may be gleaned from the public statements of Quebec political elites, including premiers Lévesque and Bourassa. Both leaders, despite their considerable differences, maintained while in office that additional foreign investment was required in Quebec for economic purposes and that this capital was not to be feared or restricted on cultural grounds. To paraphrase Lévesque's 1979 comments to a US audience, Québécois identity is strong enough to resist assimilation at the hands of foreign investment.[21]

Anglo-Canadian Nationalists View Quebec

Generalizing about how English Canadian and Quebec nationalists view their own cultures is difficult enough without entering into the complicated question of how each views the other's nationalism. Since it is virtually impossible to establish what either a representative English Canadian nationalist view of Quebec or a typical Quebec nationalist view of English Canada is, this discussion evaluates what might be termed 'glances across the fence'. To begin with the case of English Canada, what ideas about Quebec have been voiced by modern nationalist activists and organizations? How have these views changed over time?

Modern Anglo-Canadian nationalists have generally reflected a positive and sympathetic view of Quebec nationalism. In the 1968 Waffle Manifesto, for example, left-wing investment nationalists argued that the goals of English Canadian and Quebec nationalisms were complementary and mutually beneficial:

Quebec's history and aspirations must be allowed full expression and implementation in the conviction that new ties will emerge from the common perception of 'two nations, one struggle'. Socialists in English Canada must ally themselves with socialists in Quebec in this common cause.[22]

This early statement emphasized a common socialist thread between the two nationalisms and the importance of retaining the federal system; it did not explicitly mention self-determination, preferring instead to share the official NDP view of Quebec's 'special status' within the federal system.[23]

This position shifted in part during 1970-71, when the NDP leadership candidate endorsed by the Waffle, James Laxer, articulated a self-determination argument that contradicted official party policy. Laxer submitted a resolution supporting self-determination to the NDP federal convention; it was endorsed by prominent New Democrats in Quebec.[24] Delegates to the April 1971 NDP convention in Ottawa, however, rejected both the recognition of Quebec self-determination and Laxer's candidacy, endorsing instead the candidate of the party establishment (David Lewis) and the mainstream NDP argument that the Waffle's position amounted to a defence of Quebec separatism.[25]

During this same period, the Committee for an Independent Canada was established with a more moderate foreign investment strategy than that of the Waffle. Paralleling the Waffle's efforts to elicit support among New Democrats in Quebec, the CIC worked to attract prominent Quebeckers to its ranks. The editor of *Le Devoir*, which in January 1971 had published the Waffle resolution on self-determination, became co-chair of the CIC in September 1971; Claude Ryan joined his co-chair, Toronto publisher Jack McClelland, in working to press the federal government for a coherent foreign investment policy.[26] Ryan was initially very active in the Committee; with Peter C. Newman, for example, he drafted the text of the CIC's petition on foreign investment at Newman's *Toronto Star* office.[27]

Yet Ryan's commitment to the CIC, which had helped to generate concern about foreign investment in Quebec, gradually dissipated. After a leaked version of the Gray Report was released, Ryan wrote that investment nationalists tended 'to ignore almost completely the existence of two different societies in Canada'.[28] As Peter C. Newman recalls, 'Ryan never resigned from the Committee and he never turned against us. But there certainly was a waning of interest. He got too busy with what was happening in Quebec.'[29]

Events in Quebec not only turned Ryan's focus elsewhere; they also tended to distract and, to some extent, divide English Canadian participants in the CIC. Although the group's focus remained foreign investment until its dissolution in 1981, individual activists responded to the 1976 Parti québécois (PQ) victory and the 1980 referendum in varied ways. Perhaps the most important reflection of a growing ferment among English Canadian nationalists was the creation of the Committee for a New Constitution. Announced in the *Canadian Forum* in 1977, the Committee proposed that 'a dialogue on a new constitution for

Canada' unfold within the framework of three basic principles:

1.The right of Quebec to choose its own constitutional future by free and democratic means. Among the several options open to it are: continued membership in the Canadian federation, membership in a modified Canadian federation, independence and a new association with Canada, or independence.

2. The parallel rights of English-speaking Canada to define its priorities, determine its constitutional features, and protect its own legitimate interests.

3. The obligation of both communities to conduct negotiations with one another in a spirit of good will aimed at mutual accord.[30]

Signatories to the Committee's proposal called for the creation of a joint Canada-Quebec constitutional study commission and for 'a popularly elected constituent assembly charged with drafting a new constitution'.[31] Included among the approximately 45 names in the Forum statement were those of prominent activists in both the CIC (notably Abraham Rotstein) and the Waffle (including Melville Watkins).

In stating that 'English-speaking Canada exists as a viable national community', the Committee for a New Constitution drew support from cultural as well as investment nationalists. Margaret Atwood and Susan Crean signed the *Forum* proposal, and Crean went on in the summer of 1977 to begin a dialogue with *indépendantiste* writer Marcel Rioux. Their conversations produced two books arguing that Quebec and English Canada alike faced a direct threat from the United States.[32] Crean and Rioux's claim that both societies were 'subject to the cultural and economic pressures of the American empire' became the basis for a call to renew Canada and Quebec 'and resolve to reinvent the future and repatriate our souls'.[33]

The nationalist streams represented in the Committee for a New Constitution thus looked towards accommodation and understanding between Quebec and English Canada. Although they were prepared to accept Quebec independence as 'the democratic verdict of that electorate when and if it is rendered', many Committee members seemed to prefer a reformed federal system that would allow both communities to develop inside the framework of a new constitution.[34] Self-determination seemed to have become the operative term by 1980, when the *Canadian Forum* as well as a number of individuals who had signed the 1976 statement sponsored a one-page 'Declaration of Quebec's Right to Self-Determination'.[35]

There were variations and nuances among English Canadian nationalists, however. At one end of the spectrum, neither Walter Gordon nor Peter C. Newman attached their names to the statement of the Committee for a New Constitution. Newman later described his position as follows:

I was one who didn't see sovereignty-association as a practical alternative, even though Abe [Rotstein] and others did. I thought that sovereignty-association was a first step to separatism and I was very much on the 'Non' side during the referendum.[36]

At the other end of the spectrum were Watkins, Rotstein and writer Rick Salutin, who endorsed not only the Committee for a New Constitution but also the 'Oui' position in the Quebec referendum,[37] and maintained that parallel movements existed in the two cultures. In Rotstein's words, 'To those of us who were involved in this little group, two nations, two nationalisms and self-determination for each made sense. Each would be rejuvenated and allow the other to develop.'[38]

Quebec Nationalists View English Canada

While Anglo-Canadian nationalists in the 1970s and following were developing their responses to the PQ and sovereignty-association, many Quebec nationalists were actively engaged in building a sovereign Quebec. Central to their political perceptions in this period was the belief that a *péquiste* government based in Quebec City was the best defence for Francophone interests against Anglophone incursions; in this they differed fundamentally from English Canadian nationalists. If many of the latter were fascinated by, sympathetic towards and even jealous of the achievements of their Quebec counterparts, the same cannot be said of leading Quebec nationalists vis-à-vis pan-Canadianism.

Much of the indifference and, in some cases, hostility that Quebec nationalists exhibited towards English Canada and its nationalism can be explained with reference to basic we/they differences. Anglo-Canadian nationalists did not view Quebec as an out-group or perceive its nationalism as a threat comparable to that of US influences, but Quebec nationalists clearly identified English Canada as an out-group and its nationalism (especially its centralist brand of federalism) as a potential obstacle to their political project. The perception of English Canadian nationalism held by Quebec nationalists might thus be compared with English Canada's view of US patriotism: suspect, somewhat ominous and best observed from a guarded distance.[39]

Probably the best-known commentator on English Canada among Quebec nationalists, and a frequent interpreter of Quebec to English Canadian audiences, has been Daniel Latouche. A graduate of the University of British Columbia, Latouche returned to Quebec to teach political science, write and eventually advise PQ premier René Lévesque during the period of the 1980 referendum. Latouche's commitment to the independence option thus developed alongside his interest in and familiarity with English Canada.

Latouche has acknowledged publicly the indifference of Quebeckers—including Quebec intellectuals—towards English Canada:

> For a vast majority of Québécois, nationalism has been a progressive force, opening their eyes to what was going on in the rest of the world, forcing them to think about things which until recently were outside their frame of reference. As such, I find it unacceptable that they would not be interested and preoccupied by what is going on in English Canada. Nobody, but absolutely nobody shows any interest. There is a lot of envy of the new pre-eminence of Toronto and the new-found richness of Vancouver. There might even be some resentment, a touch of condes-

cendence, and some amusement, but you will not find any respect or concern. No Quebec university offers any course on English Canadian society. A seminar on Toronto's historical development or the economy of the Prairies would be unthinkable. For years, I have tried to organize a conference on English Canada, only to be told it is a non-topic.[40]

The lack of interest that Latouche describes has been accompanied by a distinct lack of sympathy. Whereas Anglo-Canadian nationalists have sometimes taken a fawning attitude towards Quebec nationalism, prominent Quebec nationalists express limited patience with the phenomenon of English Canadian nationalism. According to Latouche, English Canada cannot even claim to have a *bona fide* nationalism because, as a society, it possesses no sense of itself. Writing in 1986 for the Macdonald Commission, he set out to 'explain why this English Canada has always refused to behave as one of the country's founding nations . . . the inability of English Canada to contemplate its own existence as a national collectivity'.[41]

Latouche concluded that Quebec's existence had curiously permitted English Canada to escape from nationhood, since the French fact permitted an easy delineation between Canada and the US. In his words:

> English Canada, which does not exist, or at least which is bent on proclaiming its nonexistence, needs its antithesis to demonstrate that the Canadian reality is 'different'. In short the French-Canadian or francophone minority allows English Canada to dispense with the search for its own identity.[42]

Although Latouche acknowledged the efforts of the Waffle and the Committee for an Independent Canada to develop an Anglo-Canadian nationalism, he contended that they were futile as long as English Canada 'was unaware of its existence'.[43]

Finally, Latouche's essay for the Macdonald Commission argued that sentiment on the English Canadian left was distinctly unsympathetic to Quebec nationalism. Contradicting some evidence to the contrary, he alleged that 'during the entire referendum campaign of 1980 not one single English-Canadian left-wing group came out in support of the "yes" thesis.'[44] Ironically, this statement reiterated what Latouche described in the same essay as 'one of the most firmly entrenched ideas of the Québécois elites'—namely, that English Canada refused to accept Quebec's legitimate claims.[45]

Meech Lake and Free Trade

The victory of the 'Non' forces in the 1980 referendum, followed by the 1981-82 round of constitutional discussions and the 1987-90 debate over the Meech Lake Accord, increased the distance between Quebec and Anglo-Canadian nationalists. Whereas many of the latter viewed Meech Lake as a decentralizing initiative that could weaken the fundamental powers of the federal state, to the former Meech Lake became a bottom-line, bare-bones requirement for Quebec to remain in the federal system. If English Canadian nationalists were prepared to offer guarded support for Meech Lake because it promised to bring Quebec into the constitutional fold, they were less prepared to endorse the decentralist terms of the agreement that applied to *all* provincial governments. Many also questioned the closed-door procedures employed to reach the Accord, violating as they did the more open and participatory approach that had been proposed ten years earlier by the Committee for a New Constitution.[46] This lingering distaste for Meech Lake deepened the rift with Quebec; as Latouche reflected in his 1990 exchange with a nationalist counterpart in English Canada, Philip Resnick, 'M. Lake is no hero to us. It is only because of your objections that we have developed some sympathy towards him. If English Canada is against him, there must be something good about the guy.'[47]

Growing antagonism between what Resnick described as the statist preoccupations of Anglo-Canadian nationalism and the national roots of Quebec nationalism reached a crisis point when the debates concerning Meech Lake and free trade overlapped. As noted in Chapters 5 and 6, the vigorous and sustained opposition mounted by English Canadian critics of free trade in 1985-88 was not matched by a comparable organized opposition in Quebec. Although some elements within Quebec society, notably unions, women's groups and farmers, shared in this cause and participated in the Pro-Canada Network (PCN), Anglo-Canadian nationalists believed that opposition to free trade in Quebec was less deep-seated than in the rest of the country. In the words of one participant,

> From inside the PCN it was clear that Quebec was a province unto itself. There were always fewer people from Quebec at meetings of the PCN. There was always a risk that the labour movement would send staff people to these meetings to represent Quebec. People who were sitting in Ottawa knew that Quebec was not part of a national campaign in the same sense that the rest of the country was. Quebec really didn't have a coalition operating on its own. Without Quebec, it is clear that the deal would not have passed.[48]

This view that Quebec was largely outside the anti-FTA umbrella, and that it was Quebec voters who permitted a Conservative electoral victory in 1988, led English Canadian nationalists to re-evaluate their already guarded support for the Meech Lake Accord. As reflected most directly in Resnick's *Letters to a Québécois Friend*, Anglo-Canadian nationalists were less and less willing to endorse Meech Lake in the aftermath of the November 1988 elections, believing that Quebeckers had betrayed the cause of an independent Canada. If free trade meant the end of the nationalist dream in English Canada, Resnick asked, how could Quebec nationalists expect their Anglophone counterparts to endorse Meech Lake? Moreover, how could Quebec nationalists have joined in the pro-trade cause with the rich and powerful business interests of both cultures—essentially selling out their progressivism along with the concerns of women, farmers and unionized workers?[49]

Latouche's reply to Resnick, together with his statements at a York University conference on free trade, reiterate and expand a number of older arguments.[50] First, Latouche rejected the Anglo-Canadian assumption that Quebec made Canada distinctive, terming it 'paternalistic and insulting'.[51] Second, he argued that to a Quebec nationalist free trade was appealing for precisely the same reason that Resnick and others like him found it threatening: because continental economic integration would tend to weaken the Canadian federal state.[52] Third, Latouche suggested that Anglophone opponents of free trade had not been supporters of Quebec nationalism, and maintained that US cultural influences so feared in English Canada did not constitute a threat to Francophone Quebec.[53] In short, Latouche found little reason to apologize either for Quebec's pro-trade position in 1988 or for Resnick's sense of betrayal in the aftermath of that election.

Assessing the Evidence

As suggested at the beginning of this chapter, drawing conclusions from nationalist writings is difficult. At this point, however, it seems fair to say that the views of leading Anglo-Canadian nationalists regarding Quebec nationalism were more or less sympathetic through 1980. The positions articulated by members of the Waffle, the Committee for an Independent Canada and, especially, the Committee for a New Constitution were consistent with a co-operative self-determination approach; that is, both cultures could best be advanced through progressive nationalisms operating in each context. Some Anglo-Canadian nationalists publicly endorsed the 'Oui' option in 1980, and a few supported the 'Non' side, but many remained neutral. Co-operative self-determination seemed at that time to mean that Quebeckers would determine their own fate in the referendum, and that once the outcome was decided in Quebec, English Canada could determine its response.[54]

This relatively tolerant view of Quebec nationalism must be juxtaposed, however, with firm commitments to a strong federal state. If Anglo-Canadian nationalists at times hoped to emulate Quebec's nationally-conscious society and cultural vibrancy, they indicated little willingness to surrender *their* structural vehicle for accomplishing such ends—namely, the federal state. If English Canadian nationalists believed in co-operative self-determination for both cultures, they did not back down from their claim that Francophone Quebec was at least as threatened by US media spillover and economic control as English Canada.[55] In other words, the perceptions of Anglo-Canadian nationalists regarding Quebec nationalism suggest possibilities for accommodation as well as collision, with collision most likely in instances where Quebec nationalism either threatened the primacy of the federal state in English Canada or increased the likelihood of an immediate continental threat to all of Canada.

This collision scenario played itself out most clearly in 1988-90. Free trade and Meech Lake constituted a double blow for Anglo-Canadian nationalists, with the former upending the basic terms of in-group/out-group relations, and the latter eroding the cherished political bulwark against continental integration, the federal state. Not surprisingly, English Canadian views of Quebec nationalism seemed far less sympathetic and accommodating than in the past; Resnick's charge of 'betrayal' reflects a common sentiment.[56]

On the other side of the coin, the general indifference of Quebec and Quebec nationalists towards English Canada seems fairly consistent across time, as does a fundamental willingness among Quebec nationalists to embrace the US as a useful counterweight. In light of Latouche's rejection of the idea that English Canada even *has* a nationalism, Quebec and Anglo-Canadian nationalisms appear not so much to collide or accommodate as simply to pass as silent strangers in the night. If English Canadian nationalism provokes anything more than a shrug in Quebec, it is perhaps a sense of threat—and only if pan-Canadianism is associated with enhanced federal powers. Quebec nationalism does not share the Anglo-Canadian perception of the US as an out-group and, in Latouche's case, rejects the use of Quebec's presence in Confederation as a justification for Canada's claim to distinctiveness. The real 'them', according to this world view, remains English Canada.

In short, Anglo-Canadian nationalists seem to have been sympathetic at times towards Quebec nationalism but remained centralist in their perceptions of domestic politics, while Quebec nationalists have shown little interest in English Canadian nationalism and have been consistently continentalist in their outlook.

Mass-Level Attitudes

From 1977 to 1981
How do public opinion data square with these trends in nationalist writing? Particularly in the period of the referendum on sovereignty-association, mass-level beliefs in both cultures seemed relatively accommodating towards the other's nationalist priorities. Figures in Table 7.1 indicate that approximately three-quarters of Anglophone respondents residing outside Quebec in 1977-81 believed that enough US capital was already invested in Canada, and that foreign companies should be forced to sell a majority of their shares to Canadians. Moreover, 87 per cent of these respondents stated that new foreign firms investing in Canada should have a majority of their shares owned by Canadians.

Although these results point towards overwhelming support for the basic priorities of investment nationalism among its most promising constituency—Anglophones residing outside Quebec—they also indicate more limited endorsement for two other positions. First, when asked if they approved of government takeovers of foreign firms operating in Canada, only about 35 per cent of Anglophones outside Quebec were supportive. Second, when questioned

TABLE 7.1   PAN-CANADIAN NATIONALIST ATTITUDES BY CULTURAL GROUP, 1977-1981[a]

ITEM	YEAR	SUPPORT (%) FRANCOPHONE QUEBEC	SUPPORT (%) ANGLOPHONE NON-QUEBEC
Require new foreign firms to have majority shares owned by Canadians	1979	82.6	87.4
	1981	83.9	87.2
Enough U.S. capital now invested in Canada	1977	69.5	72.3
	1979	76.7	81.5
	1981	79.1	83.1
Require foreign firms to sell majority of shares to Canadians	1979	64.6	72.5
	1981	74.9	71.6
Government should take over foreign firms operating in Canada	1979	46.9	34.8
	1981	54.2	36.8
Effects of foreign investment in Canada are mostly bad	1977	8.2	14.0
	1979	6.9	17.5
	1981	7.6	19.0

[a] In this and the following tables, cell entries are based on non-missing cases only.

Source: 1977, 1979, 1981 Social Change in Canada surveys.

about the effects of foreign investment, fewer than 20 per cent said that the results were generally negative.

Did investment nationalist positions obtain less support among Francophones in Quebec? Data in Table 7.1 indicate that Francophone Quebeckers were less approving than Anglophone non-Quebeckers on three of the five foreign investment items, although French-English differences exceeded 10 per cent on only one item (involving the effects of foreign investment). A more interesting cultural difference was evident in the opposite direction, on the question of government takeovers of foreign firms operating in Canada: 46.9 per cent of Francophones versus 34.8 per cent of Anglophones approved in 1979, and 54.2 versus 36.8 per cent approved in 1981. This pattern contradicts conventional assumptions regarding the 'natural constituency' of government restrictions on foreign investment and could result, ironically, from the strong statist tradition in Quebec nationalism which has made government takeovers more acceptable there than in English Canada.

In terms of support for the priorities of Quebec nationalism, data in Table 7.2 show that approximately two-thirds of Francophone respondents believed that

TABLE 7.2   QUEBEC NATIONALIST ATTITUDES BY CULTURAL GROUP, 1977-1981

ITEM	YEAR	SUPPORT (%) FRANCOPHONE QUEBEC	SUPPORT (%) ANGLOPHONE NON-QUEBEC
Support major concessions by Ottawa to prevent Quebec separation	1977 1979	67.4 69.5	15.5 11.8
Provincial governments should have more power in future	1977 1979 1981	66.2 65.6 67.0	36.5 32.8 34.8
Ottawa pays too little attention to Quebec	1977 1979 1981	47.7 43.9 51.1	12.2 7.8 6.2
Favour Quebec independence	1977 1979 1981	42.5 40.8 50.7	35.0 22.4 22.2
Constitution should give Quebec special powers	1981	35.2	4.2

Source: 1977, 1979, 1981 Social Change in Canada surveys.

provincial governments should have more power in the future, and that the federal government should make major concessions to prevent Quebec from separating. These results, however, contrast with more limited support on three other survey probes, asking whether Ottawa pays too little attention to Quebec (an average of 47.6 per cent over the three surveys); whether respondents endorse Quebec independence (average of 44.7 per cent over three surveys); and whether Quebec should be granted special powers under the Canadian constitution (35.2 per cent in 1981).

Unlike the results in Table 7.1, however, where French-English differences were generally not dramatic, Table 7.2 indicates clear patterns of cultural variation in support for Quebec nationalism. Whereas about two-thirds of Francophone Quebeckers endorsed more powerful provincial governments and major concessions by Ottawa, comparable figures for Anglophone non-Quebeckers were 34.7 (average over three surveys) and 13.6 per cent (average over two surveys) respectively. Even more modest levels of support obtained in English Canada on questions of Ottawa's attention to Quebec (average of 8.7 per cent over three surveys believed too little attention was paid), Quebec independence (average of 26.5 per cent were favourable over three waves) and,

TABLE 7.3   ATTITUDINAL DIFFERENCES BY LANGUAGE AND REGION, 1979[a]

	PAN-CANADIAN NATIONALISM SCALE			QUEBEC NATIONALISM SCALE			
	MEAN	STANDARD DEVIATION	CV	MEAN	STANDARD DEVIATION	CV	(N)
Francophones in Quebec	8.29	1.45	.17	8.89	1.26	.11	(654)
Anglophones outside Quebec	8.51	1.46	.17	6.47	1.26	.19	(1 712)
Anglophones in B.C.	8.71	1.46	.17	6.49	1.27	.19	(304)
Anglophones in Prairies	8.72	1.42	.16	6.56	1.22	.18	(285)
Anglophones in Ontario	8.39	1.49	.18	6.39	1.28	.20	(877)
Anglophones in Atlantic provinces	8.47	1.35	.16	6.58	1.25	.19	(246)

[a]For information on scale construction, see Appendix to this chapter (p. 178). Results of difference of means tests are reported in text. CV, the coefficient variation, compares the variation in distributions with different means; the smaller the coefficient, the less variation relative to the mean.

Source: Social Change in Canada survey, 1979.

finally, special constitutional powers (4.2 per cent approved in 1981).

The extent to which members of the two cultural groups differed in their attitudes towards Quebec nationalism is reflected even more clearly in Table 7.3. Survey data from 1979, the year before the Quebec referendum, show that mean scores on a four-item additive scale of Quebec nationalism were 8.89 for Quebec Francophones as compared with 6.47 among non-Quebec Anglophones (p<. 001). Regional differences within English Canada were more modest; the highest mean score on Quebec nationalism obtained among Anglophones in the Atlantic region and the lowest among Anglophones in Ontario (6.58 versus 6.39; p<. 05).[57]

Aggregate differences in levels of pan-Canadian nationalism are also reported in Table 7.3. They show that mean scores for Francophone Quebeckers and Anglophone non-Quebeckers on a five-item additive scale were 8.29 and 8.51 respectively, a difference that is less in terms of magnitude than comparable scores for Quebec nationalism, but statistically significant nevertheless (p<. 01). In regional terms, Anglophones in the Prairies had the highest mean level of pan-Canadian nationalism and, once again, Anglophones in Ontario had the lowest (8.72 versus 8.39; p<. 001). This last finding, it should be noted, suggests that English Canadian nationalism extends well beyond Ontario—the 'have' province generally regarded as its core—and that support for its priorities may in some cases be stronger in other regions of English Canada.

Did nationalists in Quebec and English Canada hold distinctive views of the other nationalism and, more specifically, did Quebec nationalists tend towards continentalist and pan-Canadian nationalists towards centralist views? Using data from the 1979 Social Change in Canada survey, Quebec nationalists were defined as Francophone respondents residing in Quebec who favoured Quebec independence and who believed that the federal government paid too little attention to Quebec (N=195), while pan-Canadian nationalists were defined as Anglophone respondents residing outside Quebec who believed that the results of foreign investment were mostly bad and that the government should take over foreign firms operating in Canada (N=184).[58]

On individual items measuring support for pan-Canadian nationalism, Quebec nationalists in 1979 were substantially more favourable than a collision thesis would predict. Comparison of the results in Tables 7.1 and 7.4 shows that support for three proposals—that new foreign enterprises have a majority of their shares owned by Canadians, that foreign companies presently operating in Canada sell a majority of their shares to Canadians, and that the government take over foreign firms operating in Canada—was considerably higher among Quebec nationalists than among members of the general public in either Quebec or English Canada. On the third item, for example, 34.8 per cent of Anglophones outside Quebec and 46.9 per cent of Francophones in Quebec endorsed state takeovers, as compared with 66.3 per cent of Quebec nationalists. The only item on which the latter appeared less nationalist in pan-Canadian terms concerned the effects of foreign investment; in this case, 9.1 per cent of Quebec nationalists and 17.5 per cent of the Anglophone public believed the results were mostly negative.

On individual measures of Quebec nationalism (Table 7.5), pan-Canadian nationalists were also more sympathetic than expected, although in no case did their beliefs approximate those of the Francophone public. On the question of support for Quebec independence, for example, 32.4 per cent of English Canadian nationalists expressed approval as compared with 40.8 per cent of Quebec and 22.4 per cent of Anglophone non-Quebec respondents. Other survey items concerning Ottawa's attention to Quebec and provincial powers in the future also show the overall responses of pan-Canadian nationalists to lie between those of the Francophone and Anglophone publics. On a fourth item involving concessions by the federal government to prevent Quebec from separating, English Canadian nationalists were slightly less favourable than members of the Anglophone public (10.5 vs. 11.8 per cent).

Summary measures of these attitudes towards the 'other' nationalism are of-

TABLE 7.4   QUEBEC NATIONALIST ATTITUDES TOWARDS PAN-CANADIAN
NATIONALISM, 1979

ITEM	% SUPPORT	(N)
Require new foreign firms to have majority shares owned by Canadians	91.4	(186)
Enough US capital now invested in Canada	84.5	(187)
Require foreign firms to sell majority of shares to Canadians	82.3	(181)
Government should take over firms operating in Canada	66.3	(172)
Effects of foreign investment in Canada are mostly bad	9.1	(186)

Source: Social Change in Canada survey, 1979.

fered in Table 7.6. Comparison of the mean scores of Quebec nationalists on the pan-Canadian nationalism scale and of pan-Canadian nationalists on the Quebec nationalism scale indicates that both groups were relatively tolerant of and, in the former case, apparently sympathetic towards these aspects of the other's nationalism. The mean score of English Canadian nationalists on the Quebec nationalism measure was 6.60, slightly greater than that of the Anglophone non-Quebec public (6.47; see Table 7.3) but far less than the mean for Francophone Quebeckers (8.89, p<. 001). In the case of scores on the pan-Canadian scale, Table 7.6 demonstrates that the average for Quebec nationalists was 8.97—a level significantly greater than that of both Francophones and Anglophone non-Quebeckers in general (p<. 001).

In short, mean figures presented in Table 7.6 offer little support for the argument that on the mass level, attitudes towards pan-Canadian and Quebec nationalisms were on a collision course in the period of the Quebec referendum. Rather, the data suggest that English Canadian nationalists were more supportive of some key priorities of their Quebec counterparts than were members of the Anglophone public in general, just as Quebec nationalists were more approving of investment nationalist positions than were members of the general Francophone public. In fact, comparison of the mean figures in Tables 7.3 and 7.6 indicates that *Quebec nationalists were more favourably disposed towards these pan-Canadian nationalist priorities than were members of the Anglophone public*. If nothing else, this last finding calls into question two important aspects of the collision thesis regarding the 'natural' or 'home' constituency of pan-Canadian nationalism, and the deep-seated continentalism of Quebec nationalists.[59]

TABLE 7.5   PAN-CANADIAN NATIONALIST ATTITUDES TOWARDS QUEBEC
NATIONALISM, 1979

ITEM	% SUPPORT	(N)
Provincial goverments should have more power in the future	41.9	(167)
Favour Quebec independence	32.4	(170)
Ottawa pays too little attention to Quebec	12.7	(165)
Support major concessions by Ottawa to prevent Quebec separation	10.5	(171)

Source: Social Change in Canada survey, 1979.

After Meech Lake

If survey results from the 1977-81 period indicate possibilities for accommodation in mass-level public opinion, what can be said about the situation ten years later? The October 1990 CBC/*Globe and Mail* poll provides one of the only sources of evidence on this subject, since it addressed perceptions of free trade as well as questions of constitutional politics in the aftermath of the Meech Lake Accord. Analysis of these survey data suggest that the less accommodative and more conflictual tenor of nationalist writings in this same period also characterized some public attitudes.

As reported in Table 7.7, Francophone Quebec respondents in the fall of 1990 were far more likely than either English Canadian nationalists or members of the Anglophone public to believe that Quebec should move towards separation. Approximately 56 per cent of Francophones surveyed endorsed the idea that Quebec should move towards separation but retain some links with Canada, as compared with approximately 11 per cent of both the Anglophone public and Anglo-Canadian nationalists.[60] By way of contrast, cross-cultural differences in response to the option of complete separation were relatively slight.

It is on questions of continental free trade that Quebec nationalists in the 1990 poll reflect an intriguing congruence with Anglo-Canadian nationalist positions. As summarized in Table 7.7, Quebec nationalists were substantially more likely than members of the Quebec Francophone public to believe that free trade had hurt the Canadian economy (51.6 versus 38.8 per cent), and were only slightly less likely to hold this view than were members of the English Canadian public (55.9 per cent). Even more interesting, on the question of Canada's decision to negotiate a trilateral free trade agreement involving Canada, the US and Mexico, Quebec nationalists were *more* likely to disapprove than were members of the Anglophone public (62.3 versus 59.6 per cent).

TABLE 7.6   PAN-CANADIAN AND QUEBEC NATIONALISTS VIEW THE 'OTHER'
            NATIONALISM, 1979[a]

	PAN-CANADIAN NATIONALISM SCALE			QUEBEC NATIONALISM SCALE			
	MEAN	STANDARD DEVIATION	CV	MEAN	STANDARD DEVIATION	CV	(N)
Pan-Canadian nationalists				6.60	1.30	0.20	(144)
Quebec nationalists	8.97	1.15	0.13				(157)

[a]For information on scale construction, see Appendix to this chapter (p. 178).

Source: Social Change in Canada survey, 1979.

In short, the differences in the constitutional perceptions of Anglophone and Francophone Canadians in the fall of 1990 appeared large, suggesting quite disparate responses to the failure of the Meech Lake Accord. At the same time, however, the prospect that after Meech Lake Quebec nationalists would have little sympathy for the arguments of Anglo-Canadian nationalism is *not* confirmed by this analysis. In fact, on one item, Quebec nationalists were slightly more likely to express a position consistent with Anglo-Canadian nationalist ideas than were members of the Anglophone public.

Conclusions

In light of this analysis, can it be safely assumed that Quebec nationalism is inherently continentalist and that its proponents share little in common with pan-Canadian nationalists? Or that English Canadian nationalists tend towards centralism and intolerance of Quebec nationalist aspirations? These propositions, which follow from the collision thesis, are confirmed more by nationalist writings from the period following 1988 than they are by other kinds of evidence. In fact, the extent to which Quebec nationalists at the mass level in both the late 1970s and the early 1990s were favourably inclined towards some positions consistent with English Canadian nationalism is notable. This pattern tends to support alternative arguments regarding multiple loyalties within Canadian public opinion; in broader comparative terms, it illustrates one apparent case of mass-level accommodation within a federal society.

This alternative view offers some possibilities for re-interpreting French/English relations in the period of the Quebec referendum, and at the same time sheds light on more contemporary developments. If Canada is the 'fragile federation'[61] of textbook lore, then mass-level data from 1977-81 point towards

TABLE 7.7   ATTITUDES TOWARDS FREE TRADE AND QUEBEC'S FUTURE IN
            CANADA, 1990[a]

ITEM	GROUP	%	(N)
Bilateral free trade has hurt Canadian economy	Anglophone non-Quebec	55.9	(1 477)
	Francophone Quebec	38.8	(369)
	Quebec nationalists	51.6	(62)
Disagree with Canada's decision to negotiate trilateral free trade	Anglophone non-Quebec	59.6	(1 410)
	Francophone Quebec	45.4	(377)
	Quebec nationalists	62.3	(53)
Quebec should become totally separate from Canada	Anglophone non-Quebec	12.1	(1 582)
	Francophone Quebec	15.2	(440)
	English Canadian nationalists	13.6	(566)
Quebec should move towards separation but retain some links to Canada	Anglophone non-Quebec	11.5	(1 582)
	Francophone Quebec	56.6	(440)
	English Canadian nationalists	11.3	(566)

[a]For information on coding the nationalist categories, see note 60.

Source: October 1990 CBC / Globe and Mail poll.

a degree of communality across the cultural solitudes that is often overlooked in the literatures on federalism and public opinion. In an essay published in 1971, John Meisel wrote of the need for thinking people on both sides of the 'present options' debate to appreciate their common concerns, to focus upon the views they shared rather than those over which they differed.[62] Perhaps, in the strained period surrounding the Quebec referendum, nationalists at the mass level were prepared to tolerate—and, in survey terms, to endorse to a degree—some goals of the 'other' nationalism. While the results might have differed had the analysis focussed on more narrow and obvious points of conflict between the two nationalisms, such as language policy or the treatment of English Canadian investment in Quebec, the findings reported here do suggest some mass-level accommodation along the lines endorsed by Meisel.

It is worth recalling, however, that while the immediate crisis of the Canadian state was averted in the early 1980s, the dualist and continental tensions did not disappear. In particular, nationalist writings since the free trade debate indicate that the tolerance, even sympathy, that may have linked some proponents of Canada's two nationalisms during the 1970s and early 1980s was later replaced by a sense of impatience, distrust and even betrayal. How and if proponents of the two nationalisms can resolve their disparate claims on federal/provincial and national/continental relations remains to be seen.

Notes

[1]Philip Resnick, *Letters to a Québécois Friend*, with a reply by Daniel Latouche (Montreal: McGill-Queen's University Press, 1990), 66.

[2]Carl Berger, *The Sense of Power: Studies in the Ideas of Canadian Imperialism, 1867-1914* (Toronto: University of Toronto Press, 1970), 134.

[3]Ibid., chap. 5.

[4]Earlier in this century, however, *Le Devoir* founder Henri Bourassa articulated a version of pan-Canadianism that argued for Anglo-French unity and resistance to Americanization. See Bourassa's writings in H.D. Forbes (ed.), *Canadian Political Thought* (Toronto: Oxford University Press, 1985), 177-93.

[5]Michel Brunet, 'Continentalism and Quebec Nationalism: A Double Challenge to Canada', *Queen's Quarterly* 76 (1969), 516. This tension is framed in more scholarly terms in Michael D. Ornstein, H. Michael Stevenson and A. Paul M. Williams, 'Public Opinion and the Canadian Political Crisis', *Canadian Review of Sociology and Anthropology* 15 (1978): 'A second perspective from which to view the response of English Canadians to the nationalist movement in Quebec is to consider the conflict between English and French Canadians as a conflict between competing nationalisms, and to argue that English Canadians who are more nationalistic in their attitude to Canada will take a less conciliatory view of the "national aspirations" of Quebecers' (181).

[6]Resnick, *Letters to a Québécois Friend*, 66.

[7]Michael Stein, 'Federal Political Systems and Federal Societies', in J. Peter Meekison (ed.), *Canadian Federalism: Myth or Reality* (Toronto: Methuen, 1968), 42. Stein drew on the theoretical work of William H. Riker, *Federalism: Origin, Operation, Significance* (Boston: Little Brown, 1964).

[8]Stein, 'Federal Political Systems and Federal Societies', 41.

[9]R.A. Young, Philippe Faucher and André Blais, 'The Concept of Province-Building: A Critique', *Canadian Journal of Political Science* 17 (1984), 808.

[10]Ibid., 818.

[11]See David J. Elkins and Richard Simeon, *Small Worlds: Provinces and Parties in Canadian Political Life* (Toronto: Methuen, 1980); Mildred Schwartz, *Public Opinion and Canadian Identity* (Berkeley: University of California Press, 1967); Schwartz, *Politics and Territory: The Sociology of Regional Persistence in Canada* (Montreal: McGill-Queen's University Press, 1974); Richard Johnston, *Public Opinion and Public Policy in Canada*, Royal Commission Research Studies, vol. 35 (Toronto: University of Toronto Press for Supply and Services Canada, 1986); and Richard Johnston and André Blais, 'Meech Lake and Mass Politics: The "Distinct Society" Clause', *Canadian Public Policy* 14 (1988), S25-S42.

[12]Johnston, *Public Opinion and Public Policy in Canada*, 226. This same view is echoed in Johnston and Blais, 'Meech Lake and Mass Politics'; while suggesting that a potential for French-English conflict exists 'where common sense dictates it should be: over language policy', they maintain that important multiple identities have developed such that 'among Quebec Francophones, identification with the Quebec community and/or government does not weaken identification with the Canadian community and/or government' (S39, S25).

[13]Each of the Social Change in Canada surveys sampled approximately 3,000 persons. The project was directed by Tom Atkinson, Bernard Blishen, Michael D. Ornstein and H. Michael Stevenson of the Institute for Social Research at York University. These data were made available by the ISR at York; neither the original investigators nor the ISR bears responsibility for the analyses or interpretations presented here. The October 1990 CBC/*Globe and Mail* poll, which sampled approximately 2,260 persons, was available to the author as a member of the poll advisory board. Neither the CBC nor *Globe and Mail* bears responsibility for the analyses or interpretations presented here. For technical details, see 'How the Poll was Designed', *Globe and Mail* (29 Oct. 1990), A7.

[14]André Laurendeau, 'Is There a Crisis of Nationalism?' in Ramsay Cook (ed.), *French-Canadian Nationalism: An Anthology* (Toronto: Macmillan, 1969), 257.

[15]Ramsay Cook, *The Maple Leaf Forever: Essays on Nationalism and Politics in Canada* (Toronto: Macmillan, 1977), 125. The variety of ideas and ideologies within English-Canadian nationalism (including Tory, liberal and socialist variants) is, according to some observers, reflective of its well-defined rather than indefinite character. See Daniel Latouche, *Canada and Quebec, Past and Future: An Essay*, Royal Commission Research Studies, vol. 70 (Toronto: University of Toronto Press for Supply and Services Canada, 1986), 81.

[16]Kim Richard Nossal, 'Economic Nationalism and Continental Integration: Assumptions, Arguments and Advocacies', in Denis Stairs and Gilbert R. Winham (eds.), *The Politics of Canada's Economic Relationship with the United States*, Royal Commission Research Studies, vol. 29 (Toronto: University of Toronto Press for Supply and Services Canada), 57.

[17]See Robert Gilpin, 'American Direct Investment and Canada's Two Nationalisms', in Richard A. Preston (ed.), *The Influence of the United States on Canadian Development* (Durham, NC: Duke University Press, 1972), 124-43; Donald V. Smiley, 'Canada and the Quest for a National Policy', *Canadian Journal of Political Science* 8 (1975), 40-62; and Donald V. Smiley, 'Reflections on Cultural Nationhood and Political Community in Canada', in R. Kenneth Carty and W. Peter Ward (eds), *Entering the Eighties: Canada in Crisis* (Toronto: Oxford University Press, 1980), 20-43.

[18]See Léon Dion, *Nationalismes et politiques au Québec* (Montreal: Hurtubise HMH, 1975); Dion, *A la recherche du Québec*, vol. 1 of *Québec, 1945-2000* (Quebec City: Presses de l'Université Laval, 1987); and François-Pierre Gingras and Neil Nevitte, 'The Evolution of Quebec Nationalism', in Alain G. Gagnon (ed.), *Quebec: State and Society* (Toronto: Methuen, 1984), 2-14.

[19]It should be noted that examining the political and jurisdictional dimension of Quebec nationalism neglects one aspect of this phenomenon over which advocates of the two nationalisms would likely clash: namely, language rights. For a discussion of tension over language rights, see Johnston and Blais, 'Meech Lake and Mass Politics'.

[20]Gilpin, 'American Direct Investment and Canada's Two Nationalisms'. In empirical terms, this opposition to English-Canadian investment in Quebec complicates the measurement of 'foreign investment' in Canadian surveys. Unfortunately, existing studies do not distinguish between attitudes towards non-Canadian versus English Canadian sources of investment among Francophone Quebec respondents.

[21]See René Lévesque, 'Quebec Independence', in Elliot J. Feldman and Neil Nevitte (eds.), *The Future of North America* (Cambridge: Harvard University Center for International Affairs, 1979), 61-70; as well as Robert Bourassa's comments at the same seminar ('Quebec's Economic Future in Confederation', in ibid., 291-300). Strong support for closer ties with the United States, including Canada-US free trade, was also voiced by PQ leader Jacques Parizeau. For an historical perspective on Quebec-US relations, see Jean-Louis Roy, 'The French Fact in North America: Quebec-United States Relations', *International Journal* 31 (1976), 470-87.

[22]'The Waffle Manifesto', in Forbes (ed.), *Canadian Political Thought*, 404.

[23]John Bullen, 'The Ontario Waffle and the Struggle for an Independent Socialist Canada: Conflict within the NDP', *Canadian Historical Review* 64 (1983), 202.

[24]See ibid., 204.

[25]Ibid., 202-5.

[26]*Le Devoir* published the resolution on 19 Jan. 1971; see ibid., 202.

[27]Interview with Peter C. Newman, 7 Oct. 1989.

[28]Claude Ryan, 'The Gray Report and Quebec', in Abraham Rotstein and Gary Lax (eds), *Independence: The Canadian Challenge* (Toronto: Committee for an Independent Canada, 1972), 172.

[29]Interview with Peter C. Newman.

[30]Committee for a New Constitution, 'Canada and Quebec: A Proposal for a New Constitution', *Canadian Forum* (June-July 1977), 4. The statement was initially issued in April 1977.

[31]Ibid., 5.

[32]Susan Crean and Marcel Rioux, *Two Nations: An Essay on the Culture and Politics of Canada and Quebec in a World of American Pre-eminence* (Toronto: Lorimer, 1983); and Marcel Rioux and Susan Crean, *Deux pays pour vivre: un plaidoyer* (Montreal: Éditions Albert St-Martin, 1980).

[33]Crean and Rioux, *Two Nations*, 2, 159.

[34]Committee for a New Constitution, 'Canada and Quebec', 4.

[35]'A Declaration of Quebec's Right to Self-Determination', *Canadian Forum* (February 1980), 6. As Kenneth McRoberts observed at the time, however, 'sovereignty-association is a far cry from self-determination'. See McRoberts, 'English Canada and the Quebec Nation', *Canadian Forum* (February 1980), 13.

[36]Interview with Peter C. Newman.

[37]Interview with Rick Salutin, 22 Aug. 1990.

[38]Interview with Abraham Rotstein, 28 June 1989.

[39]A somewhat different explanation was offered in a confidential interview by one prominent left nationalist in English Canada: 'Quebec nationalism has always looked at English Canada as a pathetic entity and for entirely understandable reasons. They've seen us as a boring, tasteless, esthetically unpleasing society, but they're about 30 to 40 years out of date . . . As well, if you're a colony of a colony, that's pretty upsetting. English Canada has been one of the world's most passive societies. To discover that your political life is largely shaped by such an entity is cause for upset.'

[40]Daniel Latouche, 'Betrayal and Indignation on the Canadian Trail: A Reply from Quebec', in Resnick, *Letters to a Québécois Friend*, 118.

[41]Latouche, *Canada and Quebec*, 73, 74.

[42]Ibid., 91.

[43]Ibid., 89.

[44]Ibid., 88.

[45]Ibid., 73.

[46]See Daniel Drache and Mel Watkins, 'Meech Lake: A Wholly Undemocratic Process', *Globe and Mail* (6 June 1990), A7.

[47]Latouche, 'Betrayal and Indignation on the Canadian Trail', 107.

[48]Confidential interview.

[49]See Resnick, *Letters to a Québécois Friend*; Drache and Watkins, 'Meech Lake'; Philip Resnick, 'Free Trade, Meech Lake and the Two Nationalisms', *Queen's Quarterly* 97 (1990), 355-60; and Reg Whitaker, 'No Laments for the Nation: Free Trade and the Election of 1988', *Canadian Forum* (March 1989), 9-13.

[50]See Latouche, 'Betrayal and Indignation on the Canadian Trail'; and Daniel Latouche, 'Le petit, le gros et le moyen: l'Accord de libre-échange en perspective', in Marc Gold and David Leyton-Brown (eds), *Trade-offs on Free Trade: The Canada-U.S. Free Trade Agreement* (Toronto: Carswell, 1988), 148-59.

[51]Latouche, 'Betrayal and Indignation on the Canadian Trail', 95.

[52]Ibid., 112; and Latouche, 'Le petit, le gros et le moyen'.

[53]Ibid.

[54]Interviews with Gerald Caplan, 25 May 1990; Stephen Clarkson, 8 Aug. 1990; and Kenneth McRoberts, 25 Sept. 1990.

[55]Interviews with James Laxer, 28 Sept. 1990; Stephen Clarkson, 8 Aug. 1990; and Susan Crean, 23 May 1990.

[56]Resnick, *Letters to a Québécois Friend*, 3.

[57]This regional pattern differs from earlier findings reported in Frederick J. Fletcher, 'Public Attitudes and Alternative Futures', in Richard Simeon (ed.), *Must Canada Fail?* (Montreal: McGill-Queen's University Press, 1977), 29-32, to the effect that Anglophones living in the western and Atlantic

provinces tended to oppose the priorities of Quebec nationalism, while those in Ontario were more tolerant. Data indicating only limited regional variation within English Canada in attitudes toward Quebec nationalism are presented in Ornstein, Stevenson and Williams, 'Public Opinion and the Canadian Political Crisis'.

[58]While these criteria produced fewer than 200 nationalist respondents in each of the Anglophone non-Quebec and Francophone Quebec subsamples, they provide a more meaningful operationalization of nationalism in each culture than would have been offered by looser criteria and hence larger Ns. For a discussion of trade-offs between substantive meaning and sample size, see Mary G. Kweit and Robert W. Kweit, *Concepts and Methods for Political Analysis* (Englewood Cliffs, NJ: Prentice-Hall, 1981).

[59]This finding corresponds with those of Peyton V. Lyon and David Leyton-Brown, who argue that Francophone elite attitudes were fairly nationalist in a pan-Canadian sense during the mid-1970s and thus differed from the relatively continentalist positions of the Francophone mass public in this period. See Lyon and Leyton-Brown, 'Image and Policy Preference: Canadian Elite Views on Relations with the United States', *International Journal* 32 (1977), 640-71.

It should also be noted that Quebec respondents have been quite supportive of the cultural dimension of pan-Canadian nationalism. In 1977, for example, 72% of both Francophone Quebec and Anglophone non-Quebec respondents in the Social Change in Canada mass survey agreed that radio and television stations should be required to carry a certain amount of Canadian programming. Moreover, Gallup Poll results show Quebec respondents to be as concerned about American influence on the Canadian way of life as non-Quebec respondents, if not more (see Gallup Report, 11 Nov. 1985).

[60]In the October 1990 survey, Quebec nationalists were defined as Francophone Quebec respondents who believed that Quebec should become totally separate from Canada (N=67). English Canadian nationalists were defined as Anglophones outside Quebec who believed that Canada-US free trade had hurt the Canadian economy and who disagreed with Canada's decision to negotiate trilateral free trade (N=582).

[61]See Lorna R. Marsden and E.B. Harvey, *Fragile Federation: Social Change in Canada* (Toronto: McGraw-Hill Ryerson, 1979).

[62]See John Meisel, '"Cancel Out and Pass On": A View of Canada's Present Options', in R.M. Burns (ed.), *One Country or Two?* (Montreal: McGill-Queen's University Press, 1971), 160-7; as well as John Meisel, 'J'ai le goût du Québec but I like Canada: Reflections of an Ambivalent Man', in Simeon (ed.), *Must Canada Fail?*, 291-307; and Abraham Rotstein, 'Is There an English-Canadian Nationalism?' *Journal of Canadian Studies* 13 (1978), 109-18.

Appendix: Nationalism Scales

Two multiple-item scales were constructed using the 1979 Social Change in Canada data. The interview items and coding schemes are summarized below. Each item included in the scales satisfied not only a face relevance to the concepts of pan-Canadian and Quebec nationalism, but also a factor analysis (not reported here) which indicated their loadings on two independent dimensions of nationalist opinion.

Pan-Canadian Nationalism

The scale was computed by summing scores for the following five items, with missing data excluded from the computation:

1. There has been a lot of debate about foreign ownership in the Canadian economy in the past few years. Some people say it has helped our economy grow, but others disagree. What do you think has been the result of this foreign investment in Canada? Do you think it has had: mostly/some good effects (1); about equally good and bad effects (2); some/mostly bad effects on the country (3)?

2. Do you think there is enough US capital in Canada now (2) or would you like to see more US capital invested in this country (1)?

3. Some people think there is too much foreign investment in Canada and they have proposed a number of ways to decrease it. Could you tell me if you approve (2) or disapprove (1) of each of these proposals to lower foreign ownership . . . What about the government taking over foreign-owned companies now in Canada and running them itself?

4. Item used the same introduction as measure 3, followed by: What about making foreign companies now in Canada sell a majority of their shares to Canadians?

5. Item used the same introduction as measure 3, followed by: What about requiring foreign companies that want to start a new business in Canada to have a majority of their shares owned by Canadians?

Quebec Nationalism

The scale was computed by summing scores for the following four items, with missing data excluded from the computation:

1. What about Quebec, do you think the federal government has given Quebec too much attention (1), about the right amount of attention (2), or too little attention (3) in recent years?

2. In the future should the federal government have more power (1), things stay as they are (2), or the provincial governments have more power (3)?

3. What is your opinion about Quebec's separating from Canada and becoming independent? Are you opposed/qualified opposed (1) or in favour/qualified in favour (2)?

4. Do you think that the government of Canada should not make any concessions to prevent Quebec separation (1), make only minor concessions (2), or make major concessions to Quebec if these will prevent separation (3)?

8 | Epilogue: Nationalist Futures

It is not too late for our country. But Canadians will have to have extraordinary courage to alter what seems to be our fate. There are alternatives that will allow Canada to regain control of its destiny and recapture the values that form the base of its identity and culture. For it is in these values alone that we will find the national will to survive.[1]

The preceding chapters have tried to assess the ideas and influence of English Canadian nationalism and its complex relations with Quebec nationalism. The question remains: what of the future?

On the level of ideas, the future of nationalisms generally and of Anglo-Canadian nationalism in particular is hardly dim. Bombarded by a wide array of global influences that tend to homogenize and weaken rather than to differentiate and empower cultures—that work to erode the distinctions that make individuals feel 'part of' some larger community—people in the late twentieth century seem to be seeking out rather than rejecting collective identity. As Anthony Birch observes in his study *Nationalism and National Integration*, 'there is no evidence at all of public loyalties being transferred from national governments to supranational organizations.'[2] Nationalism continues to be a powerful force, according to Birch, because 'it has brought people the satisfaction of being governed by their own political leaders instead of by foreigners [and] has given people a secure sense of identity, status and (usually) pride.'[3]

Reaching for and affirming in-group identity have long been objectives of English Canadian nationalism. Nearly a century ago, problems of foreign influence and especially US domination of Canadian cultural life were identified by the Canada Firsters. The sense of cultural threat has hardly receded in recent years, particularly with the growth of cable, video, satellite and other technologies that make domestic control ever more difficult, and that render the goal of Canadian cultural autonomy ever more elusive. In fact, with the perception that culture in a global sense has become more Americanized, more standardized, and less open to contributions that are not American in origin and sensibility has come a view that Canada's historic predicament is analogous to that of the rest of the contemporary world.[4] Given this diagnosis of uniformity and rampant spillover, the appeal of a counter-identity, of a cultural answer to the dominant out-group, is not difficult to understand.

Viewing cultural questions in this light makes it interesting to examine the decisions of the federal Conservatives to substantially cut the budgets of the CBC and other cultural institutions.[5] How, one might ask, could any government disregard the obvious appeal of nationalist cultural policy? Why would an already unpopular federal regime risk tampering with an area as sensitive as cultural policy?[6]

This willingness to reduce spending in the cultural sector follows in part from the free trade debate. As argued in Chapter 5, this issue polarized proponents and opponents; many members of the Canadian cultural community were prominent among the latter. As the government sponsors of a free trade policy, the Conservatives tended after 1988 to reward their allies and, as demonstrated in the discussion of the National Action Committee on the Status of Women in Chapter 6, to punish their adversaries. The pattern of CBC cut-backs, then, can be in part explained in light of an us/them perspective among the governing federal elite: if the primary resistance to cultural cut-backs lies among a constituency already hostile to the Conservatives, there is little to be lost in pursuing such a policy. Moreover, if the CBC and other public-sector cultural vehicles are increasingly viewed as central Canadian, elitist institutions, then the political threat implied by cut-backs seems even smaller.

More generally, however, the fate of cultural policy in the early 1990s is tied to the dynamics of ideological polarization in Canada. Unlike the so-called brokerage era of 'classless' politics that prevailed prior to free trade, post-1988 developments read far more like an East-West showdown at the height of the Cold War. Dichotomous perceptions of good and evil, right and wrong, characterize both sides in debates over market-led versus state-led, *laissez-faire* versus interventionist, continentalist versus nationalist, and business interests versus societal alternatives. The gaps between the two sides in these debates often seem unbridgeable, as in any highly polarized situation. Moreover, those who hold the reins of power in a majority government are far more willing to provoke and even incense their opponents under polarized conditions than they would be under consensual, brokerage ones. Clearly, cultural nationalist ideas are embedded in a larger world view which is generally rejected by the federal Tories, and which directly contradicts the terms of the world view that is dominant in the governing party.

What about the ideas of economic nationalism, especially their investment and trade variants in English Canada? From a comparative perspective, Anglo-Canadian nationalists' demands for controls on foreign investment appear less compelling in the early 1990s than do their arguments for cultural independence. This may be attributable in part to a weakening of US investor interest. In fact, some studies (*not* by nationalists) cite declining foreign control in the natural resource and other non-financial sectors as evidence that, in the words of Alan Rugman, 'nearly 80 percent of Canada's industry is *not* owned by Americans'.[7] Growing Canadian investment in the US and elsewhere has also been cited as evidence that foreign investment is no longer, if it ever was, an appropriate focus of concern for Canadians.[8] Even on the political left, one hears increasingly strong arguments to the effect that what matters most to Canadians is the performance, not the national origin, of foreign firms.[9]

By themselves, contemporary questions about foreign investment seem less visceral, less politically charged, than questions about cultural identity. Perhaps this is because debates over investment tend to deteriorate into numbers games, whereas questions of media spillover and what it means to be Canadian remain at a more comprehensible level of discussion. Numbers games in the investment field seem many steps removed from identity questions; they also tend to favour the 'authoritative' sources found among mainstream economists who, for the most part, are not sympathetic towards nationalist positions.[10] Furthermore, concern about foreign investment is generally connected with larger economic cycles, and periods of economic recession are generally not promising times for nationalist arguments.[11]

This is not to suggest that foreign investment will fall off the nationalist agenda in the near future. Rather, it is likely that investment debates will remain sector-ally focussed, zeroing in on specific questions of Canadian ownership in such areas as manufacturing, high technology and natural resources. The key sectors approach to foreign investment is not new; in fact, it has been a feature of nationalist thinking in Canada since at least as far back as the 1960s Mercantile Bank affair.[12]

What is most interesting and innovative about contemporary foreign invest-ment ideas and, to a more limited extent, cultural arguments, is their integration within a larger free trade perspective. The critique of foreign investment has been folded into a larger critique of continentalist trade policy, with the implicit and sometimes explicit nationalist argument being that Canada-US free trade is far more than simply a trade deal. As a vehicle that exposes Canadian cultural policy to the possibility of open-ended commercial retaliation (under section 2005.2 of the 1988 bilateral agreement) and that severely limits federal action in the area of foreign investment, free trade is interpreted by nationalists as a fundamental threat to all three of its major streams.[13]

Yet how effectively can the specific ideas of trade and investment nationalism be articulated in the late twentieth century? If cultural arguments appeal very directly to people's sense that their communities and identities are being eroded in the face of global influences, can the same be said for economic arguments?

The answer to this second question is 'probably not'. Nationalist claims that foreign investment and open bilateral trade distort economic development and restrict Canadian autonomy are qualitatively different from claims in the cultural area, where the human impact seems stronger. Nationalists do appear to be winning the numbers game in the trade field, where the job losses attributable to free trade have been estimated in the tens of thousands by the Canadian

Labour Congress.[14] Yet this is by most accounts a hollow and depressing victory; nationalists could hardly have hoped to underestimate the damage done to Canada by free trade and economic recession.

Only when these economic perspectives are merged with cultural ones, and with the powerful argument that continentalism threatens to harmonize Canadian social policies with those of the US, do debates about trade and investment assume the emotive punch, the personal immediacy, that we associate with nationalism. Perhaps this is because English Canadian nationalism, like most nationalisms, is at its core a series of arguments about cultural distinctiveness: about the distinctiveness of Canada's harsh spatial landscape, parliamentary traditions and commitment to a developed social welfare system—as contrasted with the less rugged territory and 'minimal state' republicanism of the US.

Finally, economic nationalist arguments against bilateral and trilateral free trade have usually been predicated on an assumption that multilateral strategies are preferable, and that the GATT talks provide a better alternative for Canada. The apparent collapse of the GATT round in the fall of 1990 undermines this alternative, shedding doubt not only on the viability of global trade strategies but also on the ability of nationalists and their allies to develop a coherent economic alternative to continental free trade.

Is pan-Canadianism in the 1990s the nationalism we used to know? Modern economic nationalist ideas in English Canada tend to be ideologically coloured by the left-of-centre interventionism that most of their proponents endorse. This resistance to the neo-classical doctrine of an unfettered marketplace imparts a curious global or at least transnational dimension to contemporary nationalism. That is, English Canadian economic nationalism in the late 1980s and following has attached itself to a broader critique of neo-conservative policy, whether in Canada or elsewhere. As suggested by their description of the 1988 Free Trade Agreement as 'the Reagan-Mulroney deal', nationalists linked opposition to free trade with a rejection of what John Warnock termed 'the new right agenda', the market-driven ethos that has characterized the recent governments of both the US and Canada.[15]

With the emergence of a trilateral free trade initiative involving Canada, the US and Mexico, this transnational dimension could become even more significant. Canadian nationalists have sought to build on the shared concerns of trade union, environmental, agricultural and other interests in Mexico and the US, working towards a coalition that links opponents in all three countries. Traditional in-group/out-group categories in the English Canadian world view have thus been relaxed to some extent: since the late 1980s, the out-group has increasingly been defined as neo-conservative continentalists in Canada and their allies elsewhere, and the in-group as progressive societal interests in Canada and elsewhere—including, most notably, the United States.

English Canadian nationalism, as an increasingly transnational opposition to new right policies, has thus come full circle. Like its cultural and investment streams during the inter-war period and following, organized nationalism in the late twentieth century has returned to older international concerns with social progress, human equality and the obligations of the state to foster both objectives.

But can nationalists in Canada foster a cohesive in-group identity once their critique of out-group influences takes on an international dimension? How likely is the fragile coalition of interests that constitutes pan-Canadianism in the 1990s to thrive in these circumstances?

Liberal and right-of-centre nationalists, particularly those who were attracted to the investment issues of the 1970s and to cultural arguments for much of this century, could fall out of the nationalist fold as it moves in transnational directions. Although these elements, particularly tory nationalists, already constitute a minority within a minority, their presence has provided an important element of diversity within the nationalist coalition. Losing these moderate and conservative parts of the spectrum could make pan-Canadian ideas indistinguishable from left discourse in general.

In short, a revived and newly transnational set of nationalist ideas in English Canada may not triumph. In practical political terms, Anglo-Canadian nationalism faces many difficult challenges, each of which limits its impact in important ways. Some of these limits were noted in earlier chapters, but at this point it is useful to speculate on their future significance.

First, as noted in Chapters 1 and 7, pan-Canadianism has tried to present itself as a counterpoise to the decentralist impulses both of Quebec nationalism and of English Canadian regionalism. Following as it does from a profoundly centralist view of Confederation, Anglo-Canadian nationalism embraces strong federal powers and has little patience with political undertakings that threaten the central government. Prominent nationalists in English Canada have tried to find common ground with Quebec nationalists—particularly in periods when the two interests did not collide directly and when they shared a common left-of-centre ideology. Yet for nationalists in Quebec and provincial rights supporters in English Canada to embrace the pan-Canadian emphasis on federal supremacy is virtually unthinkable—as unlikely as the prospect that English Canadian nationalists would contemplate a diminution of federal sovereignty.

The fundamental support in the Anglo-Canadian world view for a federal bulwark against continental integration is clear and firm. This commitment means that a *rapprochement* with Quebec nationalists on jurisdictional questions is virtually impossible, at least as long as Quebec's demands are negotiated within a symmetric bargaining system that grants parallel concessions to all provincial governments. With bitter divisions between nationalists in the two cultures since the free trade and Meech Lake debates, it is difficult to imagine that much common ground will emerge in the near future. Moreover, the likelihood of bridging the distance between pan-Canadianism and regionalism is even more slight as long as regionalism in western Canada, for example, attaches itself to both right-of-centre *and* decentralist vehicles like the Reform party.

Cynics might say that, given its progressive and centralist world view, the future prospects of modern Anglo-Canadian nationalism are dependent on those of the Ontario left. Yet the outcome of the September 1990 provincial elections suggests that such a linkage is no longer the sure ticket to oblivion that it may once have been. Indeed, the accession to power of an NDP government in Ontario means that critical questions about free trade, foreign investment and cultural identity have a chance of becoming part of the official national agenda, rather than remaining confined to an opposition discourse.

Even within Ontario, though, if we set aside the larger limits imposed by Quebec nationalism and regionalism, pan-Canadianism faces some significant challenges. How effectively does it speak to the concerns of immigrant and visible minority communities, to the fragmented mosaic that constitutes urban English Canada in the 1990s? Can alliances with feminist, environmental, aboriginal and other movements succeed in rejuvenating pan-Canadianism, in attracting a new cohort of youthful activists to its ranks? It would seem that the Pro-Canada Network has served as an effective recruitment tool for organized nationalism in recent years, bringing in far more women and trade unionists, for example, than were prominent previously.[16] Nevertheless, English Canadian nationalism continues to project an overwhelmingly white, European face in 1990.

What would constitute success for English Canadian nationalism? As Robert Fulford has argued, admitting or even hypothesizing that continentalism was no longer a threat could imply failure in the next round.[17] English Canadian nationalists would no longer be able to justify either new or existing policies on communications, trade and foreign investment. Does success, then, amount to eternal vigilance, to an organized commitment to keep US influences at bay?

In recent years, pan-Canadianism has come to mean far more than simply enhancing in-group identity and limiting out-group impact. It was been increasingly tied to the broader political agenda of federal opposition parties—to opposing Via Rail cut-backs, to thwarting the federal Goods and Services Tax, to defending Mohawks on the barricades at Oka. In this polarized political environment, nationalism has taken on a distinctly anti-government, and anti-Conservative government, colouration.

If the federal Conservatives were thrown into opposition, would success be closer at hand? Liberal partisans among the ranks of the Council of Canadians and the Pro-Canada Network (which changed its name in 1991 to the Action Canada Network) will not necessarily wield influence in a new Liberal government. Any future federal regime—Liberal or New Democratic—that understood the political costs of such policies as the National Energy Program would deliberate long and hard before repeating the exercise, even if free trade were *not* an impediment.[18] An NDP federal government would also be constrained by the regional considerations noted earlier and, like a Liberal regime, might hesitate to alienate Quebec nationalist interests in the pursuit of federal jurisdictional primacy.

All told, the real-world prospects of English Canadian nationalism seem far less promising than the future of the ideas by themselves. As argued in Chapters 2 through 5, nationalist ideas can be influential when they command a strong organizational base, when they enjoy support in the federal bureaucracy and, above all, when domestic and international political actors are prepared to endorse these ideas. Yet, even with the support of Canadian media and public opinion and a revived organizational base, nationalists face the reality of a domestic party system that is leveraged by regional and French/English considerations and a US regime that is unlikely to remain passive in the face of nationalist renewal. In the case of the federal bureaucracy, nationalist preferences seem to have been purged from senior levels—a reality that is no small obstacle in itself.

Only time will tell whether the attractiveness of pan-Canadian ideas and the rejuvenation of nationalist organizations can be harnessed to a sympathetic bureaucratic state and to a sympathetic political elite at the federal level—both of which are prepared to act on their affections. What can be said at this point is that the prospects for such a linkage within Canada as it is presently constituted are daunting.

If one were to imagine a reconstituted Canada in which Quebec had either left or obtained associate status, then could English Canadian nationalism contribute meaningfully to this new entity? Would nationalist ideas prevail in a confederation along the lines of the European Community?

Such a scenario is difficult to explore because North America, with or without free trade zones, is not easily comparable to a united Europe. The United States would retain uncontested hegemony on its continent and English Canada's vulnerability on the cultural and economic fronts would persist no matter what course Quebec pursued. Introducing Mexico as a possible ally and counterweight for Canada, with or without Quebec, would not redress the asymmetrical balance of power.

Moreover, within a reconstituted English Canada, the position of Ontario could parallel the continental status of the US. As the dominant Anglo-Canadian province, one that has consistently endorsed jurisdictional centralism, Ontario has been home to many nationalist individuals and organizations. But this is not to say English Canadian nationalism starts and ends at the Ontario border. Much of the active opposition to free trade during the late 1980s developed outside that province, and survey data consistently indicate public support for nationalist ideas in western and Atlantic Canada.[19]

The problem with using this potential to build a united English Canada rests in the reality of regionalism. As long as powerful societal and political interests oppose the interventionism and centralism of the Anglo-Canadian world view, and as long as these interests work to polarize the public along ideological and regional (read anti-Ontario) lines, then nationalism's future in a reconstituted Canada will remain doubtful.

Taking Quebec out of the equation, in other words, is no solution to the problems that nationalists in English Canada face. Perhaps the only possible response is a continuation and, above all, an integration of efforts to be culturally creative despite limited resources, to point out the threats to human communities implied by homogenization and economic integration—in short, to expand in a tolerant way the world view that modern pan-Canadianism has tried to develop.

Notes

[1]Maude Barlow, *Parcel of Rogues: How Free Trade is Failing Canada* (Toronto: Key Porter, 1990), viii.

[2]Anthony H. Birch, *Nationalism and National Integration* (London: Unwin Hyman, 1989), 224.

[3]Ibid., 220.

[4]See Richard Collins, *Culture, Communication and National Identity: The Case of Canadian Television* (Toronto: University of Toronto Press, 1990).

[5]For a review of these policies, see Harvey Enchin and Hugh Winsor, 'Loss of 1,100 Posts the Deepest Cut', *Globe and Mail* (6 Dec. 1990), A10.

[6]In the period of the fall 1990 CBC cut-backs, support for the federal Progressive Conservatives in national polls was approximately 16 per cent. See Hugh Winsor, 'Malaise Deals Tory Support Another Blow', *Globe and Mail* (29 Oct. 1990), A1.

[7]Alan M. Rugman, 'Multinationals and the Free Trade Agreement', in Marc Gold and David Leyton-Brown (eds.), *Trade-Offs on Free Trade: The Canada-U.S. Free Trade Agreement* (Toronto: Carswell, 1988), 7. Emphasis in original.

[8]See ibid. as well as A.E. Safarian, 'Foreign Direct Investment', in John Crispo (ed.), *Free Trade: The Real Story* (Toronto: Gage, 1988), 77-86.

[9]See David Crane, 'Rae Welcomes Any Takeovers Offering Gains', *Toronto Star*, 16 Jan. 1991.

[10]Most academic economists in Canada, as argued in Chapter 5, tended to endorse bilateral free trade. See William G. Watson, 'Canada-US Free Trade: Why Now?' *Canadian Public Policy* 13 (1987), 337-49; and R.A. Young, 'Political Scientists, Economists and the Canada-US Free Trade Agreement', *Canadian Public Policy* 15 (1989), 49-56. For one account of the origins of continentalism among economists, see Stephen Clarkson, 'Anti-Nationalism in Canada: The Ideology of Mainstream Economics', *Canadian Review of Studies in Nationalism* 5 (1978), 45-65.

[11]See Lawrence LeDuc and J. Alex Murray, 'Open for Business? Foreign Investment and Trade Issues in Canada', paper presented at Conference on Canadian Political Economy in Comparative Perspective, Blacksburg, Virginia, May 1986.

[12]See John Fayerweather, *The Mercantile Bank Affair: A Case Study of Canadian Nationalism and a Multinational Firm* (New York: New York University Press, 1974).

[13]For a sampling of these arguments, see Duncan Cameron (ed.), *The Free Trade Deal* (Toronto: Lorimer, 1988).

[14] See Barlow, *Parcel of Rogues*, Appendix.

[15] See John W. Warnock, *Free Trade and the New Right Agenda* (Vancouver: New Star Books, 1988).

[16]These new faces included Maude Barlow and Marjorie Cohen from the women's movement as well as Bob White from the trade union movement.

[17]See Robert Fulford, *Best Seat in the House: Memoirs of a Lucky Man* (Toronto: Collins, 1988), chap. 10.

[18]On these political costs, see Barbara Jenkins, 'Reexamining the "Obsolescing Bargain": A Study of Canada's National Energy Program', *International Organization* 40 (1986), 139-65; and David Milne, *Tug of War: Ottawa and the Provinces Under Trudeau and Mulroney* (Toronto: Lorimer, 1986), chap. 3.

[19]See survey data on nationalist attitudes in Chapter 7, for example.

Appendix A

Abbreviations

ACTRA Association of Canadian Television and Radio Actors
CBC   Canadian Broadcasting Corporation
CBS   Columbia Broadcasting System
CCF   Cooperative Commonwealth Federation
CDC   Canada Development Corporation
CEW   Committee for the Equality of Women in Canada
CIC   Committee for an Independent Canada
CIPO   Canadian Institute of Public Opinion (Gallup)
CMA   Canadian Manufacturers' Association
CPA   Canadian Petroleum Association
CRTC   Canadian Radio-Television and Telecommunications Commission
DEA   Department of External Affairs
EMR   Department of Energy, Mines and Resources
ENFIN   Energy and Finance
FIRA   Foreign Investment Review Agency
FTA   Canada-US Free Trade Agreement
GATT   General Agreement on Tariffs and Trade
GNP   Gross National Product
IPAC   Independent Petroleum Association of Canada
LSR   League for Social Reconstruction
MNC   Multinational corporation
MP   Member of Parliament
MPP   Member of Provincial Parliament (Ontario)
NAC   National Action Committee on the Status of Women
NBC   National Broadcasting Corporation
NEP   National Energy Program
NFB   National Film Board
OPEC   Organization of Petroleum Exporting Countries
PCN   Pro-Canada Network
PCO   Privy Council Office
PMO   Prime Minister's Office
PQ   Parti québécois
RCSW   Royal Commission on the Status of Women
REAL   Realistic, Equal, Active, for Life
SAGIT   Sectoral Advisory Group on International Trade
YWCA   Young Women's Christian Association

Appendix B

Acknowledgement of Informants

Doris Anderson
Paul Audley
Maude Barlow
David Bell
Carl Berger
André Blais
Michael Burgess
Alan Cairns
Gerald Caplan
Stephen Clarkson
Marjorie Cohen
Ramsay Cook
Susan Crean
Donna Dasko
Stéphane Dion
G. Bruce Doern
Terry Downey
Daniel Drache
Maureen Farrow
John Fayerweather
Ernest Fraser
Roger Gibbins
Franklyn Griffiths
John Goyder
Clara Hatton
Alfred O. Hero, Jr.
Chaviva Hosek
Mel Hurtig
Réjean Landry
James Laxer
Lawrence LeDuc
Evert Lindquist
Seymour Martin Lipset

Isaiah Litvak
Ronald Manzer
Robert Matthews
Jack McClelland
Thelma McCormack
John McDougall
Kenneth McRoberts
John Meisel
Catherine Morrison
Neil Nevitte
Peter C. Newman
Kim Nossal
Maureen O'Neil
Frank Peers
Michael de Pencier
A. Paul Pross
Philip Resnick
Alexander Ross
Abraham Rotstein
Rick Salutin
Mildred Schwartz
Jeffrey Simpson
Grace Skogstad
Elizabeth Smythe
Katherine Swinton
Annis May Timpson
John Trent
Mel Watkins
Alan Whitehorn
Gilbert Winham
David Wolfe
Robert Young

Index

Aboriginal groups, xi, 110, 117, 120, 136, 184
Advertising Agency Association of British Columbia, 65
Agricultural groups, 110, 117, 120, 136, 142, 146, 163
Agriculture Canada, 122
Alberta, provincial government, 85, 86, 99, 116
Allison, Graham, 40, 44
American media influence in Canada, 9, 12, 17, 49, 52, 61-78, 181
Anderson, Doris, 138
Anti-Reciprocity League, 15
Applebaum-Hébert Report, *see* Federal Cultural Policy Review Committee (1982)
'Artists and Writers for Free Trade', 119, 120, 121
Assembly of First Nations, 117
Association of Canadian Advertisers, 65
Association of Canadian Television and Radio Actors (ACTRA), 65-66, 117
Atkinson, Michael, 48
Atwood, Margaret, 11, 116, 141, 160; *Surfacing*, 11; *Survival*, 11
Auto Pact, 17, 107, 112, 123
Axworthy, Tom, 97

Bachrach, Peter, 43, 52
Baker, W.M., 6
Baratz, Morton, 43, 52
Barlow, Maude, 117, 118, 139, 141
Bell, Joel, 90, 91
Benson, Edgar, 23
Berger, Carl, 7, 28, 154
Berton, Pierre, 116
Beuth, Philip, 66
Bill C-58, An Act to Amend the Income Tax Act (*Time/Reader's Digest* Bill), xii, 10 (Table 1.1), 12, 13, 40, 55, 56, 57, 61-78, 83, 99, 105, 110, 112, 124, 129; and bureaucratic framework, 61, 67-69, 70, 76, 77; and integrative framework, 61, 69-76, 77-78; and societal framework, 61, 65-67, 69-70, 76, 77; US opposition to, 63, 65, 70, 72, 76
Birch, Anthony, 4, 179; *Nationalism and National Integration*, 179

Blair, Bob, 88, 89
Bliss, Michael, 14
Board of Broadcast Governors, 10 (Table 1.1)
Borden, Robert, 15-16
Bourassa, Robert, 158
Bowker, Marjorie Montgomery, 141
Boyle, Harry, 68
Breton, Albert, 73
Breuilly, John, 4
Brimelow, Peter, 3
Broadcasting Act (1968), 64, 68
Brooks, Stephen, 119
Brown, Robert Craig, 7
Brunet, Michel, 155, 157
Business Council on National Issues, 87, 99, 107, 115, 136

Cairns, Alan, 48, 49
Cameron, Barbara, 142
Cameron, Duncan, 109
Canada Council, 9, 10 (Table 1.1)
Canada Development Corporation (CDC), 20, 21 (Table 1.2), 23, 24, 56, 57
Canada First movement, 7, 8, 11, 12, 13, 18, 26, 27, 28, 62, 179
Canada-US Free Trade Agreement (1988), *see* Free trade, Canada-US
Canadian Alliance for Trade and Job Opportunities, 108, 115, 116, 120
Canadian Arctic Resources Committee, 86
Canadian Automobile Workers, 116
Canadian Broadcasting Corporation (CBC), 9, 10 (Table 1.1), 12, 13
Canadian Centre for Policy Alternatives, 119
Canadian Chamber of Commerce, 107, 115, 136
Canadian Conference of Catholic Bishops, 117
Canadian Conference of the Arts, 117
Canadian Dimension, 22
Canadian Exporters Association, 115
Canadian Federation of Independent Business, 115
Canadian Federation of University Women, 137
Canadian Forum, 8, 18, 19, 22, 23, 159, 160; 'Declaration of Quebec's Right to Self-

Determination', 160

Canadian Labour Congress, 116, 136, 181-82

Canadian Manufacturers' Association (CMA), 15, 16, 17, 18, 28, 87, 107, 115, 136

Canadian National League, 15

Canadian Periodical Publishers' Association, 65

Canadian Petroleum Association (CPA), 86, 87, 88, 89, 99

Canadian Radio League, 8, 9, 12

Canadian Radio-Television and Telecommunications Commission (CRTC), 61, 64, 66, 68, 70, 77; *The Integration of Cable Television in the Canadian Broadcasting System* (1971), 64

Canadian Union of Public Employees, 116

Capital Cities Communications, 66

Caplan-Sauvageau Report, *see* Task-Force on Broadcasting Policy (1986)

Carney, Pat, 99, 126

Carter, Jimmy, 92

Catholic Women's League, 138

C.D. Howe Institute, 119

Church groups, 110, 116, 118, 136, 146

Clark, Edmund, 90, 95, 100

Clark, Joe, 84, 92; Clark government, 91

Clarke, Tony, 117

Clarkson, Stephen, 3, 92; *Canada and the Reagan Challenge*, 3, 92

Coalition Against Free Trade, 136, 140, 141, 148

Cohen, Marjorie, 140, 141

Cohen, Marshall (Mickey), 90

Coleman, William, 40, 48

Committee for a New Constitution, 159-61, 163, 164

Committee for an Independent Canada (CIC), 2, 22, 23, 25, 27-28, 56, 65-66, 85, 86, 87-88, 89, 114, 117, 157, 159, 160, 162, 164

Committee for the Equality of Women in Canada (CEW), 137

Communications industries: broadcasting, 10 (Table 1.1), 12, 56, 61, 62, 63-64, 65-66, 68, 69, 70, 77-78, 129; film, 107; publishing, 11, 56, 62-63, 64, 65-66, 68, 70, 77-78, 129. *See also* Bill C-58, An Act to Amend the Income Tax Act (*Time/Reader's Digest* Bill); Communications, nationalist policy on; Nationalism, cultural

Communications, nationalist policy on, xii, 1, 8, 12-13, 39, 61-78, 109. *See also* Bill C-58, An Act to Amend the Income Tax Act; Na-

tionalism, cultural; Communications industries

Confederation of Canadian Unions, 136

Conservative Party policies, on cultural nationalism and Bill C-58, 75; on foreign investment, 24; on free trade, Canada-US, 107-108, 116, 118, 124-26, 127, 129, 137, 140, 143-44, 149; Goods and Services Tax, 186; on National Energy Program, 95, 99, 100; VIA Rail cut-backs, 184

Cook, Ramsay, 9, 157

Cooperative Commonwealth Federation (CCF), 8; Regina Manifesto, 8

Council of Canadian Film-makers, 11

Council of Canadians, 110, 116, 117, 118, 141, 148

Council of Forest Industries of British Columbia, 115

Crean, Susan, 11, 62, 160; *Who's Afraid of Canadian Culture*, 11

Creighton, Donald, 19, 28

Crosbie, John, 112, 124

Cullen, Bud, 74

Cultural groups, 110, 117, 119, 120, 136, 142

Dahl, Robert, 41; *Preface to Democratic Theory*, 41

D'Aquino, Thomas, 115

Davey Report, *see* Special Senate Committee on Mass Media (1970)

Davey, Senator Keith, 69, 74, 75

Denison, Colonel George Taylor, 7

Department of Energy, Mines and Resources (EMR), 90, 91-92, 95, 126; *An Energy Policy for Canada: Policies for Self-Reliance*, 90, 91

Desveaux, James, 91

Devoir, Le, 27, 159

Diefenbaker, John, 19, 28; Diefenbaker government, 17

Doern, Bruce, 86, 87, 89

Dome Petroleum, 88, 89

Duplessis, Maurice, 73

Economic Council of Canada, 104, 119

Elkins, David, 27; *Small Worlds: Provinces and Parties in Canadian Political Life*, 27

Enders, Thomas, 72

Energy industry, 84, 86-89, 99. *See also* National Energy Program

Energy Pricing and Taxation Arrangement, 85

Environmental groups, 110, 116, 117, 118, 120, 136, 142, 184

Evans, Peter, 43; *Bringing the State Back In*, 43

External Affairs, 70, 104, 106, 121-22, 123; *Canadian Trade Policy for the 1980s*, 106-107, 121-22

Federal Communications Commission (US), 70
Federal Cultural Policy Review Committee (1982) (Applebaum-Hébert Report), 10 (Table 1.1)
Finance Department, 91, 122
Findlay, Sue, 140; 'Facing the State', 140
Foreign Investment Review Agency (FIRA), 21 (Table 1.2), 24, 56-57, 92, 94, 108, 114, 124
Foster, Peter, 90, 91; *The Sorcerer's Apprentices: Canada's Super-Bureaucrats and the Energy Mess*, 90
Fowler Report, *see* Royal Commission on Broadcasting (1957)
Free trade, Canada-US, x, xii, xiii, 3, 18, 26, 40, 55, 56, 100, 104-130, 136-49, 163-64, 165, 180, 181-82, 183; alternatives to, 112-14; and agricultural sector, 119; and automotive industry, 112; and bureaucratic framework, 121-23; and Canadian business interests, 107, 113-14, 115, 119, 120, 124, 127, 129, 130, 136; and Conservative policy, 107-109, 110, 124-126, 127, 129, 137, 140, 143; and cultural industries, 111, 119, 180, 181; and employment, 119, 141, 142, 181; and integrative framework, 123-28; interest groups opposed to, 110, 116-19, 120, 136-49; interest groups supporting, 115, 120-21; and Liberal policy, 106, 107, 116, 126, 127; nationalist opposition to, xii, 3, 18, 39, 40, 49, 109-121, 136, 182; and NDP policy, 116, 126, 127; publications favourable to, 106 (Table 5.1); and Quebec, 163-64; and Reagan administration, 107, 118, 124; and societal framework, 114-21; and threat to national identity, 109, 111, 114, 129; and threat to sovereignty, 111, 119; US response to, 18, 107, 123, 124, 129
Free trade, Canada-US-Mexico, 171, 182, 185
Fulford, Robert, 184

Gallagher, Jack, 89
General Agreement on Tariffs and Trade (GATT), 17, 94, 113, 122, 182
Gillespie, Alastair, 92
Gilpin, Robert, 158
Globe and Mail, 141
Gonick, Cy, 2, 22
Goodman, Eddie, 23
Gordon Report, *see* Royal Commission on

Canada's Economic Prospects (1957)
Gordon, Walter, 2, 20, 22, 23, 24, 63, 74, 75, 160
Granatstein, J.L., 15, 16, 107
Grant, George, 12, 20, 28; *Lament for a Nation*, 20
Green Paper on Communications Policy (1973), 68
Group of Seven, 7-8

Hall, Emmett, 120, 121
Halliday, Anthony, 122-23
Hartman, Grace, 138
Hopper, Wilbert, 90, 91
Horowitz, Gad, 22
Hosek, Chaviva, 138
Howe, C.D., 14, 19
Hunter, Floyd, 41
Hurtig, Mel, 109, 117, 118
Hyde Park Agreement (1941), 19

Ikenberry, John, 43
Independent Petroleum Association of Canada (IPAC), 87, 88
Independent Publishers' Association, 11
Innis, Harold, 22, 113
International Trade Advisory Committee, 108, 128
Investment Canada, 24. *See also* Foreign Investment Review Agency
Investment, foreign, *see* Nationalism, investment; National Energy Program; Free trade, Canada-US

Jenson, Jane, 46-47, 48, 49
Johnson, Harry, 3, 17
Johnson, Lyndon, 63
Johnston, Richard, 156
Joint House of Commons-Senate Committee on External Affairs and International Trade, 141
Juneau, Pierre, 68

Katzenstein, Peter, 43, 44
Kaye, Lynn, 141
Kierans, Eric, 116
King, William Lyon Mackenzie, 14, 16, 104
Kissinger, Henry, 64
Krasner, Stephen, 43-44

Labour, as interest group, 110, 116, 117, 118, 120, 136, 142, 146, 148, 163
Lalonde, Marc, 74, 75, 92, 94, 95-97, 99, 100

Lash, Z.A., 15
Latouche, Daniel, 161-62, 163, 164, 165
Laurendeau, André, 157
Laurier, Wilfrid, 14-15, 16; and reciprocity debate of 1911, 15-16, 18, 104, 111
Laxer, Gordon, 3; *Open for Business*, 3
Laxer, James, 2, 22, 110, 159
Lévesque, René, 158, 161
League for Social Reconstruction (LSR), 8, 18
Levitt, Kari, 2; *Silent Surrender*, 2
Lewis, David, 22, 159
Lewis, Stephen, 22
Liberal Party policies: on Canada-US free trade, 107, 116, 126, 127; on cultural nationalism, 63; on foreign investment, 24, 28; on National Energy Program, 83-85, 89, 91-92, 95-97; on Pan-Canadian nationalism and Bill C-58, 73-75, 76, 77
Lougheed, Peter C., 115
Lumsden, Ian, 2; *Close the 49th Parallel Etc.*, 2

McCall, Christina, 69, 70
McClelland, Jack, 159
Macdonald Commission, *see* Royal Commission on Economic Union and Development Prospects for Canada
Macdonald, Donald S., x, 115
Macdonald, Sir John A., 15, 110
McDonald, Lynn, 138
Maclean-Hunter Publications, 63, 65
McLuhan, Marshall, 12
Magazine Association of Canada, 66
Mair, Charles, 6; *Tecumseh: A Drama*, 6
Manifesto of the Toronto Eighteen, 15, 18
Manitoba, provincial government, 116
Mannheim, Karl, 5
Marsden, Lorna, 138
Massey-Lévesque Report, *see* Report of the Royal Commission on National Development in the Arts, Letters and Sciences (1951)
Mathews, Robin, 12
Media opinion concerning nationalist issues: cultural nationalism, 61, 72; free trade, 121, 127, 129, 130, 141; investment nationalism, 97; Pan-Canadian nationalism, 185
Meech Lake Accord, xi, xiii, 108, 155, 162-64, 171-72, 183
Meisel, John, 173
Mexico, 171, 182, 185
Mills, C. Wright, 41
Milne, David, 91; *Tug of War: Ottawa and the Provinces Under Trudeau and Mulroney*, 91
Moffett, Samuel, 3

Mosher, Terry, (Aislin), 116, 148
Motion Picture Association of America, 65
Mulroney, Brian, 24, 108, 110, 111, 118, 124-25, 127, 145, 182; Mulroney government, 107-109, 110, 124-26, 127, 139, 143-44
Murphy, Peter, 108

National Action Committee on the Status of Women (NAC), xii, 116, 118, 130, 136-149, 180; and free trade, Canada-US, 136-37, 140-49, 180; and integrative framework, 137; and 'Women's Equality Accord', 141
National Association of Broadcasters, 65
National Association of Manufacturers, 115
National Citizens' Coalition, 115
National Energy Program (NEP), xii, 25, 27, 40, 55, 57, 83-100, 105, 108, 111, 112, 114, 124, 126, 129, 136, 184; and bureaucratic framework, 83, 90-91, 97; and integrative framework, 83, 91-100; introduction of, 83-84; and societal framework, 83, 85-89, 97; and US response, 83, 92-94, 97, 100
National Farmers Union, 117
National Film Board (NFB), 9, 10 (Table 1.1)
Nationalism, Anglo-Canadian, xiii, 2, 16, 27, 30, 57, 73, 74, 117, 154-73; Anglo-Canadian attitudes surveyed, 166-72; and fear of US economic and cultural influences, 12, 14, 18, 19, 156, 157, 164, 181, 184; and free trade, 163-65, 173 (Table 7.7); and imperial nationalism, 6-7, 15; and limits to foreign investment, 180-81; and Meech Lake Accord, 162-63, 164; and Quebec nationalism, 158-61, 169-70, 171 (Table 7.5), 173 (Table 7.7)
Nationalism, conversion of ideas into federal policy: bureaucratic framework, xi, 39-40, 42-47, 48, 49, 52, 61, 67-69, 70, 76, 77, 83, 90-91, 97, 121-23; integrative framework, xii, 39-40, 47-55, 56, 83, 91-100, 123-28; societal framework, xi, 39-40, 41-42, 47, 48-49, 52, 56, 61, 65-67, 69-70, 76, 77, 83, 85-89, 97, 121
Nationalism, cultural, x, 4, 6-13, 39, 48, 49, 50, 52, 61-78, 109, 117, 120, 129, 180, 181; and communications policy, 1, 8, 12-13, 39, 109; history of, 6-9. *See also* Bill C-58, An Act to Amend the Income Tax Act
Nationalism, imperial, 6-7, 16, 26, 154
Nationalism, investment, 1, 2, 4, 18-25, 39, 40, 48, 49, 50, 61, 83-100, 109, 111, 112, 117, 129, 136, 157, 159, 165-66, 180-81; and Canada-US free trade, 108, 111, 113;

foreign investment and the resource sector, 24-25, 39, 83-100, 111; historical attitudes to foreign investment, 18-25. *See also* Foreign Investment Review Agency (FIRA); National Energy Program

Nationalism, Pan-Canadian: x-xi, 1-28, 154-73, 178, 179-86; and Anglo-Canadian nationalism, 2, 27, 154-73; defined, x-xi, 4-5; history of, 6-28; and identity, 1, 3, 5, 6, 7, 26; 'in' and 'out' groups, xi, 1, 3-4, 5, 7, 25-26, 155, 183; limits to, 5, 25-28; and Quebec nationalism, xiii, 27-28, 155-73; and regionalism, xi, 27, 28, 183-84, 185-86

Nationalism, Quebec, xi, xiii, 27-28, 73, 154-73, 178, 179, 183-86; and Anglo-Canadian nationalism, 161-62, 169-70; and integrationist policies re US, 156, 157; 1980 referendum on sovereignty-association, xiii, 158, 159, 161, 162, 164, 165, 168, 170, 172-73; and relations with US, 155, 158; and US investment, 158, 164. *See also* Quebec

Nationalism, trade, x, xii, 1, 4, 13-18, 39, 48, 49, 50, 61, 109, 104-130, 180; history of, 13-18; and National Policy, 14-16. *See also* Free trade, Canada-US

National Policy, 7, 13-16

National Revenue, 122

Natural resources, nationalist policy on, xii, 1, 8, 17, 19, 24-25, 39, 57, 83-100, 111. *See also* National Energy Program

New Democratic Party policies, 22, 84, 86, 95, 116, 126, 127, 184-85; 1971 convention, 159; and Ontario provincial government, 184; and Quebec, 159

Newman, Peter C., 2, 17-18, 22, 159, 160

Nixon, Richard, 17; Nixon administration, surcharge on processed materials (1971), 17, 23

Nossal, Kim, 3, 26, 157

Nova Corporation, 88, 89

O'Leary, Grattan, 63

O'Leary Report, *see* Royal Commission on Publications (1961)

Ontario Coalition Against Free Trade, 141

Ontario Federation of Labour, 116

Ontario, provincial government, 116

Organization of Petroleum Exporting Countries (OPEC), 84, 85, 90

Parkin, George, 7

Parti québécois, 159, 161

Pearson, Lester, 63; Pearson government, 17,

20, 63, 74

Peers, Frank, 13

Petro-Canada, 25, 57, 84, 85, 86, 90, 91, 92

Pharmaceutical Manufacturers' Association, 115

Pipeline debate (1956), 19

Pitfield, Michael, 90

Pollution Probe, 86, 116

Porter, Ann, 142

Pratt, Christopher, 119

Prime Minister's Office (PMO), 127, 128, 139

Prince Edward Island, provincial government, 116

Privy Council Office (PCO), 90, 91

Pro-Canada Network (PCN), xii, 110-11, 113, 116-17, 118, 119, 120, 130, 136, 140, 141, 142, 146, 147-48, 163, 184

Pross, Paul, 47-48

Public opinion concerning nationalist issues: cultural nationalism, 61, 72, 73 (Table 3.1); foreign investment policy, 98 (Table 4.3), 166 (Table 7.1), 169, 170 (Table 7.4); free trade, 121, 127, 128, 129, 130, 141, 144-45, 171, 173 (Table 7.7); investment nationalism, 24, 83, 94, 95 (Table 4.1), 96 (Table 4.2), 97, 98 (Table 4.3), 165-66, 169, 170 (Table 7.4); Pan-Canadian nationalism, 156, 165-72 (Tables 7.1-7.6), 185; Quebec nationalism, 167-72 (Table 7.2), 173 (Table 7.7)

Public Petroleum Association of Canada, 86, 88, 89, 110, 136

Putnam, Robert, 46, 48

Quebec, 16, 27, 73, 74, 116, 149; and free trade, Canada-US, 116, 127, 163-64, 171, 173 (Table 7.7); and Meech Lake Accord, 108, 155, 162-63; nationalist attitudes surveyed, 166-72 (Table 7.1); and the Quiet Revolution, 73; and separatism, 76, 159; and US cultural influences, 164. *See also* Nationalism, Quebec

Rabinovitch, Robert, 90

Reader's Digest magazine, 62-63, 65-67, 69, 72, 74-75, 78. *See also* Bill C-58, An Act to Amend the Income Tax Act (*Time/Reader's Digest* Bill)

Reagan, Ronald, 94, 110, 124, 182; Reagan administration, 107, 118, 124

REAL Women, 139, 143

Reform party, 184

Regionalism, western Canadian, xi, 28, 84, 85, 126, 184

Reisman, Simon, 108, 112
Report of the Royal Commission on National
Development in the Arts, Letters and Sci-
ences (1951) (Massey-Lévesque Report), 9,
10 (Table 1.1), 12
Resnick, Philip, 2, 155, 163, 164, 165; *Land of
Cain*, 2; *Letters to a Québécois Friend*, 163
Richler, Mordecai, 119
Riker, William, 155
Rioux, Marcel, 160
Ritchie, Laurell, 136, 141
Robinson, Paul, 107
Roe, Emery, 47, 112
Rotstein, Abraham, 2, 22, 23, 39, 88, 160,
161
Royal Commission on Broadcasting (1957)
(Fowler Report), 9, 10 (Table 1.1), 12
Royal Commission on Canada's Economic
Prospects (1957) (Gordon Report), 19, 20,
21 (Table 1.2), 23, 85
Royal Commission on Economic Union and
Development Prospects for Canada (1985)
(Macdonald Commission), x, 3, 108, 110,
115, 119, 122, 127, 140, 162
Royal Commission on Publications (1961)
(O'Leary Report), 9, 10 (Table 1.1), 13, 62-
63
Royal Commission on the Status of Women
(RCSW), 137-38; *Report*, 137
Rueschemeyer, Dietrich, 43; *Bringing the State
Back In*, 43
Rugman, Alan, 180
Ryan, Claude, 27-28, 159

Sabatier, Paul, 47
Sabia, Laura, 137
Salutin, Rick, 116, 148, 161
Schattschneider, E. E., 43
Science Council of Canada, 119
Secretary of State Women's Programs, 143
Sectoral Advisory Groups on International
Trade (SAGITs), 108, 128
Senate Standing Committee on Foreign Af-
fairs, 104, 105
Simeon, Richard, 27; *Small Worlds: Provinces
and Parties in Canadian Political Life*, 27
Skocpol, Theda, 43, 46, 47; *States and Social
Revolutions*, 43; *Bringing the State Back In*, 43
Skogstad, Grace, 48, 122
Smiley, Donald, 14, 27
Smith, Denis, 20
Smith, Goldwin, 3
Social welfare groups, 110, 120, 136

Special Senate Committee on Mass Media
(1970) (Davey Report), 10 (Table 1.1), 62,
72, 74; *The Uncertain Mirror*, 74
Spry, Graham, 9
Stairs, Denis, 2, 3
Standing Committee on External Affairs and
National Defence (1970) (Wahn), 21 (Table
1.2), 23
State Department (US), 70, 72, 94
Steele, James, 12
Stein, Michael, 155
Stewart, Ian, 90
Suzuki, David, 116
Swanson, Roger, 72
Swinton, Katherine, 64
Symons, T.H.B., 12

Task-Force on Broadcasting Policy (1986)
(Caplan-Sauvageau Report), 10 (Table 1.1)
Task Force on Foreign Investment (*Foreign Di-
rect Investment in Canada*) (1972) (Gray re-
port), 21 (Table 1.2), 23-24, 25, 85, 159
Task Force on Foreign Ownership and the
Structure of Canadian Industry (1968)
(Watkins Report), 20, 21 (Table 1.2), 22,
23, 24, 85
Thatcher, Margaret, 110
This Magazine is About Schools, 22
Time magazine, 62-63, 65-67, 69, 72, 74, 75,
78. *See also* Bill C-58, An Act to Amend the
Income Tax Act (*Time/Reader's Digest* Bill)
Time/Reader's Digest Bill, *see* Bill C-58, An Act
to Amend the Income Tax Act
Toner, Glen, 25, 86, 87, 89
Toronto Star, 22, 74, 94, 127
Tough, George, 90
Trade Negotiations Office, 108, 128
Trading with the Enemy Act (US), 20
Trudeau, Pierre Elliott, 23, 73-74, 75, 76, 84,
85, 92, 94, 95-97; Trudeau government,
20, 23, 74-75, 84-85, 92, 95-97, 99-100,
139
Truman, David, 41; *The Governmental Process*,
41
Turner, John, 111

Underhill, Frank, 8, 27
United Church of Canada, 117
United States: control of trade unions in Canada, 22; and free trade, Canada-US, 18, 107,
123, 124, 129, 130; influence of US media,
9, 12, 17, 49, 52, 61-78, 181; national security policy, 44; public policy, 43; response to

Bill C-58 (*Time/Reader's Digest* Bill), 63, 65, 70, 72, 76; response to National Energy Program, 83, 92-94, 97, 100; threat to Canadian nationalism, 12, 14, 18, 19, 156, 157, 164, 181, 184, 185; trade policy, 43, 104-130

United Steelworkers, 116

University of Toronto, 8, 20, 23

Waffle Manifesto ('For an Independent Socialist Canada'), 2, 22, 25, 27, 157

Waffle movement, 22, 23, 56, 85, 86, 95, 110, 113, 114, 117, 157, 159, 160, 162, 164

Warnock, John, 118, 182

Watkins, Melville, 2, 20, 22, 113, 114, 160, 161

Watkins Report, *see* Task Force on Foreign

Ownership and the Structure of Canadian Industry (1968)

Weber, Max, 1, 5-6; 'The Social Psychology of World Religions', 5

Williams, Glen, 3; *Not for Export*, 3

Women's groups, xi, xii, 47, 110, 116, 117, 118, 120, 136-49, 163, 184

Women's Legal Education and Action Fund (LEAF), 146

Women's Liberation Movement (Toronto), 138

Writers' Union of Canada, The, 11

York University, 164

Young, Robert, 156

Znaimer, Moses, 66